PROSTATE & CANCER

A Family Guide
to Diagnosis,
Treatment & Survival

aren't the lymph nodes important?

Sheldon Marks, M.D.

Illustrated
by David Fischer

FISHER
er
BOOKS™

Publishers:	Bill Fisher
	Helen Fisher
	Howard Fisher
Editors:	Randy Summerlin
	Bill Fisher
Book Production:	Deanie Wood
Art Director:	B. Josh Young
Illustrations:	David Fischer

Published by Fisher Books
4239 West Ina Road, Suite 101
Tucson, Arizona 85741
(520) 744-6110

Printed in the U.S.A.
Printing 10 9 8 7 6 5 4 3 2 1

Table of Contents

Foreword

When I graduated from my residency in Urology in 1987 (not that long ago!) prostate cancer was an ignored disease among both health-care professionals and patients. Little research was being done to understand the disease. Doctors and other health professionals were not that interested in it, and there were few resources for patients to turn to for information.

Over the last three years there has been a virtual explosion in the interest in prostate cancer. The prostate-cancer patient-support-group movement started in 1990 with the founding of US-TOO. Now patients and their partners could look to other survivors for advice, compassion and support. These groups soon caught the attention of organizations such as the American Foundation for Urologic Disease and the American Cancer Society, which nurtured their growth.

After a number of prominent Americans, including Senators Bob Dole and Ted Stevens, came forward to publicly proclaim that they were surviving the disease, the interest in prostate cancer continued to mushroom. At about this time, the prostate specific antigen (PSA) blood test was becoming more widely recognized and used as a prostate-cancer screening test. The stage was set and Act One put prostate cancer in play as one of the "in-vogue" diseases of the 1990s. Despite this tremendous progress in three short years, there is an ongoing need for quality education materials that patients can understand.

The book you are about to read, *Prostate and Cancer: A Family Guide to Diagnosis, Treatment & Survival,* is one such quality educational patient-oriented work. Dr. Sheldon Marks has put the contemporary, commonly asked questions about prostate cancer in an easy-to-understand patient-friendly format. In my daily practice, almost exclusively with prostate-cancer patients and their families, these are the most-asked questions. I will try to make this required homework for all my prostate-cancer patients. As in other aspects of our daily lives, an educated consumer has the best likelihood of success and satisfaction. So, too, with prostate cancer and its treatment, and this book will help to achieve that goal.

JUDD MOUL, M.D.
Director, Center for Prostate Disease Research
Attending Urologic Oncologist
    Walter Reed Army Medical Center,
    Washington, D.C.
National Advisor, US-TOO

Dedication

I dedicate this book to my patients—past, present and future—who inspired me to put all of this information together in one place; and to my wife, Brenda, who gave me the confidence, love and encouragement to take on the challenge.

Acknowledgments

Thanks to all my friends and colleagues who helped me with this book. Special thanks are due my patients and their wives, who shared their experiences so that together we could empower other patients to take control of their health care by educating and informing them.

Special thanks to my friend and publisher, Bill Fisher, for making this possible; to an outstanding editor, Randy Summerlin, for his clarity; and to a talented illustrator, David Fischer. I specifically acknowledge the invaluable wisdom and counsel of my colleagues.

Thanks to my parents for always believing in me. Special love to my children, Matthew, Jordan and Ally, who never really understood why I spent so many months at the computer working on *that book*.

Preface

Prostate cancer is fast becoming "the" cancer of the '90s. As more public figures have announced that they have cancer of the prostate, it has become a frequent news item and topic of discussion in many households throughout the country.

Prostate cancer has touched the lives of high-profile people such as Senators Bob Dole, Ted Stevens, Richard Shelby and William Roth, and actors and entertainers such as Bill Bixby, Telly Savalas, Don Ameche and Frank Zappa, to name a few.

Nearly 200,000 men will be diagnosed with prostate cancer in 1995, and close to 50,000 men previously diagnosed will die as a result of it. Prostate cancer has become the most-diagnosed cancer in America and the second leading killer of men. Articles appear in national magazines, questions are called in on radio talk shows and newspapers frequently report a new idea or breakthrough in the field of prostate cancer.

It seems the more we hear and read, the more confused we become. Even many primary-care doctors are confused about whether or not prostate cancer is a significant disease and which treatment options are best, if any.

I believe that the fear of the unknown is the most over-whelming and traumatic result of all the confusion about this disease. Unfortunately, short of spending an hour or two in personal consultation with a urologist, there is really no complete and accurate source of information available.

There are numerous books on prostate disease in general, or on men's health, usually with a chapter on prostate cancer. These books often tell you what the author thinks you should know about prostate cancer. But the topic of prostate cancer is too important and too controversial to confine its discussion to just a few pages. There are a few books about prostate cancer, but many of the patients' real questions are left unanswered.

As a urologist I spend a great deal of my time counseling, evaluating and treating patients with prostate cancer. My first and foremost concern with my own patients is answering their questions and calming their fears by educating them.

During the past several years I have compiled my patients' most commonly asked questions. I started doing this for my patients and their families—to help them better understand the disease and the pros and cons of the various treatment options. This information was in high demand. It filled a definite void. At my patients' suggestion and urging, I have taken my notes and expanded them into this book to provide the basic information necessary for an individual to make an informed decision regarding the evaluation and treatment of prostate cancer.

Many of us will spend months researching a new car or weeks reading up on the latest lawn mower. But when it comes to our health and our bodies, many of us, especially men, are satisfied with a five-minute explanation of the problem. Some men will accept the doctor's recommendations without question. The choices we make will definitely impact on the quality of our remaining years and very possibly the length of our lives.

You have a right to understand exactly what is going on with your body, the treatment options you have and the long-term impact of the decisions you make about your care. This book will educate you and answer your questions about your prostate and cancer. It will give you what you need to be an informed consumer. It will enable you to take back control and make the best decisions about your future that will impact on your health and well-being.

This book is intended to serve as a resource—to give you a foundation for informed discussion about your health with your doctor. This is not intended to replace your physician, who can individualize your particular situation while considering other factors such as your general health, family longevity and the specifics of your problem.

This book can't possibly cover all the details specific to you. Likewise, there is no way you should make decisions regarding your health based solely on my comments in this book. This book is written from my own personal experiences. It contains my interpretation of current philosophies and controversies regarding cancer of the prostate. I have also brought together the latest cutting-edge ideas and research from professional meetings and journals.

It is my sincerest hope that this book will answer your questions and thereby ease your fears so you can be your own best health advocate.

Knowledge is power.

SHELDON MARKS, M.D.
Tucson, Arizona

1

The Prostate Gland ~ Anatomy & Function

To understand prostate disease and its impact, you should have a general understanding of the normal pelvic and genito-urinary anatomy that is involved.

The function of the prostate gland is to add vital nutrients and fluid to the sperm. The prostate is a relatively small, walnut-sized gland that sits just below the *urinary bladder* in the bottom of the pelvis, surrounding the *urethra*. It is this position that leads to difficulties later in life. As the gland enlarges from normal growth or from cancer, it can cause narrowing of the urinary passage and make it increasingly difficult to urinate.

When fathering children is no longer a goal, the prostate no longer serves its main purpose. However, the gland remains and, in the presence of normal male hormones, continues to grow until at some point it may cause problems.

The prostate is actually a collection of glands encased as one organ that secretes fluid. The outside of the prostate is surrounded by a thin capsule of compressed fibrous tissue. Outside of the prostate is a layer of fat.

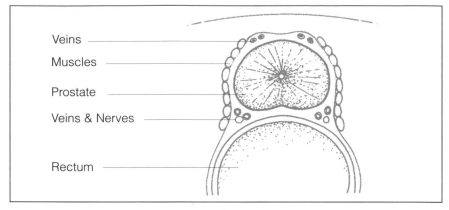

PROSTATE CROSS-SECTION: Cross-section of prostate gland shows location of nerves and blood vessels, as well as prostate position next to rectal wall.

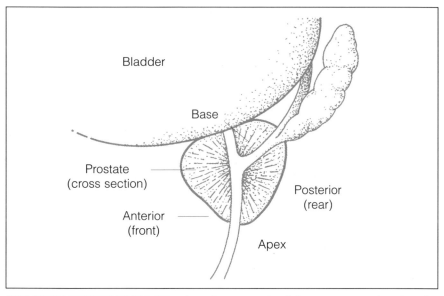

PROSTATE DESCRIPTION: Side view of prostate gland shows terms used to describe the top (base), bottom (apex), front (anterior), and back (posterior).

Below the prostate, just a few millimeters away, is the front wall of the rectum. On each side are nerves and blood vessels. These nerves are all-important when we address the treatment choices for prostate cancer and problems that can occur.

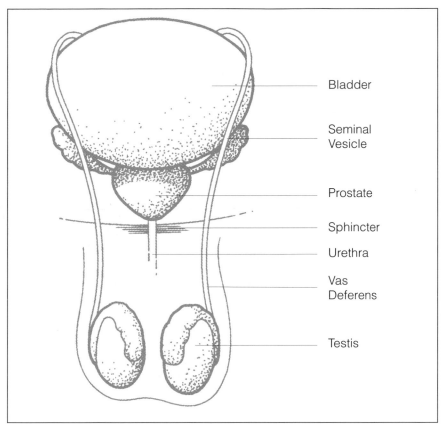

Bladder

Seminal
Vesicle

Prostate

Sphincter

Urethra

Vas
Deferens

Testis

PELVIC ANATOMY: Prostate is located immediately below the bladder in the pelvis. Seminal vesicles and the vas deferens from both testicles drain into the prostate.

The prostate is divided into right and left sides, called *lobes.* The tip of the prostate farthest from the bladder is the *apex.* The wider portion next to the bladder is the *base.* The front is called *anterior,* and the rear *posterior.*

The *vas deferens* is the tube that leads the sperm from the testicles to the urethra and empties into the urethra inside the prostate. Fluid from adjacent glands called the *seminal vesicles* also drains into the prostate. These glands are next to the prostate and below the bladder. The testicles not only make the sperm but also produce the male hormone *testosterone,* which is delivered directly into the bloodstream.

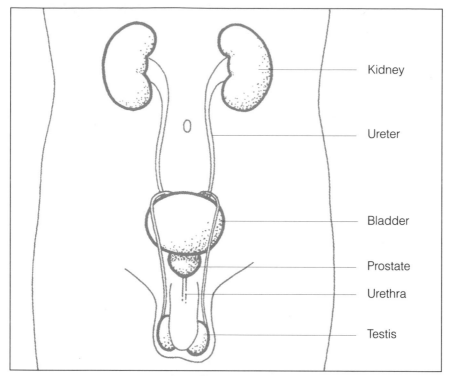

UROGENITAL ANATOMY: Kidneys filter the blood and drain urine down the ureters into the bladder. Here it is stored before coming out the urethra, through the prostate.

The bladder sits above the prostate, in the bottom of the pelvis. It serves two purposes. First, the bladder is a container or reservoir for urine, so you can build up urine and empty when you choose to, rather than when it is created. The second function is to serve as the muscle that squeezes out the urine when given the necessary messages from your brain. Urine is made in the kidneys by filtering waste products from the blood. The urine then drains down the ureters into the bladder.

The urethra is the tube that leads from the bladder through the prostate, past the *urinary sphincter* and out the penis to the opening, called the *meatus.*

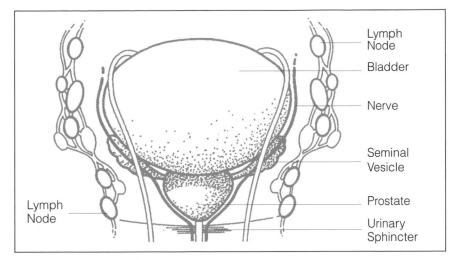

Lymph Node

Bladder

Nerve

Seminal Vesicle

Prostate

Urinary Sphincter

Lymph Node

LYMPH DRAINAGE: Lymphatic fluid from the prostate drains into lymph nodes on both sides of the pelvis. Cancer in the prostate can follow this pathway and spread to these lymph nodes.

The urinary sphincter is a collection of circular muscle fibers just below the prostate that helps to prevent leakage of urine when you cough, move or are physically active. Most of the control (called *continence*) of urine actually occurs at the bladder neck. There all of the circular muscle fibers at the bladder neck come together like a funnel.

Veins of the prostate drain blood out and up toward the heart alongside the spinal column. The *lymphatics* drain from the prostate to a number of small *lymph nodes* clustered along the wall of the pelvis on both sides.

What exactly is the lymphatic system?

The lymphatics are the cleaning system for the body. All cells of the body are "bathed" by lymph fluid—clear, slippery fluid that sometimes oozes from scrapes or abrasions. This fluid is filtered through lymph nodes, where any impurities, germs or cancers are captured. The filtered lymph fluid then flows back into the bloodstream.

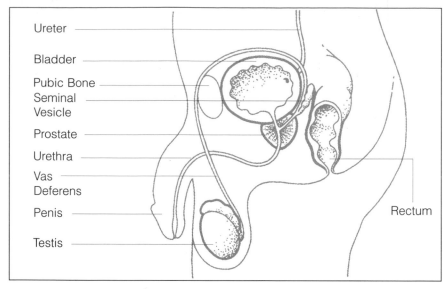

PELVIC ANATOMY, SIDE VIEW: Bladder sits behind pubic bone and immediately in front of rectum. Prostate gland is below bladder and surrounds urethra just as it leaves bladder.

Noncancerous Prostate Enlargement (BPH)

For reasons still unclear, the prostate in most men slowly grows and increases in size. This growth, called *benign prostatic hyperplasia*, or *BPH*, is not cancerous. It can seriously impact on a man's quality of life by causing blockage to the urine flow. This can result in a number of annoying and bothersome symptoms such as frequent daytime and night-time urination, dribbling and difficulty starting and stopping the urinary stream. See also list of symptoms on page 31.

For years, treatment options for BPH were limited. Most men who had the problem ultimately had surgery. During the past decade, however, new breakthroughs and advances have provided a wide range of options that can often reduce the symptoms without the risks and potential side effects of surgery.

Does having an enlarged prostate increase my odds of getting prostate cancer?

Having enlargement of the prostate (BPH) does not increase your risks for developing prostate cancer.

Do I need treatment if my prostate is enlarged but I don't have any problems urinating?

No, not at all. Unless your prostate is causing real problems with your bladder from incomplete emptying or bleeding, you don't need any treatment.

What are the options for treating the symptoms of an enlarged prostate?

There are five basic options. Each choice has definite advantages and disadvantages. These include:

1. Doing nothing.
2. Taking alpha-blocker medication such as Hytrin®.
3. Taking Proscar®.
4. Having laser surgery.
5. Having a standard surgical resection of the prostate.

How is "doing nothing" a treatment choice?

You can always choose not to treat your symptoms. If you are not bothered much by blockage symptoms, then it is reasonable to just watch and wait. You may find that you are doing better, staying the same or getting worse. Of course, if the symptoms do become a problem for you, then you should talk to your doctor about your other choices.

It is always interesting to talk to two men who have the same problems in urinating. One is miserable getting up twice each night to urinate, while the other is thrilled that he's not getting up more often.

What is an alpha-blocker?

This type of medication was originally used only for the treatment of high blood pressure. We knew this medication worked by relaxing a very specific type of muscle found in the walls of blood vessels. We soon learned that these muscles are also found in and around the prostate. When these muscles are tight, they squeeze the urethra shut and can cause the annoying symptoms often associated with an enlarged prostate. When these muscles are relaxed by taking alpha-blockers every day, the urethra and prostate open up. This can result in a dramatic improvement in urination.

What are the names of this medication?

Hytrin, manufactured by Abbott Laboratories, is the most commonly used alpha-blocker for the symptoms of blockage. In 1994 Abbott completed a study of Hytrin confirming the excellent results with minimal side effects.

The use of Hytrin over the past few years has eliminated the need for surgery for many men. Cardura® is also FDA-approved for men with urination difficulties. Others on the market, including Prazocin®, are not as widely used and are not FDA-approved for the treatment of urination difficulties.

Does Hytrin work for most men?

Most men who try Hytrin will see a dramatic improvement in their urination, with a reduction of their annoying symptoms. This usually happens within a few weeks. I have been very impressed with how well most of my patients respond in a short time. A small number may not tolerate the medication or may not experience an improvement.

Does taking Hytrin for my prostate protect me from getting prostate cancer?

No. Hytrin is an excellent medication to relax the muscles that squeeze the prostate, thus improving urination. For many, it may eliminate the need for surgery. It does absolutely nothing to reduce your risks of developing prostate cancer, nor does it play any role in cancer treatment.

Are there any side effects from taking Hytrin?

In the first few days on the medication, some men may describe a feeling of dizziness, light-headedness or fatigue. It is reported that on very rare occasions you could pass out. This can be prevented if you stand up slowly in the first few days as your body adapts to the medication. I mention this only as a precautionary note.

Does Hytrin interact with any other medications?

Because Hytrin can also lower high blood pressure, it is important for you to coordinate this medication with your primary-care physician, especially if you are already taking other medications for your high blood pressure.

How does Proscar work?

Proscar works by blocking the normal formation of male hormone byproduct in the prostate. This byproduct, called *DHT*, is a very powerful stimulator of prostate growth. When DHT is removed, the prostate may shrink in size. This may result in improved urination. As with Hytrin, if Proscar is successful, you will need to take the medication daily as long as you want to have the benefits. I offer Proscar to most men if the Hytrin is unsuccessful.

Does taking Proscar reduce my risks for getting prostate cancer?

No one really knows. A long-term research study is currently underway to look at this. Presently, it is best not to take Proscar unless you have significant problems urinating. When the results from these research studies are reported, the official recommendations may change.

What are the side effects of Proscar?

The side effects of Proscar are primarily sexual, with about 4% describing impotence and less than 4% complaining of a reduced sex interest.

Does Proscar interact with any other medications?

Proscar does not interact with any other medication and can be taken safely without worrying about interfering with other medications you take.

Can taking Proscar cause problems?

There are some concerns that Proscar can mask or hide a small prostate cancer as it grows, make it harder to identify a cancer in the early phases of growth or alter the tissue to make microscopic examination more confusing. No one really knows how Proscar affects the growth of prostate cancer over time.

How does laser surgery work?

The urologist can use a laser to destroy the prostate tissue that is causing blockage. A laser is pointed into the tissue through the urethra. Usually performed under anesthesia, this operation can be done as an outpatient procedure. The patient can return to work or normal activities the next day. The laser surgery can be done on patients who are on Coumadin®.

Are there any problems with laser surgery?

This is a relatively new treatment option, so urologists are learning exactly what technique works best for each patient. Only time will tell if it is as effective as more standard surgery. Personally, I am very happy with results for the men I have treated with the laser. It is my preferred treatment for prostate obstruction.

How is an enlarged prostate surgically treated?

The standard treatment for many years was always the *TURP*, or *transurethral resection of the prostate*. This operation is performed under anesthesia through a fiber-optic instrument. It requires no incision.

Looking through the instrument that is placed up the penis, the inside prostate tissue that has grown and is causing the blockage can be seen. It is this tissue that is literally

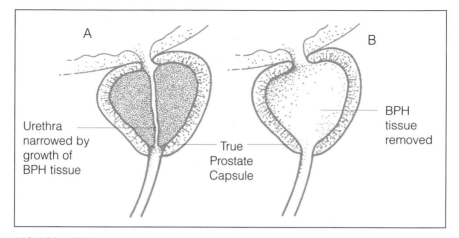

NONCANCEROUS PROSTATE TISSUE: A. *Noncancerous prostate tissue (BPH) grows and compresses the urethra, resulting in urination difficulty.*
B. *Following transurethral resection of the prostate (TURP), this nonmalignant tissue is removed, leaving the prostate capsule intact.*

scooped out with the instrument, leaving only the shell of the prostate remaining. For very large prostate glands, urologists sometimes perform an operation through an incision in the lower abdomen, but this technique is uncommon. The tissue removed is examined to be sure no cancer is present.

Does having my prostate opened up with a TURP mean I don't have to worry about getting prostate cancer?
   No. Even though the tissue causing the blockage has been removed, you are still at risk of developing prostate cancer in the rim of tissue left behind. You must get an annual evaluation to be sure no cancer is present.

Do the pathologists examine for cancer all the pieces of the prostate removed during the TURP procedure?
   No, they look at a representative sample of the tissue provided. It is almost impossible and too expensive for pathologists to analyze every piece of prostate tissue. If they look at a good percentage of the tissue, they will have a fairly good idea of how much and what kind of cancer is present, if any.

2

Cancer & the Prostate

Before we can address prostate cancer we need to review cancer in general, including its growth and causes.

What is cancer?

Cancer is *disordered and abnormal cell growth*. It is a disease of cell structure and function. Within each individual cell, thousands of microscopic *tubules* serve as a skeleton to the cell (see diagram on next page). The tubules serve as the connection between cells as well.

Tubules provide the way for cells to "communicate," or work and function with each other. With cancer, these tubules are distorted so that cells no longer function as they were intended. They no longer communicate with each other.

Normal cells have certain limits to their growth as they contact cells around them. With the tubule mechanism lost, cells continue to grow without controls. They are no longer limited by normal patterns of growth.

Most cells have a certain life span. With cancer, this can

be altered. The cells not only grow beyond their normal borders, but they also do not die as fast as they should. This phenomenon is the basic understanding of what cancer is.

Simply, cancer cells grow without the usual controls and limits. They keep growing and can spread and overwhelm the system.

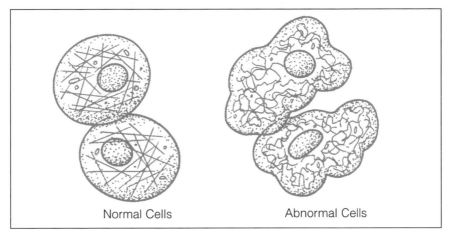

Normal Cells   Abnormal Cells

CELL STRUCTURE: Normal body cells have an organized and regular skeleton made up of microscopic tubules that allow for normal growth. Cancer cells have lost this organized pattern, with distortion of the normal microtubules and loss of the normal cell shape and growth patterns.

What is a malignancy?

A malignancy is a cancerous growth that has the potential to spread and cause injury or death.

Are all cancers the same?

No. There are hundreds of types of cancer. Each type of tissue and cell can lose the ability to grow normally. Each one has different growth patterns, properties and characteristics. Each has weaknesses that we hope to identify and take advantage of with treatment—whether surgery, radiation, chemotherapy or hormone therapy.

Does cancer always cause death?

No. Some types of cancers are almost always life-threatening, while others will rarely lead to death. Most cancers are somewhere in the middle. Prostate cancer can be very slow-growing and of minimal concern, or it can grow rapidly, spread and possibly lead to death. We use the term *aggressive* to refer to these potentially life-threatening cancers.

Is cancer contagious?

No. It is an internal cellular abnormality that starts within the cells of an individual. One person cannot "catch" a cancer from another. Cancer cannot be spread like a virus or bacteria.

What causes cancers to grow?

Cancers develop for a wide variety of reasons. Sometimes we know what can stimulate a cancer to start growing. Smoking, for example, can lead to lung cancer. With many other types of cancer, researchers have no idea what starts the cancer's growth from otherwise normal cells.

We know that many environmental chemicals and substances can start cancers growing. Research now points strongly to a person's diet as a contributing factor to many cancers, especially a high-fat, low-fiber diet over many years.

Genetics may be involved as well. Some cancers seem to run in families. Scientists have identified certain genetic weaknesses that can be passed on by parents. In certain situations, these weaknesses can cause cancers to grow.

In general, it looks as though most cancers start because of a variety of factors working together, rather than one single cause.

Why do some people fail to get cancer even when they smoke and eat all of the wrong foods, while other people who follow all of the guidelines and live healthy lives get cancer anyway?

Again, this varies from person to person. As I mentioned, some people have a genetic weakness that allows cancers to grow. Other people may have some form of genetic strength that protects them even if they are doing all the wrong things.

How does cancer spread?

As cancers grow, they begin to stimulate the growth of new blood vessels. These new vessels are known to be leaky. The cells of the cancer squeeze through the microscopic gaps and get into the bloodstream. Cancer cells then travel along with the blood throughout the body. When the cells find an environment that encourages growth, they can settle in and grow.

What is prostate cancer?

This is a malignant growth of the glandular cells of the prostate. Normally these cells are located within the glands that produce the fluid that makes up most of the semen. But, under certain circumstances, these cells can lose their normal controls and start to grow out of control.

How does prostate cancer start?

Like all cancers, it probably starts as a tiny change in just a few cells. Over many years, perhaps even 20 or more, this tiny cluster gradually enlarges. As the cancer grows, it gains momentum, growing faster.

How fast does prostate cancer grow?

In most situations, prostate cancer grows very slowly over many years, perhaps even decades. But it eventually grows faster and gets larger. Some may grow very rapidly and can be quite deadly.

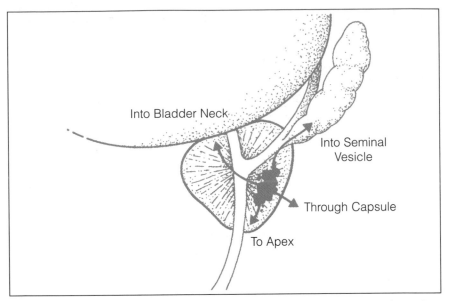

Into Bladder Neck

Into Seminal
Vesicle

Through Capsule

To Apex

CANCER SPREAD: *Prostate cancer can spread through the capsule into surrounding tissues, the bladder neck, through the apex or into the adjacent seminal vesicles.*

What stimulates prostate cancer to grow?

Prostate cancer is in a class of cancers, like breast cancer, that is *hormone-sensitive*. In the prostate, the hormone *testosterone* is converted into another very powerful hormone, DHT. In prostate cancer, these hormones stimulate the cancer cells' uncontrolled growth.

What happens when prostate cancer spreads?

As the cancer grows, it invades surrounding tissues. At first, it just grows into more and more of the prostate. When the cancer reaches the outside capsule or shell of the prostate gland, the cancer can grow through this into the fat surrounding the prostate. Cancer can also grow into the adjacent bladder or the seminal vesicles.

Where else in the body does prostate cancer spread?

Prostate cancer spreads to two main areas of the body. One, to the lymph nodes that drain the prostate, and second, to the bone, mostly of the spine and ribs. Specifically, the cancer grows inside the bone marrow—the inside of the bone where active growth of new bone takes place.

Why does prostate cancer spread to the spine?

Cancer cells leave the prostate in the bloodstream. As the blood leaves the prostate gland, it travels through a web of veins alongside and into the spine. The blood then passes into the bones of the spinal column. Prostate-cancer cells grow here because it is the first body environment the cells encounter that encourages their growth.

What are the causes of prostate cancer?

We really don't know what causes prostate cancer. Researchers around the world are investigating this now. It may be years before we have any definitive answers. However, recent evidence suggests that prostate cancers may develop because of genetic imbalances. These imbalances may be accelerated by environmental factors such as diet, which can lead to mutations over time.

We know some genes in every cell in the body prevent cancer by blocking or suppressing cancerous changes in the tissues. When these preventive genes are blocked, there's nothing to keep the cancer from starting up and growing. There are also genes that lie dormant, but under yet unknown circumstances they activate and stimulate cancer-cell growth. It appears as if all of these factors may play some role.

Is it true most prostate cancers being detected today are really insignificant and should be ignored?

Absolutely not. Reviews of patients who have been treated with surgery show that if the cancer is big enough to be detected with modern techniques, it is most often large enough to be a threat to the person's life. It should not be ignored.

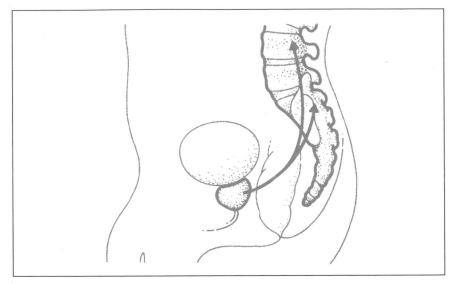

CANCER SPREAD TO THE SPINE: Prostate-cancer cells can spread up through the veins that drain the prostate from the pelvis, alongside and into the bones of the spine.

Does diet play a role?

Yes. Studies do suggest a high-fat diet somehow seems to stimulate prostate cancer to grow. This is particularly true of red meat and dairy products. Prostate cancer is far less common in countries with a lowfat diet, such as Japan and China. When men move to those countries with high-fat diets, the risks of developing prostate cancer increase and may be as high as everyone else's within a generation or two. This seems to suggest diet is probably one of the factors that enables or perhaps even encourages the cancers to grow.

How does a high-fat diet stimulate prostate cancer?

It probably serves to activate an otherwise dormant internal mechanism within a cell's own structure that directs the cell to grow without its usual limits and boundaries. Or it may block a protective mechanism, so the cell can grow without its usual restrictions.

Is there anything I can eat that will reduce my chances of cancer?

Vegetables such as broccoli, cauliflower, Brussels sprouts and Swiss chard have been shown to have powerful anticancer effects. But these can't be eaten just once in a while. These vegetables should be eaten on a regular basis over many years. In general, you should have five to ten servings a day of fresh fruit and vegetables to reduce your risks of cancer.

Early laboratory studies indicate that soy products may also have anti-cancer benefits. Maybe we should eat more tofu.

Will it do me any good to eat differently now?

Probably. It is always a good idea to eat healthful foods. Though we don't yet have any proof, a healthy lowfat diet may very well reduce the odds of developing cancer in the future or could even slow down a cancer you may already have.

Cruciferous Vegetables

Broccoli
Cabbage
Cauliflower
Brussels sprouts
Swiss Chard

I've heard about beta carotene. Is this helpful with prostate cancer?

Beta carotene is a vitamin found in leafy green vegetables and carrots. It looks very good as a beneficial dietary ingredient to reduce cancer growth. Variations are even being used as a formal treatment for some types of cancer. Beta carotene may have a protective mechanism that works to slow down the rapid cell growth that is seen with cancers. Whether it will be of use with prostate cancer is not yet proven.

What foods are high in beta carotene?

Foods high in beta carotene include: dark-green, leafy vegetables, broccoli, spinach, romaine lettuce, beets, Swiss chard, kale, carrots, tomatoes, sweet potatoes and yams.

Does taking beta carotene as a vitamin supplement work as well as eating vegetables?

Currently it is suggested that you get the nutrients you need from the fresh fruits and vegetables. There are no definite research studies showing that taking vitamins in pill or liquid form provides the same benefits we see with eating fresh fruits and vegetables.

High Beta-Carotene Foods

Dark-Green, Leafy Vegetables
Broccoli, Beets, Carrots, Kale, Romaine Lettuce, Spinach
Sweet Potatoes, Swiss Chard, Tomatoes, Yams

Does taking selenium reduce my risks for developing prostate cancer?

Early research results indicate that there may be a relationship between increased selenium intake and reduced chances for developing prostate cancer.

Is there anything else that reduces risks of cancer?

New research has identified lycopene, a natural substance that gives tomatoes their red color. It is a very powerful anticancer chemical. It reduces the risks for cancer and has been shown to prevent and slow down the growth of cancer cells. As you increase your intake of these anticancer nutrients, you may reduce your chances of developing prostate cancer. In the future this new area of research may provide medications to treat or prevent prostate cancer. We might be able to say, "A tomato a day will keep the urologist away."

Why can't we reduce the risks of prostate cancer only with diet?

An individual *can* lower his risks for prostate cancer by following correct lifelong dietary practices. However, the world population is not likely to change to a high-fiber, low-fat diet. Therefore, it is highly unlikely that the incidence of prostate cancer will ever be reduced by dietary changes alone.

Does having a vasectomy increase my risks of getting prostate cancer?

Possibly. Only one of several studies suggests there may be a relationship between men who have had a vasectomy and whether or not they are diagnosed with prostate cancer many years later. Assuming the most recent study is correct and the other studies are not, then if you have had a vasectomy, your risks of developing prostate cancer are 1.8 times greater at 20 years after the vasectomy than men who did not have a vasectomy. It is important to remember that several other studies do not show this relationship.

Scientists and researchers are unsure of an actual causative relationship. In other words, we can't explain how the body's changes after a vasectomy can later develop into prostate cancer. Urologists wonder if this is simply a statistical coincidence. It is important to remember that vasectomy and prostate cancer do not appear to be cause and effect.

Should I worry if I had a vasectomy?

There is no reason to worry because there was no increase at all in death rates in those men who were diagnosed with prostate cancer after vasectomy. You should begin to have an annual urological evaluation by your primary-care physician or urologist 10 to 15 years after a vasectomy, or if you are 40 or older.

Should I get my vasectomy reversed?

It is not recommended to have a reversal of the vasectomy for the purpose of cancer prevention, based on current information. There still is no proof that a vasectomy causes prostate cancer. And there is no proof that men who have had a reversal have a reduced risk of developing prostate cancer. In addition, the vasectomy reversal is expensive. And you would then need to find an alternative form of birth control.

Does ultraviolet radiation from the sun have anything to do with prostate cancer?

Some early studies show that as the exposure to ultraviolet (UV) light goes up (meaning more sun exposure), the rates of prostate cancer go down. Whether this has anything to do with the sun itself is unclear. We think the increased sun exposure raises vitamin D, which may help to reduce prostate-cancer risks.

What about exposure to chemicals at work? Does this increase risk?

Certain occupational hazards may play a role, but this relationship is still very weak. Men who work in rubber factories or with the chemical cadmium, as well as farmers, seem to have an increased risk. For the farmers, it may be exposure to pesticides and other industrial chemicals, or perhaps it's the high-fat diet many eat.

Why do we know so little about cancer of the prostate?

There are five reasons to explain why doctors and researchers know as little as we do about such an important cancer.

1. There has never been very much money invested in prostate-cancer research.
2. Prostate cancer takes so long to grow and progress that short-term studies really aren't of much use. Long-term studies are difficult to start up and keep going.
3. The disease is different from person to person and each variant of the disease behaves differently. It is almost impossible to compare one treatment to another.
4. Scientists, researchers and physicians have a relatively poor understanding of basic mechanisms of prostate-cancer growth and spread.

5. Most of the research that has been done has been inadequate, often with serious errors that put the results in question.

Although we do know quite a lot about prostate cancer from clinical experience, we are now seeing significant scientific studies being funded. We hope these studies will give us valuable information in the future about treatment and the disease itself.

Do all prostate cancers grow the same?

No, not at all. Many prostate cancers may look similar at any given point, comparing one man to another, but the cancers may have different rates of growth. One may grow very fast, not responding at all to treatments, while another cancer that appears to be the same might grow slowly.

Is there any way to tell which cancers may become deadly and which will grow slowly and probably not affect my life span?

There is no way to accurately tell which ones will become deadly. Until there is, most doctors believe it is appropriate for young, healthy men to pursue age-appropriate aggressive therapy.

Who's at risk?

All men are potentially at risk of developing prostate cancer at some point in their lifetime. As the population grows older, more prostate cancer is going to be detected. This is most often a disease of older men. However, young men can get prostate cancer as well. As modern medicine continues to keep us living longer and healthier lives, many of us will eventually be diagnosed with prostate cancer. In other words, if you live long enough, sooner or later you will probably develop prostate cancer. Whether or not the cancer will affect your quality of life or longevity is a different issue.

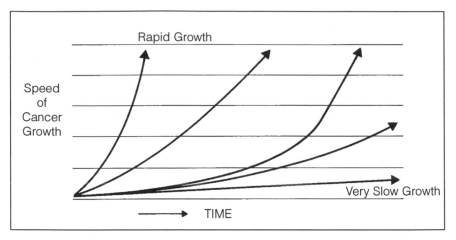

CANCER GROWTH RATES: Prostate-cancer growth can be very unpredictable. For some men it can grow very slowly throughout their lives, or very rapidly, resulting in death or any pattern in-between.

Does having a relative with prostate cancer increase my risk?

Certain groups of men are more likely to be diagnosed with prostate cancer. We know from recent studies that if there are any males in your family with prostate cancer, your risk for developing the disease are higher.

The younger the family member is when he's diagnosed with prostate cancer, the higher the risks that any other male relatives will be diagnosed with prostate cancer at a younger age.

Because my father was diagnosed with prostate cancer at age 72, does this dramatically increase my risks for getting prostate cancer?

Not really. You have some increased risks but not significantly over another man who has no prostate cancer in the family.

Does my father's being diagnosed at age 52 increase my risks much?

Yes. The younger the relative is when he is diagnosed with prostate cancer, the higher the risks that you may develop prostate cancer as well.

Author's Note: *Several years ago Michael, a 65-year-old patient, came into my office for a routine evaluation because his brother had just been diagnosed with prostate cancer. He had just seen his primary-care physician and told his doctor that his brother had prostate cancer. The doctor did the prostate exam and told him, "Yes, you have a large nodule on your prostate. Come back in a year and we'll see if it changes." Michael was not satisfied with his physician's advice and made an appointment to see me. Together we went through all the necessary exams and diagnostic tests (which I'll discuss in detail later) and we did, in a fairly short period of time, diagnose a very aggressive prostate cancer.*

Does that mean I might get prostate cancer when I'm young too?

Your odds of developing prostate cancer also at a young age are definitely increased. In this situation, prevention and early detection are most important.

Is it true black men are more likely to get prostate cancer?

For reasons we still don't understand, black men seem to have a higher chance of getting prostate cancer, and often with a more aggressive strain. In fact, black American men have the highest rate of prostate cancer of any population or group anywhere in the world. Early research suggests that a high-fat diet may play a role. Other ethnic groups may have less risks, including those men with Oriental ancestry. Hispanics have some degree of risk, though less than African-American men.

Is prostate cancer contagious (or can my wife catch cancer by having sex with me if I have prostate cancer)?

No, you cannot "catch" prostate cancer or any cancer from someone else. Cancer is a process where the cells of your body lose their self-controlling ability. This cannot affect another person through contact, sexual relations or living in close quarters. It is an internal problem of the cells of your prostate gland. It is not contagious.

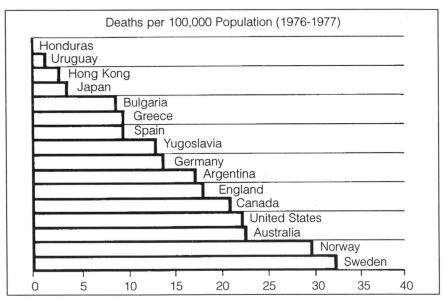

PROSTATE-CANCER DEATH RATES AROUND THE WORLD: Prostate-cancer deaths are highest per person in Scandinavia. They are lowest in the Far East and Central America. Chart courtesy American Cancer Society, 1993.

What are the official recommendations of the American Cancer Society?

All men age 50 and over should have an annual digital rectal exam and PSA blood test. The PSA test is explained in detail in Chapter 5.

Men with a family history of prostate cancer should get an annual PSA test and digital rectal exam starting at age 40.

African-Americans should have an annual digital rectal exam and PSA test starting at age 40.

Cancer Treatment Goals

Reduce number of men who develop cancer
Improve early detection
Improve treatments

Are there any substances that stimulate cancer growth in bone marrow?

A normal substance in the body, called *transferrin*, is secreted by the liver and stored in bone marrow. It is used normally in the body for iron storage for the cells. Recent studies show that transferrin in the bone marrow stimulates prostate-cancer growth. This is very new information and isn't usable yet in the treatment or prevention of prostate cancer. Understanding this substance may be one of the keys to future prostate-cancer management.

Is there anything that blocks cancer growth in the body?

Yes, a substance called *spermine* has been shown in laboratory experiments to inhibit the growth of prostate cancer. Interestingly, spermine is found primarily in the prostate itself. This could explain why prostate cancer seems to grow so fast once it has spread outside the prostate gland. While it is growing in the gland, its growth is being limited by the presence of spermine and so the cancer's growth tends to be slow.

Can a person with prostate cancer take spermine to stop cancer growth and progression?

No. It is not available as a medication that a person could take. This is simply a newly established laboratory fact. It is being investigated as a way of preventing or treating prostate cancer in the future. At the present time, however, it is years away from use.

What are some of the treatment goals for new approaches to cancer?

There are three ways a treatment can reduce the death rate from cancer. First, we can try to develop ways to reduce the number of men who get prostate cancer. Second, we can improve early detection of prostate cancer. Third, doctors and researchers can work to improve the treatments available with fewer side effects and better results.

3

Routine Evaluation & Symptoms of Concern

When you have an appointment with your doctor, you will be asked about your past medical problems, past surgery, medications you take (including the specific names, dosages and how often they are taken) and any allergies you may know about.

You will also be asked about the history of serious illnesses or health problems in your family, whether or not you smoke or drink alcohol and how much. The doctor will want to know about any problems you may be experiencing that may serve as clues regarding underlying disorders. These are called *symptoms*.

What about my physical exam?

The doctor will also perform a physical exam. The doctor wants to make sure there are no abnormal changes or irregularities indicating something could be wrong. Your urine will be checked for abnormalities (it should usually be clear), and blood will be drawn from a vein for analysis. Anything wrong that the doctor can see, feel or detect is called a *sign*.

Every man over the age of 50 should routinely have a general medical exam, a digital rectal exam, a urine evaluation and a PSA blood test. All of these can be done at the same time when you visit your primary-care doctor. The information provided by all of these functions can help your physician decide if there is reason to be concerned. If something is not as it should be, then further evaluation may be appropriate.

Symptoms of Concern

What are the warning signs that I might have prostate cancer?
Unfortunately, there are *no* classic warning signs that prostate cancer may be growing in your body. In fact, most often there are no warning signs or symptoms at all.

Prostate cancer usually grows very slowly. Because of its location in the prostate, it usually doesn't cause physical symptoms. Even when it causes symptoms, they are not specific, meaning that those symptoms could represent a number of problems other than prostate cancer. The same nonspecific symptoms of prostate enlargement could also be caused by an enlarging prostate cancer as it compresses the urethra.

Could I have prostate cancer and have no symptoms?
It is quite possible. This does occur, far too often, with men being diagnosed with large and advanced cancers even though they deny having urination problems.

How can I have cancer if I feel so good and have no symptoms?
I have this discussion weekly with patients I have just diagnosed with prostate cancer. This illustrates the point I am trying to make: there are *no* early warning signs. If you wait until something is obviously wrong, then you have most likely waited too long. The disease could be in an advanced stage. This is why a routine annual exam by your physician should always include a prostate check and a PSA blood test.

Are there any ways to know that I have prostate cancer if there are no symptoms early on?

The best way to detect prostate cancer early is by a physical exam of the prostate and the PSA blood test. Each of these alone is helpful. But together, if you have a potentially dangerous cancer, the exam and PSA are likely to indicate abnormalities. Prostate cancer, if it grows large enough, will lead to the onset of exactly the same bothersome symptoms as noncancerous prostate growth.

What are the symptoms of an enlarged prostate that might disguise a growing prostate cancer?

Some prostate-enlargement symptoms include:
- Getting up at night to urinate.
- Urinating frequently during the daytime.
- Standing a long time before the urinary stream starts.
- Lots of dribbling at the end of the stream.
- A sense of urgency to rush to the bathroom.
- Leakage of urine.
- Straining to empty your bladder.
- Returning to the bathroom to urinate again just a few minutes after completion of urinating.

If I have prostate cancer, will I have all of these symptoms?

Most likely no. You may have any combination of symptoms—just a few, all of them or none at all.

Are there any symptoms if the cancer has spread?

This depends on where the cancer has spread. Back pain, rib, hip or shoulder pain could suggest that prostate cancer has spread to the bones. Often the pains will come and go. Fatigue, weakness or generalized aches and pains could also represent prostate cancer in more advanced stages. Rarely, advanced prostate cancer can cause pelvic pain.

All of these problems are nonspecific. In other words, they don't indicate *why* you have these symptoms. Even if there is advanced prostate cancer, most men will describe only a few symptoms at any given time. Some of these aches and pains may also just be the result of a naturally aging body. This is why a routine exam is so important. Without exception, the prostate exam should always be a part of your routine annual physical.

Does blood in the urine suggest prostate cancer?

Most often when blood is seen in the urine (a condition called *hematuria*), it is not associated with prostate cancer. The blood may come from noncancerous enlargement of the prostate, broken blood vessels on the surface of the prostate, prostate or bladder infections, bladder tumors or even kidney stones. During an evaluation for blood in the urine, we often never find the source.

Is it possible to have blood in the urine if you have prostate cancer?

Yes, it is possible. Because the presence of blood may be an indication of something serious, it is very important to have a complete urologic evaluation when you have bloody urine.

Causes of Blood in Urine

- Enlarged Prostate
- Prostate Cancer
- Bladder Infection
- Bladder Cancer
- Bladder Stones
- Kidney Stones
- Kidney Cancer
- Unknown Source

Should I worry if I see blood in my semen?

Usually not. Most often blood in the semen, called *hematospermia*, is not associated with prostate cancer. Rather, it is thought to come from inflammation or irritation of the prostate or seminal vesicles. This may be seen with an infection, following straining during sexual activity or after a bowel movement. The majority of times the evaluation is completely normal, and there is no evidence of cancer in the prostate.

However, nothing is 100%, so it is always possible that blood in the semen may be a warning sign of something wrong with the prostate, such as cancer. It is always important to see a urologist regarding blood in the semen to be certain everything is normal. Don't just "assume" that nothing is wrong. The evaluation is quick, and the knowledge that there is no cancer is reassuring.

4

Signs of Concern ~ The Physical Exam

The prostate exam is an important basic procedure that you will experience with your doctor. Over a period of time, you can expect to have a number of such exams when the health of your prostate gland is being followed.

What exactly is a prostate exam?
The exam is primarily a feel of the back wall of the prostate gland. This exam goes by a variety of different names, including *rectal exam, digital exam, prostate exam* and *finger wave*. I had one patient wonder how I could do a digital exam without a computer. He thought *digital* meant *computer* and did not realize the finger is referred to as a *digit*.

To do the exam, your doctor briefly inserts a gloved, lubricated finger into the rectum to feel the back wall of the prostate gland. Some rectal cancers can be felt, providing additional potentially lifesaving information.

Does the exam let the doctor feel the entire gland?

No. The exam allows for feeling only the back wall of the gland. This is like feeling the back of your head and trying to guess what your face looks like. Much of the prostate cannot be felt during the rectal exam.

What is the doctor trying to feel?

I feel the prostate to see if there are any areas of firmness or hard nodules, lumps or irregularities. I am basically feeling to see if there are any areas that are not soft, smooth and symmetrical. If something is not right, it simply suggests that cancer *may* be present. An abnormality does *not* always mean there is cancer! A number of other things can cause abnormalities in the exam. These include previous surgery of the prostate, past or present prostate infections, previous biopsies, stones in the prostate and even noncancerous growths that can cause nodules.

If there is an irregularity, should I just wait and see if it changes over time?

No, this is not a wise choice. This approach was popular many years ago and still leads to unnecessary problems today. Even if the PSA test is normal, an irregularity in the prostate gland could possibly represent a serious but *curable* cancer. If you were to leave and return for a repeat exam six months later and the irregularity is even bigger, then you may have lost that opportunity to detect and treat the cancer while it was still confined to the prostate gland.

Should I have my annual exam done by a urologist?

Not usually. This really depends on how skilled and experienced your primary-care doctor is at performing and interpreting the exam. In my practice, most of the abnormalities picked up on the exam are felt by the primary-care doctors. They then send the patient over to me for a consultation to see if I agree.

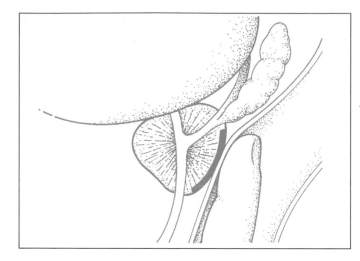

PROSTATE EXAMINATION: Digital rectal examination allows examiner's finger to feel only the back wall of the prostate, adjacent to the rectal wall. Cancers in the middle or front of the prostate might not be felt.

I still see a number of men, however, who prefer to have a urologist perform their annual exam. There is some truth to the old statement that checking prostates is what we do for a living. All things being equal, if the primary-care doctor doesn't feel an irregularity or nodule, it is not common for me to detect something they couldn't feel. Occasionally I do, but not often.

Does it matter if I see different doctors for my exam each year?

Yes. Ideally you should have your exam done by the same person each year so that if there are any subtle changes your doctor will be able to detect them. If at all possible, try to find a doctor you have confidence in and have that doctor do your examination every year.

5

PSA Blood Test

The PSA blood test and the digital prostate exam, combined, provide the best information needed to tell whether or not a cancer may be present. We know the PSA test significantly increases our ability to detect cancers early, even before they can be felt on the exam. The PSA test has mostly replaced the PAP test, which was the best test we had until the PSA came along. (See end of this chapter for a discussion of the PAP test.)

What is PSA?

PSA stands for *Prostate Specific Antigen*. It is a test of an enzyme normally produced by prostate cells, both normal and cancerous. PSA is found nowhere else in the body in significant amounts. Normally, a small amount of PSA is constantly released into the bloodstream. When the prostate is irritated or damaged, more of the PSA leaks out and can be measured by this blood test. This is why the PSA is very sensitive for identifying any abnormalities of the prostate, including but not limited to prostate cancer.

A mild to moderate increase in the PSA does *not* mean you definitely have cancer. It just suggests there is an increased *possibility* of having cancer. In fact, many times no cancer is detected. However, a very high PSA is highly suggestive of a cancer.

What is the normal range for the PSA levels?

The normal range is usually 0.0 to 4.0, although some types of PSA tests have the upper limit of normal as 2.5. Results from the two types of tests are not the same: they are two *different* types of PSA measurements. (See page 48.) The normal range is usually printed on the lab report with the PSA result. Each of the different tests looks at a slightly different aspect of the PSA, which is why the ranges are different.

How high does the PSA go?

Though most men with prostate cancer are diagnosed with a PSA level in the 10s or 20s, the PSA can go up into the hundreds and even into the thousands. A reading at these higher levels almost always means you have advanced prostate cancer. Usually additional tests will show the cancer may have spread to the bones or the lymph nodes. I have seen some men with infections that push the PSA reading up into the 60s or higher, but with treatment it returns to normal within a few months.

What can cause an increase in the PSA?

The PSA can be elevated for a number of reasons. These include any inflammation or infection of the prostate, simple enlargement or noncancerous growth of the prostate gland (there is more tissue to produce PSA), stones within the prostate, a recent urinary catheter or procedure, recent prostate biopsies or prostate or bladder surgery.

Causes of Elevated PSA

- Cancer of Prostate
- Urinary-Tract Infection
- Prostatitis (Prostate Infection)
- Stones Within Prostate
- Catheter in Bladder/Urinary Retention
- Recent Prostate Surgery
    - * Laser
    - * TURP
- Recent Prostate Biopsies
- Noncancerous Enlargement of Prostate Gland

Can infections elsewhere in the body cause an elevation of the PSA?

Infections elsewhere in the body cannot elevate the PSA. Colds, flu, pneumonia, infected teeth and recent gum surgery and all other nonurinary infections will not elevate the PSA result.

Does a urinary-tract infection elevate the PSA very much?

Yes, the PSA can go up substantially because of inflammation in the prostate gland from the infection. I have seen the PSA go as high as 56, and then drop back down to 2.5 six weeks after the infection is treated. This is well within normal limits. It is important to allow enough time for the irritation to resolve.

How long after a urinary-tract or prostate infection should I wait to have a PSA test?

First, the infection has to be adequately treated with the correct antibiotics. A urine culture is usually obtained to identify the infection. Then we can see what antibiotics will work. You should be on antibiotics for at least 10 to 14 days. Sometimes your doctor may opt to keep you on antibiotics for up to four to six weeks.

Even after the infection is over, there still is residual inflammation and irritation that needs to resolve before the PSA will drop to your normal level. The PSA should normally be checked about six weeks after the infection is over. I often do a follow-up urine test about a week or two after the antibiotic treatment is over to be sure the infection is totally gone.

I'm really afraid my high PSA isn't because of my infection. Will waiting for it to go down hurt me?

Probably not. There are no guarantees, but in my practice every single patient who had a high PSA level as well as a urinary-tract infection had a normal PSA after the infection was treated and the inflammation subsided.

Why do you have to wait so long to recheck the PSA?

I am asked this all the time. It takes a long time for the swelling and irritation of the tissues of the prostate gland to heal. If the PSA is checked while the swelling and irritation are still present, then the PSA will still be elevated and continue to confuse the issue. You should wait long enough for healing before the test is performed again.

Does smoking or use of other tobacco products affect the PSA test?

The use of all tobacco products may inhibit any changes in the PSA in spite of the presence of cancer. As a result, tobacco use can delay the discovery of a cancer until treatment options are significantly limited.

If the PSA test doesn't tell you if you have cancer, why do it?

I prefer to consider an elevated PSA as a warning sign that cancer may be present, then do further evaluation. I often use the analogy that the PSA test is like a red light in your car's dashboard. It tells you something may be wrong but it doesn't tell you what. You need to examine further. The higher the PSA level, the more likely a cancer is present and the more likely cancer will be a threat to your life.

If my PSA level is normal, does that mean I don't have cancer?

A normal PSA doesn't mean you don't have cancer. Rather, it simply means you are less likely to have cancer. I have had patients with a PSA level as low as 1.7 who had a significant cancer. On the other hand, I have a patient with a PSA over 20 with no evidence of cancer despite many biopsies over several years. The PSA test is just one investigative tool.

If the PSA level is elevated, is the prostate exam always abnormal?

No, not always. If the PSA is up, the exam could still be normal. If you have an abnormal exam, the PSA may or may not be elevated. Sometimes you will be told you have an elevated PSA, even though your exam is normal. It is very important that we not exaggerate the PSA test results in our search for cancer. It simply serves as a warning device and occasionally gives us an early clue before the exam changes.

We use the PSA as a measure of probability. If you do have cancer, the PSA test may add some information about the cancer's nature.

Why would the digital exam be normal if the PSA is high?

If the cancer is not along the back wall and is located in the middle or even the front of the prostate, then the exam could very well be normal.

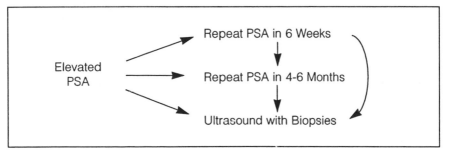

OPTIONS FOR ELEVATED PSA WITH NORMAL EXAM

Does my age have anything to do with the PSA?

Recent studies suggest that your age may play a role in your PSA level. For younger men in their early 50s, a normal PSA may be up to 3.0. As men age, the PSA gradually goes up. For men in their 70s or 80s, a normal PSA may be as high as 6.5. This is a topic of heated debate among experts.

Unfortunately, if we use these age-adjusted numbers, then too many young men will have unnecessary biopsies and too many older men will not be evaluated when they should be. For now, it appears that anything above 4.0 should be further evaluated.

Whatever the PSA level, you should have an ultrasound evaluation with biopsies if you have an abnormal exam.

At what PSA level should I be concerned?

If your exam is normal and the PSA level is within the normal range, you can probably feel comfortable. Everything is probably fine. The PSA should stay at about the same level every time it is checked. There may be a slight increase over time as you age and your prostate gradually enlarges. There will be some minor fluctuations and variability.

As an example, one of my patients was very upset that his PSA went from 3.5 to 3.9 over a six-month period. I explained that this could always represent a growing cancer, but most likely if the test is repeated, results will come back from 3.1 to 4.0, representing the usual day-to-day fluctuations in the level.

The point is, look at the general range and do not focus on the specific number. Is the PSA low, mildly elevated or high? Don't overemphasize the particular number.

My PSA has always been very low but just went up, though it is still normal. Should I be concerned?

An unexpected change in the PSA number is always of concern and warrants a complete evaluation, no matter what the number is.

As an example, I was following the progress of a man with a normal exam and a PSA around 1.0 every year for several years. A follow-up exam was still normal, but his PSA jumped up to 2.6. I checked and he had no infection or reason to explain the sudden elevation. Subsequent evaluation showed he did have cancer of the prostate. He opted for surgery, which showed a surprisingly large volume of cancer but no evidence the cancer had spread. He had an excellent long-term prognosis.

How often should I have the PSA test done?

Most men have the PSA test every year starting at age 50. Once a year is probably adequate. More often doesn't seem to help and less often may let some cancers grow too long before being detected.

What does the PSA blood test cost?

The test itself should cost between $40 and $65, depending on the location. It is almost always covered by your insurance plan. I found one plan in Minnesota that refused to pay, referring to old studies and reports from 1991 and 1992. They ignored the updates by the same sources that *reversed* the original recommendations. Time will tell if the insurance carrier will read the new information.

Almost all insurance plans realize there is a benefit to early detection and treatment of prostate cancer. The test is so important that I recommend you pay for it yourself if that's what is necessary to get it done. You may be able to find a prostate screening program which offers the test for around $15 to $20.

What if my doctor doesn't want to do a PSA test?

This happens occasionally. Many primary-care doctors have become confused by arguments about whether or not doctors are changing anything with early detection and treatment. I believe the facts today support early detection.

Your primary-care doctor may say he does not think a PSA test is needed. You can explain that you have done your own research, and although you realize it is not proven 100%, the majority of experts in the field of prostate cancer still do strongly recommend a PSA test. You can stress that you feel very strongly about having the test.

What if he still refuses to check my PSA level?

If he still refuses, you have several options. You could probably change doctors. You can also file a complaint with appropriate authorities.

At what age should I start to get the PSA test?

If you have a strong family history of prostate cancer (father, brother, grandfather), then you should definitely begin having it checked by age 40, and every year thereafter. African-American men should start checking their PSA levels by age 40. I recommend most men start getting PSA tests by age 50 if they are not at risk.

Is there an age when I should not get the PSA test?

This is a tricky question. The basic guideline I use is this: If you will not allow the doctor to do anything if a cancer is found—because either you think you are too sick or too old—then there really is no reason to undergo the blood test and any additional evaluation. Why take the risks of a biopsy and endure the anxiety if it's not going to make a difference?

At some point in your life, perhaps as you reach 80, you should sit back and realize that even if you have some prostate cancer, it probably will not cause any problems or shorten your life span. That is the point to stop checking a PSA.

As we were taught in medical school, don't take the temperature if you don't want to find a fever. I tend to stop checking PSA in men in their 80s and 90s.

Will my doctor call and remind me to get my PSA done?

Probably not. It's not reasonable to expect a doctor's

office with thousands of patients to remind each one of routine lab tests.

Take control of your own health and put it on your schedule. Don't assume you don't need a PSA recheck just because your doctor didn't call and tell you. I have seen patients who have "disappeared," only to return a few years later with extensive cancer because they assumed I would track them down to remind them about their PSA and exam.

Does it make a difference if I have the test before or after the prostate exam?

We used to think so, but studies show it really doesn't make a difference. If your doctor did not do a vigorous prostate massage, you can have the PSA test done right after the exam. If you're not sure, then wait a week or two. In general, most men can have a PSA blood sample drawn right after a routine prostate exam without concern that it may push up the level.

Does the PSA tell whether or not I should have surgery?

No, but if you have cancer the PSA can be a useful tool to help doctors decide if the cancer is confined to the prostate. A recent study showed that if the PSA is less than 4.0, it is likely the cancer will be confined to the prostate. If the PSA level is greater than 10.0, it is more likely the cancer will have started to grow through the wall and possibly outside the prostate's capsule and into surrounding fat or even into the seminal vesicles.

Does the PSA level reveal anything about the cancer if it is present?

The higher the PSA, the larger the cancer tends to be. The larger the cancer, the more aggressive the cancer cells are.

More importantly, I have seen men who had a very high PSA and underwent a full evaluation where nothing was found wrong. Then a follow-up PSA several months

eturned at a much lower level. For reasons I can't
, someone's PSA may occasionally be inaccurately
high. When in doubt, check it again. If it remains elevated,
then you should seek evaluation by a urologist.

*If I have an elevated PSA with an abnormal exam, should I
also get a recheck of the PSA?*

No, if there is an irregularity on the prostate, then that
is reason enough to proceed with further evaluation, so I don't
recommend a recheck.

*Does the PSA tell anything about which treatment options
may be best or should be avoided?*

To some degree, yes. As the PSA goes higher and higher, the chance increases that the cancer has spread outside the
prostate. Many urologists will recommend radiation if they
don't believe the surgery will be curative. But the PSA alone
doesn't give a definitive diagnosis. It's a lab test that helps the
doctor interpret all the information when making a diagnosis
and determining treatment options.

Can the PSA tell if cancer has spread?

Only if the PSA is very elevated, above 70 or more in
most men. The cancer could very well be in lymph nodes or
in bone at much lower levels, but you cannot assume that is
true in everybody unless the PSA is very elevated. Again, the
higher the PSA the more likely that the cancer will have
spread.

*What about new tests that are supposed to show if the prostate
cancer has spread?*

The most recent test is a variation of the routine PSA
and is supposed to tell if the cancer has started to spread.
These tests are still somewhat expensive and not really proven
to be effective. Only time will tell whether the tests are going
to be as effective as promised.

Does it make a difference if I've been fasting before the PSA is drawn?

No. You can have the blood drawn for the PSA test whether you have recently eaten or not.

Does the PSA go up because of what I ate the night before?

What you eat makes no difference in the PSA result.

Can PSA be used after treatment?

This is actually the best use for PSA: to monitor a treatment to be sure it has worked and the cancer is not coming back. Each treatment has different expectations for what the PSA should be.

Does having sex increase the PSA level?

There is no evidence that having sex changes the PSA level significantly.

Are there any medications that affect the PSA level?

Yes. Proscar can drop the PSA about 50%. In fact, if the PSA does not drop with Proscar, then I would be concerned that cancer may be present. Other medications that reduce testosterone levels can also drop the PSA level.

Does testosterone replacement elevate the PSA?

I'm not aware of any studies showing that testosterone replacement for impotence causes an elevation of the PSA. I am always concerned about giving testosterone to men above 50 because of the risk that it may stimulate an otherwise small and slow-growing prostate cancer to grow faster.

Can I get a PSA more often if I am really concerned?

If you are paying for the test yourself, you can have it done as often as you want. You only need to have it done about once a year. You could check it every six months if you are really concerned or at high risk.

How often should I check my PSA if it is elevated?

It depends on how suspicious your doctor is. For the average man with a mildly elevated PSA, I usually ask for another PSA test about every four to six months. If my patient is older (75 or more), or if I am only minimally suspicious or concerned, then maybe every 12 months is enough.

What if my doctor didn't check my PSA level in the past? Did he do something wrong?

No. Until recently, there was considerable debate about whether or not the primary-care doctors should even be doing the PSA test. Because the answer wasn't clear, many excellent family practitioners and internists did not routinely check a PSA level on their patients.

Can I compare PSA results from different labs?

Probably not. Most tests are done with the Hybritech® machine, with a normal range of 0.0 to 4.0. The Yang® machine has a normal range of 0.0 to 2.5. Abbott IMX® or "ultra-sensitive" PSA range is 0.0 to 4.0, but it measures a different aspect of the PSA in the bloodstream.

At low levels, you can roughly compare the IMX and Hybritech results. If you multiply the Yang result by 1.5, you can get a rough idea on a 0.0 to 4.0 scale. However, it is really best to have your PSA blood tests processed in the same lab or on the same equipment from year to year. If you are seeing the same physician or physician group, they will most likely be using the same lab over the years.

What PSA results are used in this book?

I have used Hybritech PSA levels throughout this book because they are most common.

Does it make a difference which kind of a PSA test is done?

No. They all are good and consistent. I do think it is best if you continue to use the same lab for each of the PSA tests, whether it's for early detection or following the PSA after treatment. Your doctor is most likely working with a lab that he or she trusts.

Should I have a urologist check my PSA?

No, there is no advantage to a urologist drawing the blood or doing the PSA test even if he has the machines in his office.

Are the doctor's office labs as good as the big hospital labs?

In most situations, probably. In larger labs, testing is overseen by a pathologist who specializes in this work. Big labs also are under more scrutiny and monitoring. The test itself is fairly easy to do, and it doesn't make a lot of difference who does it or where it is done. Again, you should have it performed at the same place each time to maintain continuity.

How long does it take to get PSA results back?

Depending on where the lab is, the time of day your blood is drawn and delays on weekends and holidays, results usually take 24 to 72 hours. Some labs may do them only once or twice each week. This is always a good question to ask when you are having the test. They should be able to give a fairly good idea of when they will get results back.

Should I get copies of my PSA results?

I think it is a good idea to keep copies of important results on any tests you have. Just ask your doctor or the lab when your blood is being drawn. They are usually happy to provide a copy of results to you.

Should I keep an ongoing record of my PSA test results?

Yes, this is a very good idea. Whether it's tracking your annual PSA or monitoring a PSA level every few months after a treatment, the record will keep you better informed and more in control. Occasionally, a patient will point out a trend or concern that I may not have seen. I have several patients who plot out each PSA on their computers, which makes trend lines even more dramatic. A Prostate Cancer Evaluation Log is included in the Appendix.

What is the Prostatic Acid Phosphatase blood test?

Also called *PAP*, the Prostatic Acid Phosphatase blood test was one of the original tumor markers used to identify cancer that had started to spread. It was the best, and only, test we had—but it had flaws. Nevertheless, it was used routinely. Unfortunately, results were quite variable and often inaccurate and misleading. Most specialists do not utilize this test anymore.

Why would some specialists still prefer to check a PAP in addition to a PSA test?

The PAP is very elevated when prostate cancer has spread outside the gland. If the PSA and exam suggest there may be widespread disease and that the cancer is no longer confined to the prostate, checking a PAP may simply add one more piece to the puzzle. In my practice, I have found the PAP to be so inaccurate that I no longer use it.

What about having an alkaline phosphatase test?

This test is even less accurate than the PAP. When the level is elevated, it simply suggests rapid bone growth. Though this can be seen with widespread cancer in the bones, it is not specific to any particular disease or prostate disorder.

6

Screening

Prostate screening is the process of looking specifically for prostate cancer in a large number of men. The tests used are usually available widely and easily to anyone. Clinics, doctors' offices or hospitals will often advertise free screening for the public. Men are given a digital rectal exam and PSA blood test to see if there are any abnormalities that suggest prostate cancer.

Why is prostate screening so controversial?

There is some debate about the cost to society of this screening, compared to the results achieved. This is because for many of the men who are evaluated, some will need to undergo additional testing. Of these, only a small number will actually have cancer and require treatment. All of this effort and testing costs someone money.

The real question being asked is, does it cost society too much money for widespread prostate-cancer screening, evaluation and treatment when it really only benefits a few?

I think screening has an important role today and should be continued.

What is the difference between screening and early detection?

Screening means looking at large numbers of men for signs of prostate cancer, including many who may not be ill or even suspect a prostate abnormality. Screening is usually done through advertising to the mass population and is usually free.

When an individual goes to his physician for routine care, the doctor's examination of the prostate and drawing blood for a PSA test is referred to as *early detection*.

Does screening make a difference?

Initially there was much debate on this question, but it now appears screening does increase the chance of finding a cancer before it has spread. The final statistics aren't yet in, but the early results of screening hundreds of thousands of men over the past several years suggest a definite advantage to finding cancers early, especially in men between 45 and 65 years old.

Why should I participate in prostate screening if I feel fine?

There are several reasons why screening for prostate cancer is important to you and society. First, despite what you may have heard or read, prostate cancer is a killer—50,000 men will die of prostate cancer in 1995. This makes it the second leading killer of men by cancer in the United States. The cancer may be slow-growing in many men, but it can still be fatal and should not be ignored.

Second, prostate cancer can be present without any symptoms. Many doctors believe that the early discovery of cancer, especially in high-risk groups, results in improved long-term outcomes and better survival.

It used to be that about a third of men diagnosed with prostate cancer had advanced disease, often already spread to the bones. Now, with screening, early detection and awareness, only about 5% of all men diagnosed with prostate cancer have disease that is advanced.

Why is early detection important for prostate cancer?

First, prostate cancer does kill. Second, there is no curative treatment for advanced prostate cancer. And third, all cancers begin as small, organ-confined lesions with a small volume—something that is treatable.

What will happen if I go for a prostate-cancer screening?

Usually prostate-cancer screening is simply a digital rectal exam. The office or clinic will often ask many questions regarding any difficulty urinating. They will also ask for your address and phone number so they can follow up with you and notify you in writing if there is a concern on the exam.

Sometimes the screeners will even do a free PSA blood test. Other places may charge you their cost to perform the blood test, about $15 to $20.

At screenings, what kind of physician does the exam?

At most screenings, urologists do the exams, although primary-care physicians occasionally are involved. The ability to identify cancers through digital rectal exams depends on the experience and skill of the examiner, regardless of his special medical training.

Is the PSA blood test a good screening test to detect prostate cancer?

I believe that it is. I have seen men whose cancers were found as a result of an elevated PSA level during screening, even though their rectal exams were quite normal. The PSA, though expensive, can be a valuable tool to help identify cancers early.

7

Prostate Ultrasound & Biopsy

If anything suspicious or concerning is discovered on your prostate exam or PSA blood test, your doctor will recommend that you have a prostate ultrasound with biopsies.

This relatively new technique allows us to visualize the entire prostate gland with ultrasound waves. It gives us information about the actual size of the prostate gland and whether or not there are suspicious areas or gland distortions caused by a possible cancer.

Most importantly, the ultrasound focuses the biopsies more accurately on areas that may be suspicious for cancer.

The prostate ultrasound is a recent advance that has helped to dramatically improve the urologist's ability to detect cancer in an early, curable stage. In the days of my residency training, we blindly used our finger tip to direct biopsies of the prostate. This was fine at the time, because it was all we had. Many cancers were missed, simply because the technique—even in the best of hands—was relatively crude. Now with ultrasound guidance, we can detect even tiny abnormalities and direct the biopsies right to them.

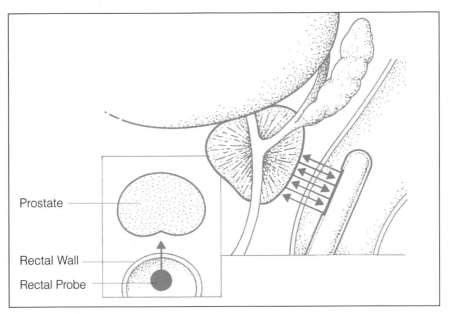

PROSTATE ULTRASOUND: Prostate ultrasound is performed by placing an ultra-sound probe in the rectum, just behind the prostate. Sound waves are bounced into and off of the prostate and surrounding tissues and reflected back to the probe. Closeness of the probe to the prostate itself allows for good visualization of the internal architecture.

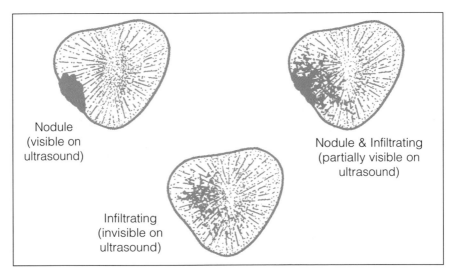

CANCER ON ULTRASOUND: Prostate ultrasound is best when trying to see large nodular cancers. Infiltrating prostate cancer that is evenly spread throughout the tissue may not be clearly visible on ultrasound. Cancers that are a combination of both may appear to be much smaller than their actual size.

How is a prostate ultrasound done?

A lubricated ultrasound probe is gently inserted into the rectum. Sound waves are emitted from the end of the probe. They bounce off the prostate and are detected by the probe. These sound waves bouncing off different tissues are transformed into a picture. This allows your doctor to see the entire prostate.

Does the ultrasound of the prostate hurt?

It is very uncomfortable initially when the probe is inserted into the rectum. For some men, it can be painful, especially if they have a scarred or very tight rectal sphincter muscle. Men who have had hemorrhoids repaired in the past may have scarring that can prevent placement of the probe. This pain is only momentary, lasting just a few seconds. To make it more comfortable, I use an anesthetic lubricating jelly and try to massage the sphincter to relax, then slip the probe in gently.

Afterwards, most men say the procedure wasn't as bad as they had expected, although it clearly is not something they want to do again unless necessary.

Can I just have an ultrasound, or do I really need biopsies as well?

The ultrasound alone is not as precise as we would like it to be. Although it may show us definite areas of concern, about 20% of the time cancer can be present but not visualized on the ultrasound. This may reflect the machine's quality, a technical problem or a lack of experience by the doctor reviewing the scan.

Sometimes the type of prostate cancer can't be seen on the ultrasound scan. Whatever the reason, it is considered standard practice to do at least a series of random biopsies even if the ultrasound appears normal. I like to look at the ultrasound as a scope on a rifle—it lets you focus on your target, but it doesn't capture your information.

> **Author's Note:** *I saw a patient who was being cared for by a urologist and was concerned about cancer because of an irregularity on his prostate exam and a mildly elevated PSA. Once a year he saw this urologist who performed a routine ultrasound without any biopsies.*
>
> *Each time no ultrasound abnormalities were noted. The urologist therefore assumed nothing was wrong and sent him home, with instructions to come back in one year.*
>
> *After several years of this, I saw the patient for what had become a very high PSA and a very hard, abnormal prostate. We went ahead with an ultrasound and biopsy. The ultrasound was still normal, but the biopsies all came back with a very aggressive cancer. Subsequent testing showed the cancer had spread to his bones. The lesson: A normal ultrasound alone means nothing.*

What if I had an ultrasound and I was told nothing was seen, but no biopsies were done?

It depends on the level of suspicion. If the PSA is elevated and/or there are definite abnormalities on the exam, then I would still want tissue samples. I would feel very uncomfortable assuming that a normal ultrasound means no cancer.

Does it make a difference who does the ultrasound evaluation?

The ultrasound is most often done by the urologist at the time of the prostate biopsies. There are some institutions

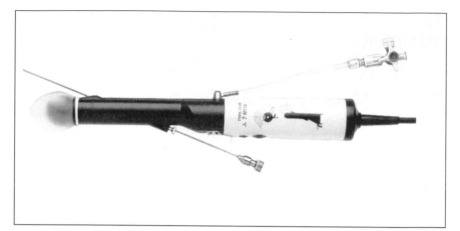

PHOTOGRAPH OF ULTRASOUND PROBE: *This probe accurately directs sound waves into the prostate. The reflection (bouncing back) of the sound waves, depending on the different tissues, creates a picture of the entire prostate gland. Most probes allow the biopsies to be done directly through the probe, under ultrasound guidance. This allows for a quick and accurate sampling of the prostate. Photo courtesy of B and K Medical.*

where a radiologist may do the ultrasound portion of the study. Before I could afford to buy a machine for the office, I had my patients meet me at a local hospital to do the study. There, because of hospital policy, a radiologist was in attendance and oversaw the ultrasound component of the study. In this setting, the ultrasound procedure was actually done by a technician, and I simply did the biopsies.

Why aren't all prostate ultrasounds done at the hospital?

Many are, but most are done in the urologist's office. In my situation, I found that it took too much time for me to drive to the hospital, get the patient ready, wait for the usual hospital paperwork and delays, do the ultrasound and then get back to the office. Now I do these in my office. I can see patients during the setup portion and continue to see patients immediately afterwards. In other words, having the equipment in the office allows me to be much more efficient in the use of my time.

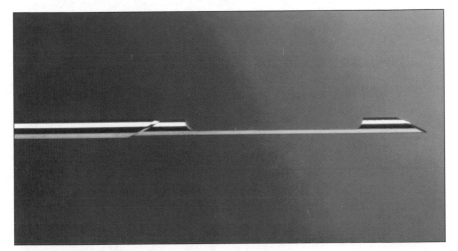

BIOPSY NEEDLE: *New biopsy needles are small and very precise in removing tiny slivers of prostate tissue for microscopic analysis. This is a highly magnified view of a needle which is only 1.2mm in diameter. Closed needle enters tissue. Sheath slides open and closes onto a sample of tissue and the needle is withdrawn.*

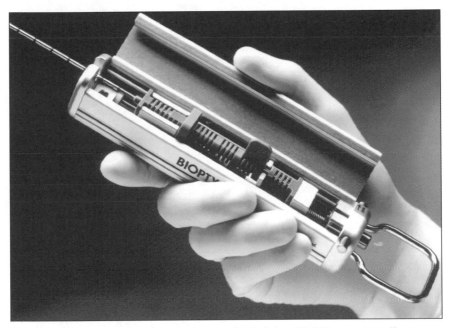

PHOTOGRAPH OF BIOPSY GUN: *Spring-loaded, hand-held biopsy gun allows very rapid and accurate removal of prostate biopsies in just a few thousands of a second. Photos courtesy of C.R. Bard, Inc.*

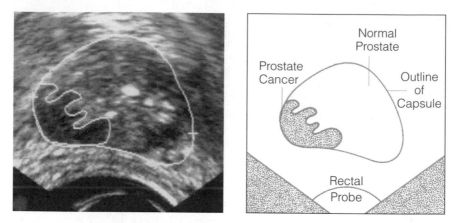

ULTRASOUND IMAGE: Ultrasound image at left is actually a continuous picture, with still photographs taken to document the findings. Here the cancer is seen outlined as an irregular area of darkness. Biopsies confirmed this to be a rather aggressive prostate cancer. Diagram at right clarifies what is shown on ultrasound image.

In addition, I can check a urine sample to make sure you haven't developed an infection. The cost is substantially less than if done at a hospital.

Do I have to worry that I'm being told to have a biopsy that I really don't need?

No. It is fairly standard to do an ultrasound with biopsies if there is either an abnormal exam or an elevated PSA.

If both are normal, then there is no reason to have an ultrasound and biopsy. Using this technique to screen for a hidden cancer when digital rectal exam and PSA levels are normal is not effective and may perhaps be doing a bit too much.

Is there any radiation exposure with ultrasound?

No, ultrasound uses harmless sound waves to generate a picture on the screen. Different tissues reflect sound waves differently, creating a picture of the inside of the body.

What does the probe do?

The probe not only emits sound waves in a certain

pattern but also receives reflected waves. The waves then are visible on the machine, forming the picture we see on the monitor.

Aren't there other ways to ultrasound the prostate than through the rectum?

Scanning through the abdomen doesn't provide the clear picture or allow for biopsies. Scanning the abdomen would allow for evaluation of the bladder, but not the prostate because of its location down behind the pubic bone.

Another less acceptable option is a urethral probe to look at the prostate. This would be like a catheter, placed up your penis. Again, it doesn't provide as good a result as the rectal probe.

What exactly is a prostate biopsy?

In a biopsy of the prostate, multiple tiny sliver-like pieces of tissue are obtained for microscopic analysis to ascertain if cancer is present. These pieces are obtained through a long but very thin needle, specially designed to open inside the prostate, take the sample and then close.

Originally these tissue samples were all taken by hand without anesthesia, which was a slow and painful process. I was lucky if the patient would allow me to obtain more than a few samples. I would often take men to surgery and under a general anesthetic, with the patient asleep, perform the necessary biopsies.

Then several years ago a high-speed "biopsy gun" from Scandinavia was introduced, which allows biopsies to be done with a much smaller needle. Each biopsy can take just a few thousands of a second.

For most men, biopsies can be done as an outpatient office procedure without anesthesia and with usually only temporary discomfort. Now we can get a good representative sampling of the entire gland with minimal trauma to the gland.

What is a transrectal biopsy?

For a *transrectal* biopsy, the needle is inserted into the prostate through the rectal wall. The rectal wall is thin, so it is possible to place the needle more accurately and with less injury to other tissues. Because of its simplicity and accuracy, this is by far the most common technique used.

What is a transperineal biopsy?

Another uncommon technique is to do what is called *transperineal* biopsies. Instead of putting the needle through the rectal wall, the skin under the scrotum is numbed with a local anesthetic. The biopsies are then performed through this tissue, with less risk for infection.

This procedure is much less accurate and requires the needle to be placed through a more sensitive area of the body. Some urologists still do this, although they numb the skin with a little local anesthetic. This allows them to obtain as many samples of tissue as they want without pain. Today, the gold standard remains the transrectal biopsies done at the time of the ultrasound.

Are there any other methods of obtaining prostate tissue for biopsy?

For a few years, urologists tried simple aspiration where tissue was sucked up into a syringe through a very thin needle. But with the development of the biopsy gun, this technique has become very rare. It is much easier to analyze actual cores of tissue than small cluster cells.

Do I need sedation to relax me for the biopsies?

No. The procedure takes just a few minutes, and for most men it isn't so unpleasant that sedation is needed. I wonder if the risks of sedation are worse than those of the biopsy.

Will I need a ride home?

Although it is not necessary, I usually ask that you have

a ride home arranged just in case you are uncomfortable. Y
may be sore and distracted by the discomfort, so it is best if
someone else can drive you home safely.

Can I play golf or tennis the next day?

Yes, there should be no real limits on your activity the
following day.

How soon can I drink alcohol after the biopsy?

I ask that you hold off on alcohol for a few days until
all the antibiotics you were provided have been taken. This is
to prevent any potential interaction between alcohol and
drugs. In addition, alcohol can sometimes increase the risks
for urination difficulties after a biopsy.

How many biopsies need to be done?

Studies show there should probably be at least six separate biopsies at the time of the procedure to get an adequate
sampling of the gland. Some experts now call for additional
biopsies of deeper areas in the gland, where some cancers can
be present and occasionally missed.

If specific areas of concern are seen or if there is a
definite nodule found on exam, then biopsies should also
be directed to these spots. Sometimes, finger-guided biopsies will be done as well as ultrasound-guided. The average
number is between six and eight, although some urologists
do more.

Does having a biopsy allow the cancer to spread?

No, there is no evidence that cancer spreads simply
because of the biopsy. Though it might seem like doing a
biopsy could release cancer cells into the system, it appears
that this does not happen.

What are the risks of a prostate biopsy?

The main risks are severe bleeding and infection. These

are quite rare, occurring in less than 1 in 100 men. But it is important to be aware so that if you have any problem afterward, you'll be able to notify your doctor and take appropriate steps to prevent serious problems.

How likely will there be bleeding afterwards?

Some bleeding after prostate biopsies is very common. This is because the needle passes through the rectal wall and into the prostate gland, which can be surrounded by many veins. This is why I tell my patients before and after that they should expect to see some blood in the urine, semen and with bowel movements, on and off, sometimes up to a few weeks.

Occasionally, blood can be seen in the semen for a few months after prostate biopsy. This is expected and should not cause you to worry. We only are concerned if the bleeding is heavy and prolonged, as it can lead to difficulty urinating, requiring placement of a catheter or rarely surgery under anesthesia to find the bleeding spot.

If there is blood in the semen, does that mean cancer cells are present?

No. Blood in the semen is a direct result of taking tiny slices of tissue with the biopsy needle. Occasionally there will be bleeding into the seminal vesicles or into the prostate. When these glands then secrete the fluid during ejaculation, blood may be seen. There is no relationship between blood in the semen and whether or not cancer is present.

How can a biopsy cause an infection?

Infection can occur because of the introduction of a needle through the rectal wall into the prostate gland. With appropriate antibiotic preparation and antibiotics afterwards, infection is very rare. Rarely, tiny amounts of germs can be taken into the gland and can result in the development of an infection of the prostate and urinary tract.

Even more uncommon is an infection in the blood-stream, with high fevers and shaking chills, called *sepsis*. This can be quite serious and needs urgent medical attention! If you develop high fevers, you most likely will need hospital-ization and powerful antibiotics. You must not delay contact-ing your doctor or going to the nearest emergency room.

How common are these risks?

Fortunately, these serious side effects are quite rare. Most men are surprised just how well they did. I call my patients within a day or two to see how they are doing. Most say they are doing fine without any complaints.

What can be done to minimize the risk for bleeding?

To lower the chances for bleeding, we usually ask you to stop taking aspirin and aspirin-containing products for seven to ten days before the biopsy. You also should stop tak-ing ibuprofen, Advil®, Motrin® and other non-Tylenol® pain and anti-inflammatory medications three days before a biopsy. If you are unsure what you should or shouldn't take, ask your doctor. Also see anti-inflammatory list on page 175.

Why won't my doctor do the biopsies if I'm taking aspirin?

Aspirin keeps normal clotting mechanisms from work-ing. It blocks the blood product called *platelets* from func-tioning and from stopping bleeding. This means you can have an increased risk of bleeding.

How long in advance do I have to stop taking aspirin before the biopsies are done?

I ask my patients not to take aspirin for 10 days before biopsies. If there is a good reason to stay on aspirin, I will do biopsies if the patient is off aspirin for five days—with the understanding of rare but possible increased bleeding risk.

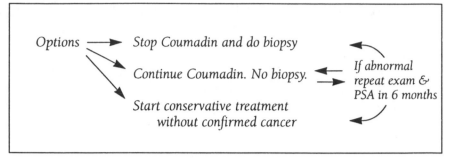

SUSPICIOUS EXAM WITH ELEVATED PSA—PATIENT ON COUMADIN BLOOD THINNER

Why won't my doctor do a biopsy if I'm on Coumadin blood thinner?

Coumadin® acts to thin the blood so it won't clot and stop bleeding. If you cut or scrape yourself while taking Coumadin, you will bleed much more than if you were not on the blood thinner.

If I were to biopsy the prostate of a patient on Coumadin, there would be an increased risk of severe bleeding. This can be quite significant and even require hospitalization or surgery to control.

If you need a biopsy, you will need to be taken off Coumadin by your cardiologist and/or primary-care doctor. I prefer to get permission from all your doctors before I ask you to stop important medications such as Coumadin.

What options do I have if I'm on Coumadin and have an abnormal prostate exam or PSA?

You could stop the Coumadin and have the biopsies, or you may want to repeat the PSA and exam in six months. If there is not a dramatic change in the PSA or exam, you might be able to avoid a biopsy and the risks of stopping the blood thinner.

What is done to stop the bleeding during a biopsy?

Under anesthesia, the urologist would perform a cystoscopy and cauterize any bleeding spots if blood were seen in the urine. If severe rectal bleeding was observed (which I have never seen), then that source of bleeding would have to be located and cauterized.

Can anything be done to stop the bleeding without surgery?

In the vast majority of biopsies, the bleeding will stop on its own. To help this along, I ask you to drink lots of fluids and to avoid strenuous activity. You should avoid sex or becoming constipated. Both can prolong any bleeding.

What can I do to prevent infection?

To reduce the risks for infection, we first make sure you do not have an infection when we do the biopsy. We check the urine for bacteria or white blood cells, the cells your body uses to fight infection. We also give you antibiotics to take by mouth before the biopsy and for several days afterwards. Many urologists will also give you an injection at the time of the biopsy to be sure that antibiotics are at a peak level in the tissues and bloodstream.

Are there any other problems that can develop?

Very rarely, one can have some swelling of the gland and have difficulty urinating. This can result in urinary retention. You would be totally unable to urinate and your bladder would continue to fill and fill. This is very painful. It requires placement of a small rubber tube, called a *catheter*, to allow urine to drain out. How long it stays in depends on a number of factors, including how much urine is in your bladder when the catheter is placed.

Can I become impotent after a prostate biopsy?

This is very rare. I did a biopsy on a retired doctor several years ago, and he related that he had a problem with impotence for several months following the study. I am at a loss to explain how this could happen. I suppose swelling and inflammation alongside the prostate where the nerves travel could temporarily cause a problem. It would be quite rare to have enough significant inflammation and swelling on both sides to impact on erections.

After a biopsy some patients have expressed concerns and fears about ejaculation, pain and bleeding that could potentially impact on erections from a psychological point of view.

Do the ultrasound and biopsy hurt?

Not most people. It is quite uncomfortable to have the ultrasound probe placed, and the biopsies do sting a bit. Each biopsy feels similar to a rubber band being snapped against the skin, just inside the rectum. Usually the first few biopsies are tolerated well. It becomes more uncomfortable and even a little painful with the last few biopsies. Some men describe a cramping sensation that usually passes in a few minutes. I am always surprised when most patients say afterward that it wasn't as bad as they had anticipated.

What if my doctor just wants to do a finger-guided biopsy without the ultrasound?

Sometimes if a small nodule is present or if a substantial portion of the prostate feels like cancer, I might choose to pass on the ultrasound. Occasionally I will do the biopsy away from my office, so the only way to do a quick biopsy is finger-guided. In general, though, I prefer to do my biopsies with ultrasound guidance.

Who usually does the ultrasound-guided biopsies?

In most situations, this is done by the urologist. Occasionally a radiologist can participate or even do the biopsies.

Who looks at the tissue samples?

The cores of prostate tissue are sent off to be prepared

and analyzed by a pathologist, who will look at the tissue under a high-power microscope to see if malignant cells are present. Often, the cells will actually be seen by several pathologists, who must all agree before a report is issued. If there are any questions, the tissue can be sent to another group of outside pathologists who may have more extensive experience. Because of the number of pathologists who look at the tissues, mistakes are extremely rare.

How long does it take to get biopsy results back?

On average, it takes about 48 hours for most labs to get results to my office. Some pathologists can have results back in 24 hours, while others may take three, four or more days to process the specimens and generate a report. If the pathologist is out of town at an outside lab, then extra delays are common. Some outside labs, though, will process specimens and fax or call the result back to the office. Weekends and holidays slow down everything.

Can the doctor select the pathologist he prefers?

With so many patients belonging to an HMO or other health plan today, we really have less and less control over who we send specimens to for analysis. Many of the larger insurance plans and HMOs have contracted a particular laboratory (often to the low bidder) for all pathology work, including blood-test results as well as biopsies. For Medicare patients and some insurance plans, the doctor can still choose the pathologist.

Is there a chance that someone else's specimens will get mixed up with mine in the lab?

Extraordinary measures are taken to be sure that what the urologist sends to the lab is accurately identified. I'm not aware of any such mix-up occurring with prostate biopsy specimens in all my years of practice or in conversation with urologists from around the country.

Should I have tissue specimens sent off for a second opinion?

If you and your doctor really don't have a lot of trust in the pathologist, this is always an option. The glass slides that have the tiny slivers of tissue can be sent anywhere in the world, but it may cost you several hundred dollars that might not be covered by your insurance plan. If you have any doubts or questions, talk to your urologist. Sometimes the pathologist will have additional questions and will ask your urologist for permission to send the tissues out for additional opinions.

If the biopsies return showing no cancer, does that mean I don't have to worry?

No. The pathologist can only look at those bits of tissue he is given to analyze. If a cancer is present, but simply missed by the biopsy, then naturally the report will come back negative, showing no cancer. This is called *sampling error*. There is no way one can safely and accurately biopsy every part of the prostate without removing the entire gland. Remember, the pathologist can only describe and evaluate what he is given. From that analysis, we try to project what is left behind.

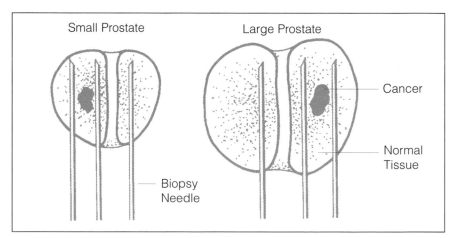

SAMPLING ERROR: Occurs when cancer is present but missed by the biopsies. It is easier to miss a cancer in a large prostate.

If I have had a biopsy that shows no cancer, what are the odds cancer is present but was simply missed by the biopsies?

A relatively small percentage—about 15%—of men with a negative biopsy still have cancer of the prostate and may need repeat biopsies and close, regular follow-up. Unfortunately, there is no way to know which patients are the 15%. We need to follow everyone who has an abnormal exam and an elevated PSA with a negative biopsy.

What if the report isn't sure there is cancer?

Sometimes pathologists don't have enough tissue to give a definitive answer. We don't want them to guess. When this happens, the pathologist will often recommend that you follow up with your urologist in two to three months and possibly repeat the biopsies.

What actually is written on the biopsy report?

The prostate biopsy report is how the pathologist relays to doctors what is seen under the microscope in the tissue taken from the prostate biopsies. The big question is whether or not cancer is seen. If it is identified, how much and what grade of cancer is reported. Is it invasive into surrounding tissues or is it just a little speck? From this report, we try to get the true clinical picture. We take into account the PSA level, past PSA levels, the exam, symptoms and so on to ascertain what the situation is and what treatment options are best.

The pathologist usually describes what is seen with the naked eye. The cancer can be described as extensive, invasive or no mention at all of volume of cancer seen. Some specialists think this is important, but I still see occasional patients who had very tiny specks of cancer on the biopsy, only to have a rather large amount of cancer found when the entire prostate gland is removed.

In a most recent example, the entire gland was filled with cancer, from right to left, front to back, and yet the biopsy showed only a small speck of low-grade cancer. This suggests that the volume of cancer seen on the biopsy may not be an accurate predictor of the actual volume of cancer in the prostate. This is an area of continued debate among specialists.

Should the treatment I select be based on how much cancer is seen in the biopsies?

Some doctors have gone so far as to decide what treatments, if any, should be recommended based on the volume of cancer seen on the biopsies. The biopsies are randomly sampled, very small slivers of tissue from a walnut-sized or larger gland. In the same way that looking at a few still pictures can't explain the plot of a movie, so too I believe that biopsies can not be used as an accurate predictor of cancer volume.

What will the prostate biopsies cost?

This depends a great deal on where the specimens are processed. If the pathologist who performs the analysis is in a big city, it can cost quite a bit more than if the laboratory is in a smaller, more rural area. Also, the number of specimens sent out will partially determine the cost. The cost can range from about $150 up to several hundred dollars or even more.

What does it cost to have a prostate ultrasound with biopsies?

It can cost from $300 to $1,500, depending on where the study is done (hospitals are more expensive) and who is involved. If a radiologist participates with the urologist, costs can be higher. As with most medical services, big cities and both coasts tend to cost more.

Why does it cost so much?

You are being charged for use of ultrasound equipment, which can cost up to $100,000. You also pay for the disposable biopsy needle, a $1,500 biopsy gun, the urologist's time, skill and expertise in interpreting the ultrasound pictures, and the knowledge where to direct the biopsies.

8

No Cancer is Found

A prostate biopsy may have a negative result (show no cancer), but there is always a chance the biopsy could have missed a cancer present in the prostate gland. Depending on how concerned your doctor is, you should probably have a repeat rectal exam and PSA blood test in four to six months.

What is sampling error?

When cancer is actually present, but the biopsies do not find it, we call that *sampling error*. This happens because the needles missed sampling the cancer within the prostate! This detection error occurs about 15% of the time. Because of the possibility of sampling error, we can only say that we do not find any cancer in the biopsied tissue. We can't completely rule out the possibility of cancer. Consequently, it is essential you continue to see your urologist regularly.

Does a negative biopsy mean I don't have cancer?

No. It only tells us that no cancer was seen in the tissue analyzed.

Does the repeat biopsy, the second or third time around, ever show cancer?

Yes, occasionally it does. The more biopsies you have that are normal, the less likely that additional biopsies will show anything.

Should I have repeated biopsies?

This depends on the level of suspicion and the trend of PSA levels over time. If the biopsies return as "normal" with no cancer seen, and your doctor is very suspicious that there may be cancer present, he may want to repeat the biopsies in a few months. He may believe there is a good chance cancer is in the prostate but that it was missed with previous biopsies. If your exam continues to change, or if the PSA level continues to rise, then he may also want to repeat the biopsies.

The first round of biopsies will detect 85% of cancers. If you go back for a second pass, there is only a 15% chance of detecting a cancer. Only rarely do we need to do more than two sets of biopsies. The most I have ever done to a patient is five separate sets of biopsies, over a two-year period. That patient had an abnormal prostate nodule, and his PSA level was not increasing. We ultimately did find cancer, which was treated successfully.

How should I be monitored after the biopsies if all comes back fine?

It depends on your age and the level of concern by you and your doctor. Most often, I recommend a recheck of the PSA level in about four to six months. If the PSA level is about the same, then I would repeat it six months later. If it is still unchanged, then probably a repeat level every six or 12 months would be fine.

What if they find PIN on the biopsies?

PIN stands for *prostatic intraductal neoplasia*. This term is used by many pathologists to describe suspicious abnormal areas seen on biopsied tissue. Other pathologists use the term *dysplasia*. They mean the same thing. These areas are not cancer, but they are not normal either.

PIN may represent a premalignant, or precancerous change. If given enough time, these areas may eventually develop into a cancer. PIN may also be found adjacent to cancer, suggesting that the biopsies were very close but just missed hitting a cancer in the prostate.

My doctor told me I have PIN 2. Is that important?

The pathologist can take PIN a step further and grade these areas as PIN 1, PIN 2 or PIN 3. Grade 1 is low grade and of minimal concern. Grade 3, on the other hand, is often associated with prostate cancer. Grade 2 is somewhere in the middle.

Normal Cells	PIN 1	PIN 2	PIN 3	Cancer Cells

PIN CONTINUUM: Normal cells can turn into very low-grade changes called PIN 1, which can continue to progress and ultimately become PIN 3, a suspicious premalignant change. Ultimately, they will turn into cancer. Finding PIN 3 on a biopsy raises serious concerns about cancer adjacent to the tissue biopsied, requiring close follow-up and probably repeat biopsies.

What should I do if I have PIN identified on biopsies?

If you have PIN on a biopsy, especially if it is PIN 2 or 3, then you should at least be followed more closely with exams and PSA tests, about every four months. At the slightest hint that the PSA is going up or the exam is changing, repeat biopsies are a good idea. If I am really suspicious, I will often repeat biopsies six to eight weeks after the original biopsies. This allows time for swelling and inflammation to heal.

If I have PIN 3, why can't I just go ahead and have surgery or radiation?

Even though this is often related to cancers, I believe that PIN 3 itself is not a threat. Therefore, it would be inappropriate and too aggressive for me to treat you just for PIN 3. If we identify a true cancer, then we can talk about curative treatment options.

9

Cancer is Detected on Biopsy

When cancer is detected in biopsied tissue, the challenge then is to make an educated guess about how much cancer is left behind in the prostate. This is done by judging from the few tiny bits of tissue that we've examined. Your urologist must look at the big picture, taking into account the PSA, trends in the PSA levels over time, how suspicious the exam is and any other signs or symptoms.

Will the cancer kill me?

Probably not. This is not a time to panic—it's a time to gather information. Whether or not this cancer will be significant and impact on the quality or length of your life depends on a number of factors. Further tests may be necessary to help your doctor decide if this cancer is a threat and how best to respond.

What happens next?

With this information, your doctor will decide which additional tests and studies are needed. This will depend on your age, health, PSA results and the specifics of the biopsy tests. Then you and your doctor can discuss the treatment options and decide what to do next.

Does the amount of cancer in the biopsies tell us how much cancer is in the prostate?

This is an area of debate. Many researchers do suggest that the amount of cancer in biopsied tissue may be an accurate reflection of the volume of cancer in the prostate gland.

In my experience, there is usually *more* cancer in the prostate than we would guess from the biopsy report. We know this from looking at specimens removed during surgery and comparing them to the presurgery biopsy results. A critical concern is just how much cancer is really present, or what is the tumor volume.

What is tumor volume?

Tumor volume is the term used to describe how much cancer is present in the prostate. The more there is, the more concerned we become. We usually refer to tumor volume in cubic centimeters.

Tumor volume is initially estimated based on the examination, PSA level, ultrasound and biopsy results. The only accurate way to measure tumor volume is after the prostate is removed and the pathologist can measure the size of the cancer.

Why is tumor volume important?

Tumor volume is an important factor in determining the prognosis and options available for managing prostate cancer. The larger the cancer, the more aggressive it usually is. This means risks are greater that it has started to grow outside the prostate.

10

The Grade of Cancer

To describe the degree of a cancer's malignancy, we refer to its *grade*, which is a standardized measurement. As with most cancers that can occur elsewhere in the body, there are various grades of prostate cancer.

Some cancers are very aggressive, with the cells looking nothing like original tissues. These are called *high-grade*, or *poorly differentiated*. Other cells may resemble normal cells except for a few key points. These are called *low-grade*, or *well-differentiated*. Some more middle-of-the-road cells are called *intermediate*, or *moderately differentiated*.

Does the "grade" mean the same thing to all doctors?
Most pathologists and urologists use a special grading scale to help make prostate-cancer evaluation more standardized. This way, two doctors across the country can talk about a patient and both will understand the grade of cancer in question. This also allows for a standardized approach to evaluating and treating patients around the world.

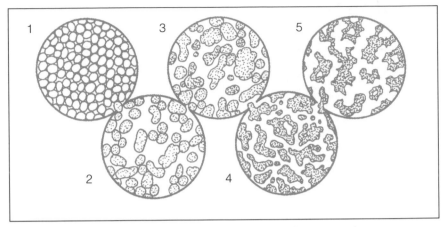

GRADE OF CANCER / GLEASON SCORE: The Gleason grading system is a standardized method of determining the grade of cancer. This technique utilizes cell shape and arrangement as part of the score.

What is the "Gleason scale?"

The most common grading scale for the comparison of cancers is the Gleason scale. In this grading system named after a pathologist, cancer cells are assigned a certain point value based on well-accepted standard criteria. These criteria describe and rate the cancer cells in two ways: 1) how the cancer cells look, and 2) how they are arranged together. Each component is given a number from 2 to 5, with the sum of the two numbers being the Gleason sum. Your urologist may refer to a cancer as a "Gleason 7" or simply "a grade 5." The higher the number, the worse the cancer.

My doctor told me my cancer was "grade 1 out of 3." What does that mean?

There are a few hospitals and institutions that insist on using their own grading system. For their own reasons, they prefer the old system that was used at that institution before the Gleason system became widely used. They still rate the cancers on a 1, 2 or 3 out of 3 scale, with 1 being the best, 3 being the worst.

How do you use the Gleason grade of cancer?

Like using cancer volume and the PSA level, the grade of cancer is an important indicator. In fact, all three are related. Larger cancers and higher PSA levels usually equate to more aggressive cancer cells. Left untreated, the cancer will continue to grow. As it grows it will secrete more PSA, and the cells will become more aggressive. Like a snowball rolling downhill, the cancer grows faster and faster.

This rapid development is why it is important to learn as much as possible by using the PSA test, prostate exam, ultrasound findings and biopsy results to decide what to do and when to do it. Ideally, we can use this information to cure you of your cancer during the window of opportunity.

What is the window of opportunity?

This is the time from the point of discovery of cancer until the time when the cancer begins to spread outside the prostate (see diagram below). During this time, you have more options to choose from, including choices that are potentially curative, such as radiation and surgery. When the cancer grows outside the prostate, options available will focus on cancer *control* rather than *cure*.

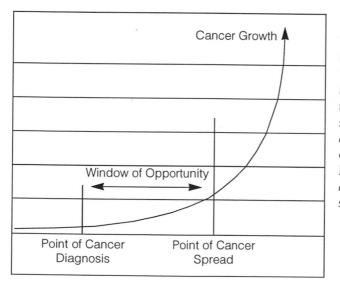

Cancer Growth

Window of Opportunity

Point of Cancer Diagnosis

Point of Cancer Spread

WINDOW OF OPPORTUNITY: The time from when the cancer is diagnosed until it has started to spread is called the window of opportunity. *During this time curative treatments should be successful.*

What is a low-grade cancer?

Low-grade prostate cancer is the least-dangerous type. Cancer cells look the most like the normal cells from which they came. They tend to be slow-growing. They can be called *well-differentiated*. On the Gleason scoring system, low-grade cells would be 2, 3 or 4. This is the cancer to have. Probably this is what the more aggressive cancers started as, before they had time to grow and enlarge.

What is a high-grade cancer?

These cancers are the least like normal prostate cells. In fact, some can be so wild and aggressive that the pathologist might not even be able to tell what the original cell type was. The pathologist may ask the doctor where he took the tissue from. These high-grade cancers are rapid-growing, very aggressive and quick to grow into surrounding tissues. They can spread into the lymph nodes and bone.

High-grade cancers are the deadly ones. These are responsible for those rare stories of very rapid growth in relatively young men, such as the entertainers Bill Bixby and Frank Zappa. These cancers tend to be large. They are called *poorly differentiated* and are graded on the Gleason scale as 8, 9 and 10.

High-grade cancers may be hard to treat and quick to come back. Some don't even respond to hormone therapy at all. The absolute worst are so wild that they may not even secrete the PSA enzyme, but this is rare.

How do the intermediate-grade cancers fit in?

As you might expect, they are somewhere in the middle, between the low-grade and high-grade cancers. Intermediate-grade cancer is what most men have when they are diagnosed with prostate cancer. These are called *moderately differentiated* and are graded as 5, 6 or 7 on the Gleason scale. These cancers can behave like either low-grade or high-grade cells, depending on how much tumor volume is present and how high the PSA is.

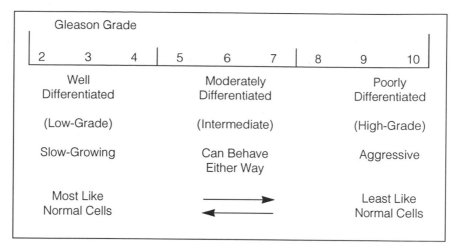

GRADE OF CANCER: *Terms to describe each grade and its behavior are compared here to the Gleason system of grading cancer cells.*

Do the cancers stay the same or do they always get worse?

Many are so slow-growing that they may very well stay about the same over many years. Some, however, may reach that unknown critical mass where the volume gets so big that they begin to grow faster and faster, becoming more aggressive and secreting more PSA into the bloodstream. It is thought that this volume of cancer may be about 1 cubic centimeter, or about the size of a cranberry. To get this big may take 20 years or more of slow and steady growth.

How often are pathologists wrong about the grade of cancer?

Not very often. There may be some minor disagreements, but in general they are usually fairly accurate.

Does it make a difference if I'm a grade 5 or 6?

The exact number really isn't important. Sometimes the pathologists will disagree about minor points, but it is important to look at the big picture. Is the cancer low-grade, high-grade or somewhere in between? This is what really makes a difference.

Does the grade of the biopsies tell what the grade of the cancer is in the prostate?

Most often, yes. We know that a surprising number of times we find that the grade of cancer in the prostate is actually *worse* than what was biopsied and analyzed by the pathologists. This is called *undergrading.* I try to take this into account when counseling patients regarding the available options.

Why is the grade of cancer important?

The grade of cancer tells us a lot about the nature of the cancer and its potential behavior. It is the high-grade cancers—scores 8, 9 and 10—that are the most aggressive and most commonly associated with rapid cell growth and death. The low-grade cancers—scores 2, 3 and 4—are least likely to cause problems. The intermediate-grade cancers—scores 5, 6 and 7—can behave either way. This type should be treated as if the potential for aggressive growth may be there.

I try to direct the treatment to the potential threat of the cancer, as suggested by the Gleason grade as well as the PSA, exam and stage. Stages are explained in Chapter 12.

Does the grade of cancer change over time?

Yes, as the cancer grows and becomes larger, it tends to become more aggressive. With prostate cancer, more advanced cancers tend to be largest, with the highest risk for spreading. This is why early detection can be so important.

What is ploidy status?

Ploidy status is a special study of the genetic material within prostate-cancer cells. This tells if the cancer cells are likely to respond to treatment. *Diploid* cancer cells are most likely to grow slowly and not spread. *Aneuploid* cells have the potential to "behave" aggressively and not respond as well to treatment. *Tetraploid* cells are somewhere in the middle.

11

Cancer Workup

After the diagnosis of prostate cancer, you and your doctor will want to discuss treatment options. But first, your doctor needs to know whether or not the cancer has spread outside the prostate. He also needs to determine the stage of the cancer.

There are several tests available to help us detect cancer outside the prostate, but none are perfect. This means there could be a cancer present outside the prostate that is too small to be detected with current testing methods.

These tests provide valuable information about your cancer that will help us determine the most appropriate treatments. Whether or not we recommend a specific test depends on how suspicious we are that the cancer has grown outside the prostate and what information each test can provide.

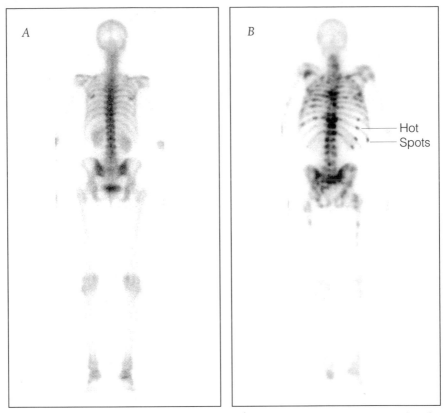

BONE SCAN: A. Normal bone scan with no "hot spots" to suggest cancer spread to the bones. B. Bone scan showing evidence of multiple areas where prostate cancer has spread and is growing in the bones.

Bone Scan

What is a bone scan?

A bone scan is a nuclear-medicine body-imaging technique where a tiny amount of radioactive substance is injected into the bloodstream. The substance circulates throughout the body and is absorbed by the bones. Certain abnormalities, including cancer, can be identified by this test.

The bone scan is the most sensitive imaging technique available today to identify cancer in the bones. The spine is the most common site outside of the pelvis for cancer growth. The scan often detects cancer in the bones long before regular X-rays can.

The bone scan doesn't show cancer, but it does show areas of rapid bone growth. Prostate cancer, when it spreads to the skeleton, typically has a classic pattern of random and variable *hot spots* that show up on the scan. This occurs frequently along the spine, ribs and skull. For reasons we're not sure of, the arms and legs seem to avoid cancer deposits.

My doctor has scheduled me for a bone scan. What is that used for?

The bone scan is used to detect whether or not the prostate cancer has spread. The spine and other bones are among the most common locations for the spread of prostate cancer.

Can anything else cause similar spots on the bone scan?

Other problems, both cancerous and noncancerous, can also show up on the scan, but often with different patterns. It is the interpretation of these results that leads the radiologist to tell whether or not the images suggest the spread of prostate cancer, or some other process, or nothing at all. The report can only say whether or not the results look like metastatic cancer.

One of the most common irregularities is an old injury or fracture of a rib. For example, back surgery or a broken shoulder will show on a bone scan the same way a cancer would show.

Arthritis of the spine and bones and Paget's disease can also show on the bone scan. That's why it's important for your urologist to know your medical history so that he and the radiologist can best interpret the bone-scan results.

Can any other X-rays be done to see if the spots are from old injuries or broken bones?

You may need a few regular X-rays to see what the areas in question look like. If I am really concerned, I might order an *MRI scan* to look at the bone itself. This special scan, discussed later in this chapter in more detail, can let us get a better look inside the bones to see if it looks like cancer or not.

How can you tell if the spot on the bone scan is or isn't cancer?

If there is an area on the scan that does not look like it is caused by cancer, the radiologist will most often ask if you have had any injuries or fractures in that area. This way we can correlate any past history with irregularities on the bone scan.

So the bone scan can't prove for sure that cancer has spread?

No, it only gives us evidence that it *probably* has spread. This information is then reviewed together with the rest of the known facts to see if these findings are worrisome.

If the bone scan doesn't show anything, does that mean there is definitely no cancer spread to the bones?

No, it only means there are no cancer spots in the skeleton large enough to be detected by the equipment. There is no question that the equipment is very sensitive, but the cancer in bone marrow has to be present long enough with enough increase in bone growth to be seen on the scan. A negative bone scan is a fairly good indication that most likely there is no spread of cancer into the bones. A tiny cluster of just a few cells won't show up on the scan. This is the limitation to the study.

Even if I had an injury many years ago, it can show up on the bone scan?

Yes, sometimes old injuries show up even 50 or more years later.

Can't we just recheck the scan in a few months and see if it is growing?

Yes, this can be done if we really aren't sure. Most often, however, I am trying to determine what treatment options to recommend. Holding off a few months is not usually a good idea.

If it is cancer, is it always prostate cancer?

It probably is. There are several cancers that can spread to the bone. Prostate cancer is the most common. It would be very uncommon for a different cancer to show up on the bone scan when you are already known to have prostate cancer with a PSA level high enough to signal that spread to the bone is possible. Some other cancers that spread to bone include cancers of the breast (yes, even in men), bladder and colon.

What if there is only one spot on the bone scan, rather than the usual pattern?

Again, the radiologist would need to look at your past history and probably want to compare the bone scan with regular X-rays to see if there is evidence of an old injury. If there are still questions or concerns, an MRI scan can help to provide detailed information. Even then, if we're really uncertain, orthopedic surgeons can biopsy the bone and take out a piece of tissue for analysis.

What is a superscan?

In the usual bone scan, the kidneys show up as the radioactive substance is excreted. When there is so much widespread metastatic cancer that the kidneys don't even show up, this is called a *superscan*. This results because all of the radioactive material is going to the bones, so none is left to be filtered out of the blood by the kidneys. It is obviously not good to have so much cancer in the bones. This suggests a poor prognosis.

What does a bone scan cost?

As with everything, much depends on where in the country you have the scan done. The range in price could be from $500 to over $1,000. Insurance and Medicare usually cover this expense, minus your deductibles.

Can I be admitted to the hospital to have this done?

No. It is an outpatient test that does not require you to be hospitalized.

Why is it always done at a hospital or in a big clinic?

The equipment used to perform the bone nuclear scan is quite large and relatively expensive, costing hundreds of thousands of dollars. It is not the kind of equipment that every doctor can have in his office. It is therefore usually based at a large facility that can generate enough testing volume to justify having it around. Some communities have the equipment brought in frequently on a large truck.

Does the bone scan hurt?

No. After the injection you wait an hour or so. Then you lie on a flat table and the imaging takes a half hour or so.

Will this hurt other organs or will I be radioactive afterward?

No. The amount of radioactivity injected is very tiny and will not hurt you or anyone else that you may be in close contact with.

If you fly cross-country a few times each year or live in a high-altitude community, you are exposed to more radiation on a yearly basis from background radiation in our atmosphere.

Will a bone scan increase my risks for getting other cancers?

No. There is no evidence to suggest that having a bone scan increases your risk of getting a new or different cancer later on.

CT Scan

What is a CT scan?

A CT scan, also called a *CAT scan*, which stands for *computerized axial tomography*, is a fairly new technique of evaluating the internal organs of the body with computerized X-ray pictures.

A machine that revolves around you generates a series of pictures. The computer then translates this information into pictures that look like cross-sections of your body. It is like being able to look at the internal organs without surgery.

X-rays are taken both *without* and then *with* dye in the veins to help identify blood vessels and internal structures. The intravenous dye can cause hives, itching and/or a warm sensation throughout your body. You usually also have to drink a "shake" of liquid dye to make the intestines visible. This liquid dye may cause diarrhea.

Rarely, a patient may experience a type of allergic reaction. If you have any allergies, you should notify the radiologist before you undergo the procedure.

For years, the CT scan was used routinely to help identify enlarged lymph nodes in the pelvis that might represent the spread of cancer. This has not turned out to be very effective. Most of the time, what we see with the CT scan doesn't provide accurate information regarding the lymph nodes. Sometimes the nodes will look fine, yet turn out to be full of cancer. Other times, the nodes will look enlarged and "suspicious" with no cancer identified by the pathologist at the time of surgery.

Most urologists no longer order a CT scan before considering a radical prostatectomy. If you are going to choose radiation therapy for your cancer, then a CT scan is needed. The CT scan is used to help calculate how much radiation to deliver and where exactly in your body to deliver it.

What if my urologist wants me to have a CT scan before surgery?

There is always a small chance that something more serious than prostate cancer can be picked up by the CT scan, such as cancer of the pancreas or liver. If that were to happen, then there would be no reason to have prostate surgery.

If you are going to have to deal with a serious and life-threatening cancer other than prostate cancer, then you don't need to undergo the potentially serious side effects of prostate-cancer surgery. This is especially true if the prostate cancer will probably not be the dominant threat to your life.

In other words, as I often tell my patients, if you are driving down a steep mountain road and your brakes are failing, don't worry about whether or not the dome light works.

Does the CT scan hurt?

No, not at all. You just lie on a flat table that slowly moves you through the inside of the CT scanner, which is like going through the middle of a giant doughnut.

Will I be exposed to a lot of radiation?

No. There is more radiation with a CT scan than with a bone scan or even a chest X-ray, but it really isn't significant as long as you're not having one frequently.

What does a CT scan cost?

The cost is quite variable but can be from $500 to $1200 or more for a scan of the abdomen and pelvis.

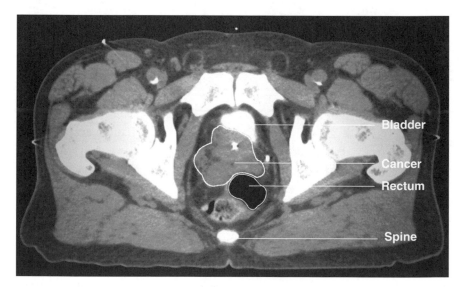

CT SCAN: Shows a very advanced and enlarged prostate cancer with local growth into base of bladder, seminal vesicles and around the front of the rectum. Cancer outline includes prostate and cancer with seminal vesicles.

MRI

What is an MRI?

MRI stands for *magnetic resonance imaging*. It creates high-quality pictures of the internal organs. Each molecule in your body has certain characteristics and responds differently to very powerful magnetic fields. When your body is exposed to these intense magnetic waves, the molecules that make up the cells give off specific amounts of energy. This energy is detected with sensitive scanners and computerized to generate a cross-section image of the inside of the body. This result is similar to the CT scan, but MRI doesn't use X-rays.

Is MRI useful for looking at prostate cancer?

Most experts don't routinely order an MRI when trying to determine the stage of prostate cancer. MRI provides excellent pictures, but it doesn't tell us any additional information about lymph nodes or surrounding tissues that we can rely on.

Why did my doctor order an MRI after a bone scan wasn't clear about a spot?

The MRI has an advantage: It is excellent for looking into the internal makeup of bones and the spinal cord and brain. Sometimes an MRI can tell us if an abnormality in the bones is cancer or something else.

Does an MRI hurt?

No. It requires you to be inside a long and narrow tube for the duration of the study. If you are claustrophobic, this may be a problem for you. Most men get over this in a few seconds, or they can take a mild relaxant before the test. The test can be quite loud, which is upsetting to some people.

What does an MRI cost?
    About $800 to $1,400.

Why does my doctor want to do an MRI with a rectal probe?
    It is believed by some experts that this special technique may provide additional information in the initial evaluation. Still controversial, it is not available in most communities.

Other Diagnostic Tests

The following tests are among those that your urologist may order while treating you for a variety of problems. They are not usually used during the course of prostate-cancer evaluation, but your urologist may be evaluating you for other urologic complaints as well.

IVP

What is an IVP?
    An IVP, short for *intravenous pyelogram*, is an X-ray frequently used by doctors to give a general view of the kidneys and ureters through which urine drains down from the kidneys into the bladder. It is really best used when looking for irregularities in drainage of urine.
    Dye is injected quickly into the veins. It is absorbed by the kidneys and excreted into the urine. X-rays detect this dye, giving a fairly good indirect way of looking at the organs and function of the urinary system.
    Kidney stones, blockage by scars or cancer, some kidney cancers and changes of the normal location of the organs are best seen by the IVP. For this reason, some doctors order an IVP as part of the initial routine evaluation.

Should I have an IVP as part of a cancer workup?

Not really. If some information is needed about the kidneys or ureters, many times a CT scan will be done and provide more information.

What does an IVP cost?

About $250 to $400.

Lymphangiography

What is lymphangiography?

This is a fairly old and rarely used test to evaluate the lymph nodes for metastatic cancer from the prostate. Dye injected between the toes goes up through the lymph system into the lymph nodes of the pelvis. X-rays are taken, and the pictures are interpreted by a radiologist.

Originally this test was thought to show lymph nodes that contained cancer. The procedure and its interpretation are very much dependent on the skill of the operator. There is a high percentage of incorrect results. Therefore, this test is almost never used in the evaluation for metastatic disease.

What if my doctor wants to do a lymphangiogram?

I would ask what the urologist expects to learn and if this information can be obtained with other more accurate and less invasive tests. This test isn't used much today to determine the stage of prostate cancer.

Kidney Ultrasound

Is there a role for an ultrasound evaluation of my kidneys in the workup for my prostate cancer?

No. I don't order an ultrasound evaluation of the kidneys as part of the prostate-cancer evaluation.

Cystoscopy

What is a cystoscopy?

A cystoscopy (or *cysto* for short) is a procedure in which the urologist looks inside the urethra, prostate and bladder using an instrument called a *cystoscope*. This procedure is not usually part of the standard workup for prostate cancer. It is used when blood is seen in the urine, primarily when looking for bladder cancers.

Rarely, someone may have both prostate and bladder cancer. This is important to know ahead of time, because it may change your treatment options. If no blood is seen in your urine, most doctors will not perform a cystoscopy.

Should I have a cystoscopy?

Maybe. Most urologists do not routinely do a cystoscopy unless there is a reason to expect a bladder tumor, stone or other irregularity.

How likely is it that I may have something wrong with my bladder like a cancer without any warning signs?

About one out of 100 men will have an abnormality seen during a cystoscopy. I had two patients recently who developed bladder cancer several years after a radical prostatectomy. One had widespread cancer, but not invading into the bladder-wall muscle. He required several operations to remove the cancer. The other man had very aggressive high-grade bladder cancer growing through the bladder wall. We later discovered his bladder cancer had spread throughout his body.

Is bladder cancer the same as prostate cancer?

No. Bladder cancers grow from the lining of the bladder, as compared to prostate cancers, which start in the glands of the prostate. They are two separate cancers that just happen to be next to each other in adjacent organs.

Does a cystoscopy hurt?

The procedure is only minimally uncomfortable. It can be done in the urologist's office in just a few minutes. Time and again my patients have told me how scared they were before the procedure, only to be pleasantly surprised it wasn't that bad. It can be done with a flexible cystoscope, which is better tolerated but reduces the visual details slightly. The other option is the older rigid cystoscope, which causes more discomfort but provides better visualization of the bladder and prostate lining.

What does a cystoscopy cost?

The range is $150 to $400. The instrument can cost up to $8,000 or more and is very expensive to maintain and service.

Is it done in the hospital or office?

Almost all simple cystoscopies are done in the office. A cystoscopy at the time of prostate surgery could be done after you are asleep. Urologists do the cystoscopy to be sure no other serious abnormalities are in the bladder, such as an unexpected cancer or stone. Some urologists look into the bladder to see where the ureters open into the bladder in preparation for the bladder-neck reconstruction portion of prostate surgery.

What if I want sedation?

Many patients expect to receive either a pill or intravenous sedation at the time of the procedure. This is not because the cystoscopy is so painful but rather because so many patients are extremely anxious and don't understand what the procedure involves.

12

Stages of Prostate Cancer

When we talk about *how much* cancer is in a patient's body and exactly *where* it is located, we are referring to the *stage of the cancer*.

The stage describes whether the cancer is small and confined to the prostate or large with spread to any other tissues or organ, such as the bones.

How is the stage determined?

The stage is determined by information from the biopsies (whether or not the cancer is on both sides of the prostate), the PSA level, the exam and any additional tests and studies that may be done to help determine the stage.

What does the stage tell us about long-term results?

Basically, the more cancer that is in your body, the more potential for spread and the less effective the treatments are likely to be. Likewise, the more aggressive the cancers are, as judged by the grade of the biopsy, the more likely the cancer will spread.

Stages of Prostate Cancer

Stage A   Cancer found incidentally or because of
            elevated PSA

Stage B   Cancer found because of abnormal digital rectal
            exam; cancer confined to prostate

Stage C   Cancer spread to tissues outside of prostate

Stage D   Cancer spread to lymph nodes or bone

Therefore, the worse the stage, the less optimistic we can honestly be about long-term results and survival. Some physicians would consider a worse stage as reason to hold off on aggressive treatments, because the treatments probably won't be effective. Others argue that if there is an aggressive cancer, it is best approached with an aggressive treatment if there is any chance of a successful therapy.

What are the stages of prostate cancer?

The classic system uses Stages A, B, C and D. We initially use a clinical stage to describe the cancers. That means we use whatever we know to tell us where we think the cancer is located, based on clinical tests and results of biopsies. We only have accurate information when the prostate has been removed and the pathology results are available.

Is it better to have one stage than another?

Definitely yes. It is always much better to have a small-volume, low-grade tumor than a larger, high-grade cancer. The smaller it is, the less likely it will be able to spread.

What do the different stages mean?

Stage A is when the cancer is found incidentally at surgery for prostate enlargement. This means that it was *not suspected* when the man went in to have his prostate hollowed out to allow him to urinate better. This finding used to happen 10 to 15% of the time, but now it is very rare. We would receive the final pathology report from the pathologist looking at the presumed nonmalignant tissue and see to our surprise that cancer was found. How much cancer and what grade it is divides Stage A further into Stage A1 and A2.

Stage A1 is usually low-grade disease in small volumes. This is most often the type of prostate cancer where we simply monitor your PSA results. Treatment is not usually required. Regular follow-up is a must, however.

Stage A2 is when the cancer is high-grade and aggressive or seen in more than a few small specks. If there is a lot of cancer, whatever the grade, it is A2. Men with Stage A2 are usually treated, because most often a significant cancer is indeed present and only a small piece was identified.

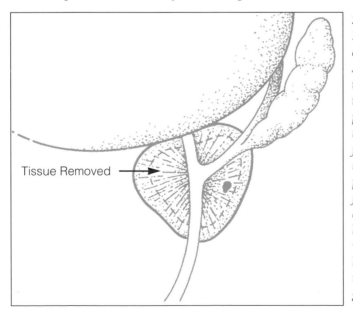

Tissue Removed →

STAGE A1: Prostate cancer is described as Stage A1 when cancer is unsuspected and identified by the pathologist in the tissue removed following a transurethral prostate resection for blockage. The cancer should have a small volume and be low-grade or intermediate-grade.

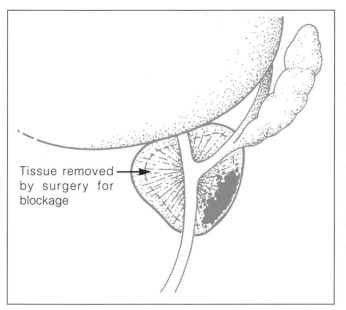

STAGE A2:
Prostate cancers
are also unsus-
pected and found
during TURP
surgery for block-
age, but have
higher-grade can-
cer and larger
volume than
Stage A1.

Tissue removed
by surgery for
blockage

Stage A3 is when a cancer is identified because of an elevated PSA alone. Most often these cancers are substantial.

Stage B is when the cancer is detected because of an irregularity or nodule found on the prostate exam. Usually the cancer is relatively small and most often confined to the prostate. This is further divided into two categories.

Stage B1 is a prostate cancer located on just *one side* of the prostate.

Stage B2 is when the cancer is on *both sides* of the gland, but with no evidence of spread outside the gland or to bones or lymph nodes.

Stage C is where the cancer has started to grow *outside* of the gland, but with no spread to bones or lymph nodes. It can be seen growing into the fat that surrounds the prostate, or into the seminal vesicles or even into the base of the bladder.

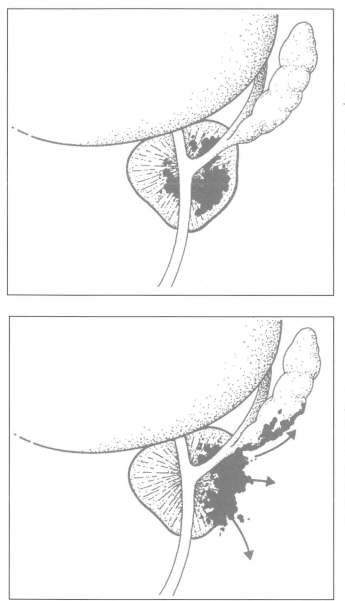

STAGE B: Cancer found by abnormal examination or elevation of the PSA that is still confined to the prostate gland is referred to as Stage B.

STAGE C: Cancer growing outside the prostate gland and into surrounding fat, tissues and adjacent organs such as the seminal vesicles.

Stage D is what we use to describe cancer that has spread either to lymph nodes or to the bones.

Stage D1 is local spread of the cancer to the lymph nodes, confined within the pelvis.

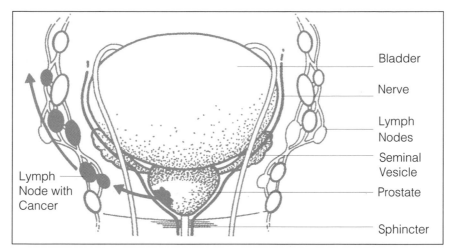

Bladder

Nerve

Lymph
Nodes

Seminal
Vesicle

Prostate

Sphincter

Lymph
Node with
Cancer

STAGE D1 PROSTATE CANCER: Prostate cancer has grown outside of the prostate and traveled into the lymphatics and the lymph nodes of the pelvis.

Stage D2 is when the cancer has started to spread to the bones.

After surgery for prostate blockage (TURP, as explained in Chapter 1), how do you know if there is any cancer left behind when you only removed the core of the prostate?

We really don't know. If cancer is found in the tissues, then we need to decide if there is any cancer remaining. I have done prostate biopsies and a repeat TURP in the past. Now, I usually recommend that we follow the PSA levels if the amount of cancer is very small. If the amount is significant, then I recommend a more aggressive treatment for what we assume is cancer still remaining.

But my doctor said I was a "T2N0M0." Is that a different way of describing the stage of my cancer?

Your doctor is using the TNM grading system. This is an international system to replace the old A, B, C, D staging system. The TNM system is thought to be more accurate. It gives doctors worldwide a more standardized way of discussing and understanding the stage of a specific cancer case.

What does the T, N and M stand for?

T—describes the cancer itself, with different numbers explaining how large the cancer is. N—stands for nodes and tells us if the cancer has spread to the lymph nodes. M—tells if the cancer has spread, or become metastatic.

Which system is better?

The TNM system is becoming more and more accepted around the world. Technically, it provides more specific information that everyone can use. This new system is slowly being adopted.

13

Options for Treatment

Men who have been diagnosed with prostate cancer have five categories of treatment from which to choose. Each category may include several options. Each choice has definite pros and cons. The patient should carefully think through each one to see which is most appropriate for his particular situation.

It is imposible to decide what treatment is best for you based on the clinical stage of cancer alone. So many factors that cannot be addressed here must enter into your decision regarding treatment.

Each patient should look at what the risks are up front and what the long-term risks and benefits are. The more risks he takes today, the more potential for the best long-term results. Why is this so? Because in general, the more aggressive the treatment, the better the chances are for cure. And it is the aggressive treatments that have more risks to the patient.

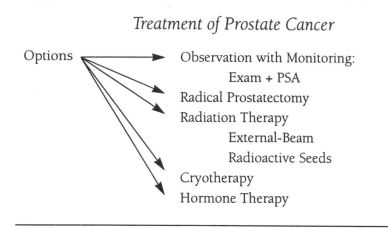

Treatment of Prostate Cancer

Options ⟶ Observation with Monitoring:
Exam + PSA
Radical Prostatectomy
Radiation Therapy
External-Beam
Radioactive Seeds
Cryotherapy
Hormone Therapy

The five basic treatment options are:
1. Simple observation with monitoring of PSA levels.
2. Radical prostatectomy (abdominal or perineal).
3. Radiation therapy (external-beam or radioactive seeds).
4. Cryotherapy may also be an option.
5. Hormone therapy (monthly hormone injections or removal of the testicles).

Which options fit into which stage classification of prostate cancer?

Stage A1   disease is where there is a small volume of low-grade cancer. The main treatment choices are between simple observation with close and regular follow-up vs. one of the "curative" options, such as radical prostatectomy or radiation therapy. (Radiation therapy is discussed in detail in Chapter 18 and 19; radical prostatectomy in Chapter 21 and 22.)

I look at the general health and age of the patient and try to get a feeling for how comfortable he is with no treatment. The large majority of men in this category will not die of their cancer even if nothing is done.

However, if you are young enough, in your 50s or early 60s, then you may live long enough for a small cancer to continue growing. It might possibly lead to your death. Up to 15% of men who live long enough will die of the cancer if left untreated.

I routinely encourage my younger patients with prostate cancer to consider radical prostatectomy as the best long-term treatment. If they are not a candidate for surgery or choose not to have a prostatectomy, then radiation may be an effective second choice. Older men can decide for no treatment and monitoring of the PSA level.

Stage A2 is a different situation altogether. When a high-grade and aggressive cancer is found in the tissue removed during a TURP, we know it is likely that there is still a significant amount of cancer remaining in the prostate. In this case, aggressive treatment is warranted.

Men under 70 should consider having a radical prostatectomy. Men over 70 should have radiation. Only very old men in poor health should have no treatment or hormone therapy with close monitoring of their PSA level.

Stage A3 is becoming more and more common, as men with normal exams are being found to have cancer simply because of an elevated PSA level. These may or may not be cured by aggressive therapy. In this category, your age, general health, PSA level and the grade of the cancer may play a role in helping you decide what treatment is best.

Stage B1 is the ideal stage for curative treatment. If you have a normal life expectancy of seven to ten years or more, then radical prostatectomy is probably the best first choice.

The cancer should be confined to the prostate, which means removing the gland would be curative. Radiation will also work well for B1 disease. Observation may be acceptable if you are elderly and ill (by this, I mean in your 80s and with a limited life expectancy of just a few years).

Hormone therapy (discussed in detail in Chapter 24) may be a reasonable option if you are older and not very healthy but want to have something done.

Stage B2 is also best treated with aggressive surgery or radiation. Some of these cancers will actually turn out to be Stage C, with some of the cancer outside the gland. A small percentage of Stage B2 patients may even have cancer in a lymph node.

If there is any question and you are young, I usually opt for surgery. If you are older (70 or older), then I may lean more toward radiation. Because of the tumor volume seen in B2 disease, I am reluctant to just observe these cases, because if you live long enough, sooner or later these cancers will progress.

Again, hormone therapy may be reasonable if your life expectancy is less than five years and you want something done.

Stage C My philosophy for men in their mid-60s and older is that these cancers are best managed with radiation therapy, because the radiation treatments often are focused on enough surrounding tissue to include any local spread. Stage C cancers are often quite large, which can make the radiation less effective. Occasionally the cancer cells may have already spread beyond the area treated by radiation.

I tend to give the benefit of the doubt to men in their early 60s and younger with Stage C disease. I may suggest a prostatectomy on the possible chance that it may turn out to be curative. Simple observation is risky if you will live more than a few years. Hormone therapy may be fine for those with a limited expected life span of five years or less.

Stage D is the stage when the cancer has spread outside the prostate, either into the lymph nodes, bone marrow or elsewhere. This stage is further divided into whether or not the cancer is confined within the pelvis (Stage D1), or outside the pelvis, as with bone involvement (Stage D2).

Treatment for this stage depends on the usual factors: age, general health and expected survival. I personally believe in early treatment of advanced disease, rather than waiting until the cancer is causing symptoms, as some physicians propose. Early treatment prolongs the time until the cancer comes back and may prolong the life span to some degree.

At this point we know of no effective cure for prostate cancer that has spread to the bones or lymph nodes. The treatment goal with Stage D is to control the cancer by eliminating the male hormones from the body. This is done because the male hormone stimulates the growth and spread of prostate cancer.

A small minority of experts believe in *debulking*, or eliminating a lot of the cancer with radical surgery, even if it clearly is advanced and even in elderly patients. They believe that if the total volume of cancer in the body can be reduced dramatically by removing the prostate, the remaining small volume of cancer can be better controlled with hormone therapy. This philosophy is not widely accepted. It may even be considered by some experts to be overly aggressive.

My philosophy is that for men in their early 60s or younger, if they are found to have a small volume of cancer in the lymph nodes at the time of node dissection, I may go ahead with the prostatectomy. My thinking is that the small speck or two in the nodes may be all there is, and perhaps there will be a chance for good long-term results. If instead we go ahead with hormone therapy, then there is no chance that long-term results will be good.

In other words, for very young men, I tend to be aggressive in treatment with the thought that they have more to lose. There really is no second place in this race. In older men, I tend to be more conservative, because the risks of the treatment go up with advancing age. It is important to consider the quality of life as well as longevity.

What should I do if the biopsies show very aggressive cancer, but the bone scan and CT scan are normal?

This is a topic of recent discussion among experts. With a high-grade cancer that is poorly differentiated (rapid-growing), the odds are fairly good that the cancer has already spread outside the prostate, probably into the pelvic lymph nodes.

For very young, healthy men there is a chance that surgery may make a significant difference. There may be no evidence of spread of the cancer. In this situation, I would probably recommend the evaluation of the lymph nodes for cancer. If no cancer is seen, then I would go ahead with radical prostatectomy.

14

Who Decides?
Your Role in Decision-Making

This area of discussion is usually left out when you are talking to your doctor. The usual scenario is for you to meet with your doctor so he can tell you what is wrong and what he wants you to do. The review of options is brief and often biased towards whatever he has decided is best for you.

Some physicians leave very little time for your questions and concerns. Rarely are you encouraged to think about the various choices. A decision is almost always expected right then and there. In fact, sometimes the doctor goes so far as to schedule your treatment or surgery before you even arrive for your appointment.

Who decides what treatment option is best for me?

You should take an active role in deciding what you will do. For many years, the doctor "knew" what was best for his or her patients. He would proceed with the treatment without really involving the patient in decision-making. Fortunately, those days are long gone.

Today, the doctor's role is to gather information necessary to provide a fair and reasonable review of the facts and present a detailed discussion of the treatment options. He or she should encourage you and your family to get involved in decisions. After all, you are the one who has to live with the outcome of the choice.

Ultimately, you are the one who must decide which treatment is best for you. You can give this power to your doctor, but again this is your choice. Whether or not your doctor agrees with your decision, he should still be there to work with you and support you and your right to decide.

I must admit that for me, as a physician, it is sometimes very frustrating and upsetting to see a patient make what I believe to be a wrong decision. This is often the case when someone makes a final decision before he has all the facts, often after talking to a friend, relative or neighbor. In my experience, this is the absolute worst thing you can do.

You will hear lots of advice, horror stories and disasters, often having nothing to do with your specific situation. I can't tell you the number of times I've heard men refuse to consider radiation for prostate cancer because of what it did to Aunt Nellie after breast-cancer treatment 35 years ago.

Remember, the person giving the advice is basing his recommendations on his own personal experience, or hearsay—not on actual statistics and the facts particular to your case. These "friends" usually know little if anything about your specific problem.

But what if my doctor doesn't agree with my decision?

Be wary of the doctor who quickly "shoots down" what you believe to be a reasonable and acceptable option. Some doctors just aren't used to having someone disagree with them. There may even be other factors that enter into your doctor's recommendations.

Author's Note: *I recently had a 62-year-old man diagnosed with what I believed to be a potentially significant prostate cancer. After a complete consultation and initial moves toward a radical prostatectomy, he expressed an interest in trying a strict "anticancer" diet. This diet would best be described as nontraditional. I felt it probably wasn't going to work. But after a full discussion with my patient, I realized he truly understood what he was doing, and he knew the associated risks and possibility for cancer progression. I agreed to work with him and support his decision. Only time will tell if he made the right choice.*

If your doctor will not respect your decision, you may need to find a doctor who will. However, in all fairness, there should be an open line of communication between you and your doctor. Be sure to listen to his or her reasons for not supporting you—they may be very legitimate.

Why do some doctors become angry when I tell them what I think is best for me?

Many patients make decisions based on incomplete or inaccurate information. This is extremely frustrating for the physician. I know one cancer specialist who jokingly says that all of his patients are "cancer specialists." After all, they read a magazine article or a book! And who is he but a mere board-certified, highly trained, well-respected medical oncologist.

Although this is a bit sarcastic, it illustrates an important point. No matter what you've read (yes, even this book), your urologist is the one who deals with prostate cancer every day of every year. Your doctor's recommendations are based on personal experience and the combined experiences of urologists around the world. Use this book and other resources as a basis for increasing your understanding by opening the doors of communication.

How can I take back control?

By reading this book, you have taken the first step to understanding what we know and more importantly what we don't know about prostate cancer. Medicine is still more an art than a science. We treat individuals based on statistics gained from the cases of large numbers of men.

What works for many may not work for you. Ask questions and expect answers. Write them down. Talk to specialists. Talk to nurses. And when you have as much information as you need to make a decision, go ahead and choose the treatment you feel is best for you.

Don't let information-gathering become your goal. And don't fall into the trap of deciding what you want the doctor to say and then start doctor-shopping until you locate one who will tell you what you want to hear. Listen to the answers. Listen to the questions your doctor asks you.

It is very important not to let the process carry you away. I've known a few patients who took up to six months to talk with expert after expert. Within a short time they were so confused and overwhelmed that they needed a break to just let it all sink in. Only then could they make a decision.

Should I try to keep my own medical records?

Yes. This is an excellent way to keep control over what is happening to you, in all aspects of your health. As you get PSA test results, record them on a log. See Appendix for a

Prostate Cancer Evaluation Log. Keep copies of your X-ray records, consultations, etc. If something concerns you, then you have records for reference. Most doctors will be more than happy to send copies of your test results as they come in.

Having records is also helpful when you travel. If you have a medical emergency in a different city, doctors treating you will know your past medical history and be able to take better care of you. I suggest that you take *copies* of your notes. If you should lose them, you still have the originals.

15

Your Wife's Role

In the excitement that follows after your doctor tells you that you have prostate cancer, it is not uncommon to forget to involve your wife or "significant other" in the long process of cancer evaluation, treatment, recovery and life after treatment.

Whatever path you choose, and no matter what happens, she will have to watch it from the sidelines. She will have to live with the results of your decision. It is sometimes easier to be the patient, because you are aware of what is happening every step of the way.

From the first time you step into the urologist's office, through all the long appointments, tests, waiting for results, long discussions about treatment options and controversies, treatment, recovery period and then as you begin your life again—hopefully cured—there is your wife. She is often quietly sitting and waiting, trying to stay calm and support you while an almost overwhelming fear of the unknown silently torments her.

As women usually do so well in times of crisis, she

may serve as the stable pillar for the family during your illness. Or she may function as your 24-hour nurse when problems develop at home.

Think about this for a minute, and then take the time to include your wife in the decision-making. Ask her what she thinks. What sounds good. What scares her. Bring her with you to talk with your doctors. Take her to the hospital for preoperative testing. Ask her to get on the phone when your doctor calls to talk. Give her an opportunity to ask questions. Let her know that her input is important and listen to what she has to say. In these situations, women tend to have more common sense and a better ability to step back and look at the total picture.

I remember one time I was in the middle of discussing treatment options with a patient and his wife. The gentleman stood up and interrupted our discussion to declare that if there was a chance he might lose erections, he would just rather die. His wife calmly looked over and reminded him that although their occasional sexual relations were nice, she would much rather have him around several more years than be a lonely widow simply because of an occasional lost erection. He stopped, thought about this and then asked me to continue talking about the options. As it turned out, he opted for surgery and had excellent pathology results. He did eventually regain the ability to have erections.

Prostate cancer is a very personal disease. From the moment your cancer is identified until it is either cured or controlled, it is essential that you include your wife. Share your feelings with her. Openly discuss your fears and concerns with her about how this might affect your sexual relationship. You may find that this issue is less important to her than making you well and extending your life. I am always happy to see my patients bring their wives or companions with them to their appointments.

What if my wife doesn't want to be involved?

There are some wives who don't feel it is their place to participate in the discussions and decision-making regarding their husband's care. All we can do is try to include her. Even if she won't participate in the discussion, she should be encouraged to at least listen so she can better understand what is happening to you.

16

Family & Friends

If you are diagnosed with prostate cancer, the decision to tell your friends and neighbors about it depends on your relationship with them.

I have words of caution about human nature and cancer. For reasons that no one really understands, whenever the word gets out that you've been diagnosed with prostate cancer, anyone who has had prostate cancer or knows of someone with cancer will seek you out to tell you their horror stories.

Even if it's not prostate cancer, they still feel it is their responsibility to tell you how miserable Aunt Nellie was after she had radiation for breast cancer 30 years ago, or how many problems Cousin George had with his prostate cancer. I have very strong opinions about these "friendly" bits of advice. I have witnessed the damage they can do to my own patients' morale. I strongly encourage you to consider some things about you and your situation before heeding the advice of friends and family.

Treatments for any disease in the past have nothing to do with treatments today. Even radical prostatectomy, which is surgery to remove the cancerous prostate gland and surrounding tissues, has been much improved. The operation men are having today has significantly better results and is much better tolerated than the same operation seven years ago.

Recently, a patient who had a radical prostatectomy was discharged after only 48 hours in the hospital. A few years ago that same patient would have just been getting out of the intensive care unit, with another seven to ten days of hospitalization ahead of him.

Should I tell my colleagues at work about my prostate cancer?

This depends on your relationship with your co-workers and your position at work. Unfortunately, there are still many misconceptions about all forms of cancer. Telling your co-workers will definitely have some effect. It could potentially jeopardize a contract, a promotion or your day-to-day working relationships because of people's fears and confusion.

On the other hand, sharing such personal information could help you identify others who have been through similar experiences. It could also make your co-workers aware of the importance of early detection for themselves. Only you can decide if it is best to discuss your cancer with co-workers.

Several of my best friends were treated for cancer with good results. Why shouldn't I do what they did?

Every cancer is different, every person is unique and each patient will respond differently to each treatment. Whatever worked for someone else probably won't have relevance in your case.

I continue to hear from patients who decided on a particular treatment because of the experience of someone they know. Sometimes it was even for a different cancer, in a different area of the body, a long time ago. All I ask my patients to do is to delay making decisions until we talk and discuss all of the options and risks specific to them. Don't let preconceived notions based on hearsay and the experience of others prevent you from making the right decision for you.

Even when talking specifically about prostate cancer, several themes keep coming up when talking with others who have had treatment. Most often the stage of the cancer is different, so Cousin George's cancer may have been more or less advanced. Even if the cancers were exactly the same stage and grade, one must also consider your health, age, family history and other social and medical factors that may make your best option for treatment different.

Everyone responds differently to treatments. The best thing that you can do when talking to others is to take everything they say with a grain of salt, smile, thank them for their concern and file the information away. If it is of concern, then ask your urologist about what you heard and discuss whether it is a valid concern for you.

17

Observing & Waiting

Observation, also called *watchful waiting, deferred therapy* or *active surveillance*, is a reasonable option for many men in selected situations as long as each understands exactly what he is choosing to do. Observation does not mean we are going to forget about the cancer and hope nothing happens. Rather, this is an active program of regularly monitoring the cancer.

I have had a number of patients who incorrectly believed that because they opted for watchful waiting, they could just go home and never return for follow-up exams or PSA blood test. It is reported that up to 30% of men with prostate cancer choose observation. But this is not without potentially serious risks. In the right patients, observation may very well be the best option. For others, it can be quite dangerous.

What exactly does "observation" mean?
Observation means to choose no treatment for the cancer.

Why would I choose to do nothing?

When you choose this option, you and your doctors are agreeing, in essence, that you will probably die of something else before the prostate cancer can grow and cause problems or kill you. This obviously depends on a number of factors including your age, your general health, family longevity and a little luck. This treatment is best if the cancer is a low-grade, small-volume disease. It is these little cancers that are the least aggressive and the slowest-growing.

What is the problem with observation?

The concern with this strategy is our frequent underestimation of the grade and volume of cancer. In other words, there are times when we think the cancer is small and of little threat, when in reality it is larger and more aggressive. If you select observation based on incorrect assumptions, there is a good chance that if you live long enough, you will have to deal with an advanced and rapidly growing cancer.

Everything I have read says prostate cancer is best watched with no treatment. Is this true?

There has been quite a lot of media attention regarding this philosophy, suggesting that prostate cancer is benign and will not hurt you and for many is best left untreated. Although there is some truth to this for some patients, it unfortunately will doom many young men to an unnecessarily early death.

We know many men have prostate cancer and are never affected during their lifetime. Most don't even know they have prostate cancer. But it is believed by urologists who specialize in prostate cancer that if we detect prostate cancer because of an abnormality on exam or because the PSA level is elevated, there is most likely a significant cancer present.

If you live long enough, and if it is allowed to grow unchecked, the cancer may very well cause symptoms. It could even result in death. Even if it is slow-growing, it will gradually reach that unknown volume when it starts to grow rapidly and spread.

What are the chances I might die of prostate cancer if I choose to do nothing?

Assuming you do not have advanced or aggressive disease, 15% or more of men who do nothing will eventually develop advanced prostate cancer and die from it within the first 10 years. If you live longer than 10 years, the chances for rapid growth and spread of the cancer and death go up dramatically.

Who is a good candidate for "watchful waiting?"

The ideal person for simple observation is an elderly man in his late 70s or 80s with a limited long-term life expectancy. Likewise, men in their 60s and early 70s with other potentially life-threatening health problems should probably avoid treatment. As noted earlier, the treatment should never be worse than the disease.

The answer to the question—what's going to get you first?—is simply a guess, an odds game. On one extreme, you want to avoid unnecessary treatment. At the other end, it is always sad when someone chooses a conservative approach only to succumb later to the disease. This sometimes happens either because they lived longer than they had anticipated or because the cancer was more significant than they had assumed. If you live long enough, an untreated cancer may very well kill you.

What aspects of the cancer should encourage me to consider observation?

Observation may be a reasonable choice if:
- You have less than five years of life expectancy.
- The cancer is low-grade and well-differentiated.
- You have low PSA levels.

On rare occasions I have found a tiny amount of cancer at a TURP (prostate resection) and recommended simple monitoring of PSA levels. If you are in your 70s or 80s and generally quite ill with a number of other health problems, then the cancer can be a higher grade or stage and observation may still be a good choice. In this situation, the treatment may actually be worse than the disease.

Who should not choose observation?

Again, it depends on the specifics of the cancer and your health. If you think you will not live long enough for the untreated cancer to cause a problem, then opt for observation. But if you are young (early 70s or less), healthy and will most likely live for several years, then it would be in your best interest to choose some form of treatment. If left to grow long enough, even many small cancers can become potentially dangerous, spread and kill.

But what if my cancer is one of those that really is not significant?

Then you don't need any treatment. But be forewarned: It is difficult to decide with certainty if you are the rare man with a prostate cancer that doesn't need any treatment at all. Most often, a cancer is large enough to warrant some kind of treatment.

How will my progress be monitored?

You will need to have the PSA blood test on a regular basis. In addition, you should have periodic prostate exams, plus urinalysis to check for blood and a brief review of symptoms or concerns.

How frequently do I need to be monitored?

This depends on how concerned you and your doctor are about progression of the cancer. It is probably reasonable to check the PSA every four to six months. The longer you have a stable PSA, usually the longer you can wait between intervals of each PSA check. This is something you will decide with your doctor.

Why can't I check the PSA level more often so we can tell earlier if it starts to grow?

If you check a PSA too often, such as every month or two, you may end up getting excited over some minor but usual fluctuation from test to test.

While I am in observation, do I need a repeat prostate ultrasound or biopsy?

No. We know you have cancer and it won't just fade away. But we are hoping it will remain small and slow-growing. Having additional studies won't add any significant new information.

Should I get a repeat bone scan?

Only if the PSA level begins to climb rapidly, suggesting fast growth. Otherwise the PSA and exam should be adequate to monitor the cancer and be sure it is not growing.

What about those news reports saying most men with prostate cancer will not die of it?

This is a true but somewhat misleading statement. Autopsy studies on men who died of other causes have shown that a large part of the aging male population will have prostate cancer at the time of their death and not even know it. But this includes even tiny specks of low-grade disease, as well as those with large volumes of cancer and metastatic disease.

More important is what happens to those men who are diagnosed with a significant cancer, as determined by the PSA, exam, biopsies and ultrasound findings. If these men live long enough, the cancer will continue to grow unchecked and ultimately can spread. If there is a "significant" cancer but you are older with only a few years to live and if you are in poor health, then it is reasonable to opt for no treatment and just monitoring of the PSA.

Another factor we have to consider is how fast the cancer is growing. We call this *doubling time*. This tells us how long it takes for a set amount of cancer to double in size. Fortunately for many men, this is so slow that the cancers are seldom detected and the men live a full life, never being diagnosed or treated for prostate cancer. Because this represents the majority of men, it skews the statistics and that results in confusion. It is generally accepted that if we find a cancer, it is significant and should be treated.

What if I want treatment but my primary-care doctor and urologist want me to pursue watchful waiting?

This usually means your doctors are worried that the treatments are potentially more threat to your health than the disease. I have had a patient with multiple serious health problems who wanted radical prostatectomy. I was able to convince him to consider other options, and he finally consented to have radiation. As expected, he did well with the radiation, although he continued to have problems with his heart and even a series of strokes.

If your doctor and urologist are trying to talk you out of an aggressive treatment, then you should listen to what they are saying. If you don't understand why they are trying to convince you to avoid therapy, ask them!

What if my primary-care doctor and my urologist both want me to have surgery or radiation but I want watchful waiting?

This means just the opposite of the previous question. Here, your doctors believe the cancer is significant enough to be a threat to your life and worth taking whatever risks are involved. This might be based on the PSA, the biopsy results, your age or your general health. You may think you're old with a limited life span, when you actually are in great shape and may live a lot longer than you realize. If you are the only one leaning toward observation, I would suggest you reevaluate and perhaps seek additional opinions.

What if my primary-care doctor says I shouldn't do anything, but my urologist is recommending aggressive surgery or radiation?

This is a potentially sticky situation with no clear answer. It's difficult to know what each physician's opinions and recommendations are based on.

In my experience, this conflicting advice most often occurs because the primary-care doctor doesn't understand the potential seriousness of the cancer or the limited risks of therapy. Many doctors believe the surgery or radiation is far worse than it really is. Most often, the primary-care doctor has been influenced by the news reports that suggest prostate cancer is a benign disease. They may even consider the urologist's advice as "self-serving" or inappropriate.

Occasionally I hear of a urologist who recommends that an elderly patient with serious health problems undergo a surgical removal of the prostate or radiation therapy when the patient's life span is quite limited. I'm not sure who or what that urologist is treating. This is a situation where a second opinion can help clear up the confusion.

Whenever there is confusion or conflicting advice, I advise patients to seek an additional opinion from a urologist who deals with a large number of prostate-cancer patients.

While I'm under observation, how will we know if there is continued growth of the cancer?

Usually there will be a regular trend of increasing PSA levels over time. I prefer to have two or three PSA checks done over several months to be sure that an elevation is not just lab fluctuation. Sometimes the exam can change with a nodule becoming larger or harder.

If the cancer appears to be growing during my observation,
would I then need to have treatment?

This depends on how fast the cancer appears to be
growing and your general health. If I become worried that the
cancer is starting to act more aggressively, and if I am concerned that the growth may cause problems or ultimately kill
you, then I would recommend the start of treatment. This is
why observation is sometimes called *deferred therapy.* We
will wait and see if the cancer may be a threat to you.

If I choose watchful waiting, at what point would treatment be
started if the cancer does start to grow?

There is no exact answer to this question. In my practice, I like to look at two or three PSAs two to three months
apart, depending on how high the levels are and whether they
are increasing. A persistent elevation, with each PSA being
higher and higher over time, worries me. If the PSA and exam
suggest cancer is growing, then I would recommend you start
a treatment that is appropriate for your age and health.

At what point is it clear that something needs to be done and
that observation is not effective?

The big question (and at the same time the big problem) with watchful waiting is: What is the end point we are
waiting for? At what point do we agree that, despite our
hopes that the cancer is insignificant, it appears there are significant changes that suggest tumor progression?

Is this end point a change in the digital exam or perhaps an increase in PSA levels? How much of a PSA elevation
makes us worried? At what point along the course of elevation do we admit that observation is no longer appropriate
and consider options for treatment? Do we wait, as some suggest, until symptoms develop?

My preference would be to agree that a continually ele-
vating PSA is consistent with tumor growth, assuming there is
no urinary-tract infection, and early treatment will hopefully

result in better long-term results. That is when I would want to start treatment.

If we watch the situation and at some point there is evidence of cancer growth, will the options be different from those that existed when the cancer was first diagnosed?

We hope not. We would like to think that in the ideal situation, a healthy male who is on the borderline between treatment and watchful waiting will not go beyond the curable phase if he chooses to wait until there is early evidence of cancer progression.

However, recent studies show the best time to treat many prostate cancers is when the PSA level is 4.0 or less. If we wait until the PSA is greater than 10.0, for example, the odds that the cancer has started to spread through the wall of the prostate go up dramatically.

For many men, the treatment choices would be the same, although the odds of being successful in removing or treating all the cancer may be less.

Could the cancer actually go to the lymph nodes or the bones while it is being watched closely?

This is always a possibility. We have no way to know for sure that the cancer is remaining confined to the prostate gland. The PSA check is only a very rough estimate. The problem with waiting until there are definite signs of growth before you start treatment is that we may wait too long. Whether or not we pass that critical point when the cancer starts to spread varies from person to person. It is always possible that the cancer will spread to the surrounding tissues or to the lymph nodes or bones during this time.

If left untreated and the cancer continues to grow, how long until it causes problems?

If we had the answer, we would know who should and who shouldn't be treated and which treatment is best. This uncertainty is the dilemma of prostate cancer. Many men will not live long enough for the cancer to be a threat to them, while others may have rapid growth or live long enough to have problems because of the cancer.

Recent long-term studies show that if you live 10 years or more after diagnosis of cancer, and you have not had any treatment, your odds of dying from prostate cancer begin to increase dramatically. Even if you live only a few years and have chosen to do nothing, the cancer may cause problems. The cancer may grow, spread and require some treatment, possibly years before the 10-year point.

In general, if you have just a few years of expected survival, and the cancer is not advanced, you may want to at least consider watchful waiting.

18

Radiation ~ External-Beam Therapy

Radiation therapy is a well-established technique of killing cancer cells with one of two different types of radiation that are used to treat prostate cancer today. The most accepted is called *external-beam therapy*, also known as *teleradiotherapy*. It is considered the "gold standard." No other form of radiation treatment has been shown to be better than external-beam.

There is also *interstitial radiotherapy*, in which radioactive pellets are placed within the prostate. This technique, also known as *radioactive-seed therapy*, is discussed in the next chapter.

How does radiation work without hurting normal tissues?

Most malignant cells are less efficient in repairing radiation injury than normal cells. Therefore, most malignant tumors can be destroyed by amounts of radiation that spare normal tissues. Some normal cells do die, but the body can handle this with normal cell growth and replacement.

	External-Beam	*Radioactive Seeds*
Treatment Time	7 weeks	1-2 days
Anesthesia	No	Yes
Hospitalization	No	Yes
Fatigue	Yes	No
Pain	Not Usually	Temporary
Bleeding	Possible, Delayed	Infrequent
Incontinence	Infrequent	Infrequent
Impotence	25%-50%	25%
Bladder/Rectal Irritation	10%-15%	10%-15%
Severe Reaction (Bleeding, Fistula, Pain)	1%	1%
Long-term Effectiveness	Good Recurrences 7-10 years	Unknown, Controversial

COMPARISON OF EXTERNAL-BEAM RADIATION VERSUS RADIOACTIVE SEEDS

Can radiation hurt me?

In uncontrolled amounts, radiation can be quite dangerous and even deadly. But radiation therapists use information from your CT scans and knowledge about your particular cancer and anatomy to custom-design a pattern and dose of radiation. This approach maximizes the killing of cancer cells with minimal damage to normal tissues. This is why everything is so precisely calculated.

External-Beam Therapy (Teleradiotherapy)

What is external-beam radiation therapy?

This is the term for a specific radiation technique used to treat many types of cancers in the body. Beams of high-energy radiation are focused from outside the body (hence *external-beam*) onto the target area.

How should I decide if radiation therapy is best for me?

You will need to consult with a radiation therapist, who is a physician trained and experienced in treating cancer with radiation, including prostate cancer. At that time you will review the important facts regarding your situation to decide if you are a candidate for radiation. You will also discuss potential risks and side effects, as well as the possible benefits.

What happens to me if I choose external-beam therapy?

You will have what's called a *simulation*, where special X-rays are taken to help determine the dose and focus the radiation. Shortly thereafter, you will start your treatments based on a set schedule, usually at the same time every day, until completed.

How quickly could I start radiation treatments?

When you have decided to proceed with radiation, you should be able to have a simulation and start treatment within a few days.

What is the length of treatment?

The full course of external-beam therapy takes about six and a half to seven weeks, Monday through Friday. Because of the radiation technique and the nature of cancer-cell growth, the time it takes to complete the radiation cannot be shortened.

Occasionally, the number of treatments during each week can be reduced to three. Although this sounds easier, it actually is less effective and increases the risks for complications and side effects, because it requires higher amounts of radiation with each treatment. So, although five times a week is more of a nuisance, it really is better for you.

How much time does the radiation treatment take every day?

Radiation takes just 10 to 15 minutes each day.

Why is it given only Monday through Friday?

This schedule allows normal body cells to recover during the brief time off each weekend. This results in better killing and disabling of cancer cells gradually over time.

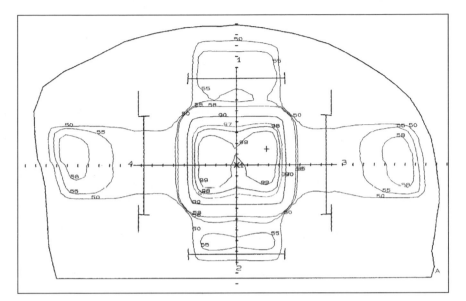

SIMULATION FOR EXTERNAL-BEAM RADIATION: *Computerized drawing of prostate from different angles, showing exact dose of radiation that will be given to the prostate and surrounding tissues in subsequent radiation therapy.*

Who actually does the radiation treatments?

Treatments are performed by radiation therapists who are specially trained to treat cancers. These physicians have completed a residency of several years in radiation therapy for cancer treatment. The doctors work closely with physicists, radiation-therapy technicians and radiation nurses to determine exactly how to treat and monitor you throughout and after the therapy.

What are the short-term results?

The main goal of radiation treatment is to control cancer growth and prevent the spread of cancer. There continues to be debate as to whether radiation kills the cancer cells or simply "stuns" them. It really doesn't make any difference so long as you live a normal life span without signs or symptoms of the cancer, even if the cancer cells are alive but inactivated.

What are the advantages of radiation therapy?

Radiation offers good treatment for the right candidate without the standard risks that go along with surgery and anesthesia. There is no risk of surgical bleeding, no hospitalization, usually no pain, no heart attacks, strokes or blood clots. I believe radiation is a very effective conservative approach.

It is ideal for the man who cannot or will not have his prostate removed, or whose health for some reason makes his surgery risk higher than that for other men. Radiation provides survival results equal to surgery for a man with a life expectancy of about seven to ten years.

External-Beam Radiation Therapy

Advantages	Disadvantages
No surgery, no anesthesia	No lymph-node analysis
No transfusion risk	Possible irritation of bladder
Less impotence than surgery	and/or rectum (10-15%)
Incontinence (less than 5%)	25% to 50% possibility of impotence
Good control of cancer	Rare risk of serious complications (1%)
	Monday through Friday for 7 weeks
	Possible local return of cancer
	in 7-10 years

What are the main side effects of radiation?

The most common side effect is fatigue in some men, which appears toward the end of treatment. There also is about a

10% to 15% risk of developing some degree of bladder and/or rectal irritation. Irritation to the bladder can cause symptoms similar to a bladder infection, such as burning with urination and the sense of urgency to urinate.

Sometimes blood in the urine can be seen after radiation. This bleeding can occur at any time after the treatment is over, even many years later. However, it is very important not to assume that any blood in the urine is from prior radiation. A complete evaluation by a urologist is necessary if blood is seen.

Some patients also experience frequent bowel movements, diarrhea and/or stomach problems.

There is a 30% to 50% risk of developing problems with erections, including total impotence, because of radiation damage to small blood vessels and the nerves responsible for erections. There is less than a 5% risk of urinary leakage, which can be serious.

What about rectal problems that can happen?

Radiation injury of the rectum or rectal wall, called *radiation proctitis*, can result in irritative symptoms, including pain, frequency of bowel movements and urgency to have bowel movements. It can result in bleeding, chronic burning and rectal discharge or leakage.

What can be done to treat the diarrhea and stomach upset?

Most often these symptoms are only mild to moderate and will go away on their own. Occasionally the radiation doses or frequency of treatments must be temporarily reduced until your symptoms start to go away. Certain medications can often be given to help with symptoms.

What can be done to treat bladder irritation?

Sometimes your doctor will prescribe medications to help to relax the bladder and make it less irritable. These include Levsinex™, Ditropan™, Urispas™ and pyridium for burning on urination.

Are these side effects permanent?

Side effects usually go away with completion of treatments. Although it is uncommon, some men do complain of continued problems with urinating, with bowel movements or with lingering fatigue.

Why have I heard about hair loss with radiation?

Hair loss occurs only in the area that is receiving the largest dose of radiation. Radiation of the prostate does not cause hair on your head to fall out. You might see some changes in the hair on your lower abdomen or pubic area, but that's about it.

Is there a problem with nausea during radiation?

This is associated with radiation to the abdomen or chest, where the intestines and stomach might be radiated. With radiation of the prostate, because of its location, nausea is almost unheard-of as a side effect.

Does radiation therapy hurt?

No, there is no pain associated with the radiation therapy itself. The exception would be if the radiation injures or irritates the bladder or rectum.

Does radiation burn the skin?

No. Modern radiation techniques do not result in skin damage that was common with radiation treatments decades ago.

Does it make a difference how soon radiation is begun?

As long as treatment begins within a reasonable time after the cancer is diagnosed, there should be no serious problems. A delay of a month or two or even a little more shouldn't affect long-term results in most men. Your long-term results depend more on your particular situation, plus the grade and stage of the cancer. I usually counsel my patients to proceed relatively soon with the treatment, just to be sure.

What are the disadvantages of radiation therapy?

The length of treatment—nearly two months—can be a real nuisance and inconvenience for many men. If you live close to a radiation-treatment facility, then it may be convenient. Unfortunately, some men may live a long distance from a treatment facility. Most men can't move near a facility for two months. Few have the financial resources to take off extended time from work.

Another disadvantage of radiation is that it offers no opportunity to evaluate the lymph nodes to be sure the treatment is indeed the correct one. If we are suspicious that cancer has spread to the lymph nodes, then there may be a role for laparoscopic lymph-node dissection before starting radiation. (See Chapter 20).

Perhaps the most controversial disadvantage is that radiation therapy is believed by many experts to be not as effective as radical surgery for patients who may have a life expectancy longer than seven to ten years.

What are the long-term results of external-beam therapy?

Most experts will agree that radiation therapy is as effective as radical prostatectomy for the first seven to ten years after treatment. There is some debate about long-term treatment results.

Will radiation therapy cure me?

The goal of radiation treatment is to kill cancer cells. Studies show that sometimes the cancer can still be present but inactive, or dormant, even years after treatment. The presence of cancer shouldn't be a problem as long as it stays inactive. This is why you always need to be monitored with the PSA blood test following radiation. Then, if the PSA level starts to go up, suggesting that cancer is growing again, the doctors can get a better idea of how fast it is growing and if there's any reason for concern. It may grow so slowly after radiation that it will never be a problem to you during your lifetime. Many doctors believe the radiation may not "cure you," but it may "stun" the cancer and render it inactive.

How does radiation cause urine leakage, or incontinence?

Radiation can cause scarring and injury to the muscle fibers located at the bladder neck or at the sphincter. This is usually a slow process and for most men being treated is relatively uncommon.

When these tissues are damaged, they can no longer "snug up" tightly. Also, the muscles of the bladder neck can't squeeze effectively at the sphincter. This means that some urine may leak out. This is most commonly associated with coughing, sneezing or straining. Some men are aware of leakage only when they stand up, run or move around. Although this leakage is permanent, most men don't regard it as a significant problem.

Can radiation cause impotence?

Yes. One-third to one-half of men treated by radiation may experience some degree of decreased erections. The condition may take a year or more to manifest itself, but impotence is a definite problem that cannot be avoided for some men. It may cause decreased erections by damaging the small blood vessels or nerves that play a role in erections.

Will radiation affect my desire for sex?

As the treatments go on, fatigue could impact on your desire for sexual relations. Some men are reluctant to have sex during treatments because of fears regarding the cancer. Truthfully, there is no medical reason to abstain from having sex.

Over time, for some men, the ability to have an erection may diminish or even go away totally. This is not usually associated with a lack of interest, but is a physiological problem.

How soon can I go back to work?

If you are one of the few who develops some lasting fatigue, you may need to take a few weeks or more off until your strength returns. One of the advantages of radiation treatment is that many men can continue to work or participate in activities such as golf, hiking, swimming or tennis during and after the treatments. Some patients find that a daily nap enables them to carry on their normal routine.

Do I need repeat biopsies after radiation?

No. The results of a repeat biopsy would not affect my care plan for my patient, so I don't see any need to put him through an uncomfortable and unnecessary test.

What kind of follow-up will happen after my radiation treatment?

I follow my patients closely with PSA tests and prostate exams.

What can be expected to happen to the PSA level after radiation?

With prostate cancer-cell death or injury, the PSA level should drop, ideally below 1.0, over a period of several months.

What if the PSA level doesn't drop after radiation?

This usually means that there are cancer cells elsewhere in the body that were not affected by radiation.

Does it make a difference if my PSA goes down slowly after radiation therapy?

Even though it seems that it would be better for the PSA level to drop rapidly, some experts believe that the slower the PSA drops, the better the long-term results.

Options if PSA Increases After Radiation

- Repeat PSA in 3-4 months

- Possible bone scan

- Hormone therapy for presumed recurrent/metastatic disease

- Salvage prostatectomy — high risk

Is radiation therapy a good treatment for aggressive high-grade cancers?

No. Radiation therapy is less effective with aggressive cancers. It should still be considered as a treatment option, because surgery and hormone therapy are also less effective with this type of cancer.

Author's Note: *Jim K. was diagnosed with prostate cancer that was confined to the gland. He was relatively young at 66 and in excellent health. He acknowledged that radiation wasn't really the best treatment option for him. But he was the sole caretaker of his ill wife and had to be there for her every day. He felt he could neither take off the time associated with surgery nor assume any serious risks, no matter how small, that might leave his wife alone. So Jim chose radiation therapy with excellent results.*

*Can I do anything to give me better results if I have a
high-grade cancer and decide to have radiation therapy?*

For some men, eliminating the male hormones in
addition to radiation therapy actually provides better long-
term results.

Can radiation actually stimulate the cancer's growth?

No, but it can sometimes appear to do so. If there is
cancer outside the field of radiation, it would continue to
grow and lead to problems or even death.

*Will the large size of my prostate influence how well the
radiation will work?*

Yes. Radiation works less effectively for very large
prostates. This is why many radiation therapists try to shrink
the gland with monthly hormone injections before radiation
to make the radiation more effective.

Should I have surgery to make the prostate smaller?

No. Surgery simply to reduce the prostate size before
radiation doesn't work well and may even increase the potential complications. In addition, you would be taking on additional risks of surgery and anesthesia.

*If I get hormone therapy before radiation, should I stay
on it afterward?*

For patients with very aggressive cancer, this may be a
reasonable option. Some early studies suggest this may be
very effective, when compared to radiation alone. This combination is ideal for the patient for whom radiation by itself will
most likely fail to control the cancer.

*If I have difficulty urinating, will radiation make it
easier or worse?*

There is usually some initial swelling of the prostate
with radiation treatment. If the enlargement is already causing

problems, then radiation can actually make it worse before it gets better.

What can happen if I don't have a TURP and I go ahead with radiation?

The worst complication is that your prostate will swell so much that it will prevent urine from leaving the bladder, and you will end up in urinary retention, requiring placement of a catheter to allow urine drainage from your bladder. Use of a catheter can increase the risk of scar formation in the urethra, and it can delay the radiation treatments.

Most radiation therapists do not like to give treatments when a catheter is in place, because of increased risk for scars and strictures in the urethra.

What can be done to take care of the urinary retention?

One solution is to stop the radiation and perform a TURP to relieve the blockage. But doing that may lead to increased symptoms and more risk for scarring and injuries, not to mention reduced effectiveness of the radiation.

Another approach is to teach you how to catheterize yourself every four to six hours to keep your bladder empty, rather than leaving the catheter in all of the time.

How soon after a TURP can I start the radiation?

Usually within four to six weeks you can begin radiation, when the irritation and inflammation of surgery have subsided for the most part. Stay in touch with your doctors to decide when starting radiation therapy is appropriate.

Does having a TURP increase my risk for developing side effects from radiation?

Yes, it does. Your risks for urinary incontinence, urinary frequency, urgency, burning and getting up at night to urinate all go up with radiation after a TURP. This is why it is best to avoid a TURP unless it is necessary.

Will there be any problems if I want to take a break halfway through radiation treatments?

Yes, this could seriously reduce the effectiveness of the radiation treatments. Again, they are calculated to provide the maximum killing dose and to reach all the cancer cells in critical phases of growth during the treatment time. If you stop mid-treatment for a while, you may end up with worse long-term results. It is advisable to plan your schedule so you can complete treatments as prescribed by the radiation therapist.

Does it make a difference if my doctor wants me to have a TURP, instead of a biopsy, to look for cancer?

If you have problems urinating and potentially have cancer, do the biopsy first. If it comes back showing cancer, then you can have your prostate totally removed and solve the blockage problem. If the biopsies are all normal, then you can address the blockage with your doctors.

Are there any very serious complications with radiation?

There is a 1% chance that radiation may result in severe pain or bleeding, or the development of an abnormal connection between the bladder and rectum, called a *fistula*. If a fistula develops, it requires surgery for urine drainage to a bag (called a *urostomy*) and/or for intestinal drainage to a bag (called a *colostomy*).

Can I have radiation if I am taking Coumadin blood thinner?

Yes, although you will need to discuss this with your doctors. Delayed bleeding from the bladder is one potential side effect that may not happen for a few years after radiation. If your doctor tells you not to stop taking Coumadin for any reason, then you should probably not have radiation. This is a point on which all experts do not agree. If you are considering radiation and you take Coumadin, talk to your radiation therapist.

How long after radiation can I expect to see blood in my urine?

This can occur right away but is most common a year or more after treatments are over. The blood can be just little clots, a discoloration of urine or it could be quite severe.

Why is there bleeding so long after the radiation is over?

Bleeding is from radiation damage to the normal tissues and blood vessels in the bladder and prostate. This makes the blood vessels very fragile and easily broken. Sometimes the bleeding starts after straining to have a bowel movement. Sometimes bleeding starts for no reason.

How is the bleeding treated?

First your doctors need to evaluate where the bleeding is coming from. Although it is common to see blood in the urine after radiation, blood can also come from a bladder cancer, kidney tumor, kidney stone or a number of other problems. Sometimes you may need to have an IVP X-ray (intravenous pyleogram, explained in Chapter 11) to look at the kidneys, ureters and bladder. You almost always will need a cystoscopy (also explained in Chapter 11) and possibly biopsies. If the bleeding is severe, the urologist may want to cauterize (burn with electricity) the bleeding spots, usually under anesthesia.

Treatment for Bleeding After Radiation

Do Nothing
Cauterize
Alum Irrigations into Bladder
Formaldehyde
Hyperbaric Oxygen
Surgery

What if it continues to bleed?

Other treatment choices include rinsing a solution of alum through a catheter into the bladder. This solution uses the same substance as a styptic pencil that stops bleeding on your face after shaving. Some doctors put a formaldehyde solution into the bladder under anesthesia to chemically seal all blood vessels.

Some studies have shown that briefly putting the patient inside a hyperbaric oxygen tank every day for a week or two can also reduce and prevent future bleeding. Unfortunately, these special oxygen devices are usually found only in large medical centers. Hyperbaric oxygen is increased oxygen under pressure, as used for deep-sea divers suffering from the bends.

For severe bleeding the radiologist can block off blood vessels that are bleeding. In rare cases, an incision may be needed under anesthesia for the surgeon to identify and tie off arteries that take blood to the bladder. Even more dramatic would be the removal of the bladder entirely, though this is very rare.

19

Radiation ~ Radioactive Seed Implants

Also called *interstitial radiotherapy* or *brachytherapy*, radioactive seeds were very popular several years ago as an alternative therapy for prostate cancer. These little rice-sized "pellets" are specially treated to be radioactive. They work by giving off a certain amount of radioactivity around them.

Ideally, when these seeds are placed inside the prostate gland, radioactivity from the seeds will kill the adjacent cancer cells without the problems and lengthy treatment time that are experienced with external-beam radiation.

Originally, *gold* or *iodine* seeds were placed surgically, but men continued to have problems with return and spread of the cancer. Newer seeds were developed, including *iridium* and most recently *palladium*. Each of these types of radioactive pellets gives off a known amount of radiation. With this information, radiation therapists can calculate how many seeds are needed and at what dose to adequately treat a specific prostate cancer.

Why are there different types of radioactive pellets?

Each seed type has definite advantages and disadvantages with its use. For example, palladium seeds are the most powerful and may offer the best ability to kill surrounding cancer cells. But the very same energy level that may make them good could very well lead to radiation irritation of the rectum or bladder. Though rare, the radiation given off from the seeds can irritate or burn sensitive tissues of the rectal wall, which lies adjacent to the prostate. In very rare cases, this can lead to a colostomy.

Why isn't everyone with prostate cancer being treated with interstitial therapy?

It is generally believed by experts who have access to all treatment options that the seeds provide a definite advantage as far as the treatment time required. But they also believe seeds may ultimately fail to give as good long-term results as external-beam radiation therapy. Some experts go so far as to label radioactive seeds as *ineffective,* while others consider them an acceptable option. It would be nice to have a quick, easy, low-risk treatment such as radioactive seeds, but for many men the old tried-and-true external-beam therapy provides better long-term survival.

How are the seeds put in place?

Most often they are inserted through the skin of the perineum, just under the scrotum and in front of the anus. Because this procedure would otherwise be painful, it is done under anesthesia. This could be either *general* anesthesia where you are put to sleep, or a *spinal* or *epidural* anesthesia where just the area below the waist is anesthetized.

Each seed is carefully placed in a predetermined location and depth as follows: A specially designed plastic template steers the pre-loaded needles into correct position. The position is confirmed with rectal ultrasound that is used to monitor the seed placement. The radioactive seeds are then inserted through these needles.

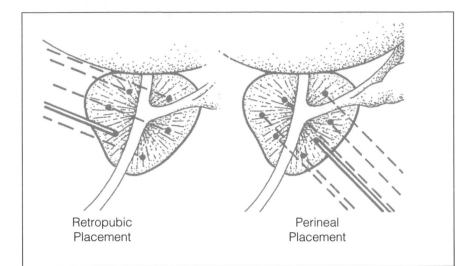

Retropubic
Placement

Perineal
Placement

PLACEMENT OF SEEDS: Radioactive seeds are placed through needles, directly into the prostate gland.

How long will I be in the hospital for placing the seeds?

Usually no longer than overnight, if that long.

How long does it take to insert radioactive seeds?

The average time to insert the seeds, including preparation and care afterward, is about one and a half to two hours.

How long am I asleep?

You will sleep for the entire time the seeds are being inserted. You first wake up from anesthesia and become aware it is all over when you are in the recovery room, or even in your hospital room.

Does it hurt to have seeds inserted?

The seeds are inserted through tiny holes in the skin under the scrotum while you are under anesthesia. Most of your pain may be soreness or discomfort in the perineal area for a week or two.

What are the main complications and side effects of seed placement?

Most often the biggest problem has to do with irritation of the urinary tract. Symptoms include an urgency to urinate with little warning, increased need to urinate frequently, possible burning or irritation with urination and blood in the urine. In addition, some men can experience similar irritation of the rectum with pain, burning, frequency and urgency to have bowel movements. There is a chance of impotence. Other potential problems include prostate infections or urinary retention.

How are these symptoms treated?

Some medications can be prescribed to reduce these symptoms and soothe an irritated bladder or rectum. Sometimes stool softeners can help as well. Occasionally pain medication can reduce symptoms, and even steroid enemas have been used to reduce symptoms associated with irritation.

Do the symptoms start up right away?

Not always. Some men complain of increasing symptoms of bladder and/or rectal irritation even 12 to 18 months after treatments are over.

What are my risks for leaking urine after seed implantation?

If you've not had a TURP, then the odds of incontinence are very low—almost zero. If you have had a TURP, then you have about a 15% chance of urine leakage.

What else can I expect following seed placement?

Some men complain of seeing blood in their semen, called *hematospermia*. Other uncommon problems include soreness of the testicles and very rarely, pain with ejaculation.

Will there be pain with ejaculation following placement of the seeds?

Yes, there can be. This is probably temporary irritation of surrounding tissues from the needle placement of the seeds and from inflammation caused by radioactivity. It usually passes with time over several weeks.

What are the odds of becoming impotent after seed placement?

This is quoted as about 25%, but it really depends more on how good an erection you are getting before any treatments. The better your erection is before treatment, the better it will probably be after treatment. The actual rate of impotence varies from 25% to 61%.

What about evaluating the lymph nodes?

Interstitial seeds can't deliver radiation to the lymph nodes that drain the prostate. If the cancer is low-grade and the PSA level is less than 10, then it is not likely the cancer has spread. In such case, the nodes would go without evaluation or treatment. The seed technique alone is best for those men who most likely do not have cancer in the lymph nodes. If there are concerns, a laparoscopic lymph-node dissection (See Chapter 20) may be a reasonable procedure to have prior to seed treatment.

Can I have the seeds removed if there is a problem?

No. After the seeds are inserted, they have to be left in place.

Is radiation from seeds a threat to my pets, wife or friends who may be near me?

No, not at all. The dose of radiation is calculated to affect the prostate tissues immediately adjacent to the pellets.

How many seeds are placed?

This depends on the type of seeds selected and the size

of the prostate gland. The number of seeds can range from 15 to 125, with the average about 45.

How long are the seeds radioactive?

This depends on the type of seeds selected and how much radiation needs to be delivered to the prostate. Some pellets may have a long radioactive life, but they won't be as powerful as other types that may have more energy to give off in a shorter time. In general, it is safe to say the seeds are usually radioactive for weeks to months.

What is the youngest age a patient should be to consider radioactive seeds?

This would depend on a number of factors, including specifics of the cancer (grade, stage, PSA levels, exam findings, volume of disease) in addition to patient's age, health, longevity and access to other treatment choices.

Is seed therapy a good option if I do not live near a radiation facility for external-beam therapy and cannot or will not have surgery?

Yes, this would be a great choice as long as you understand that you are taking less risk up front, with the chance that the cancer may come back sooner.

Is there an age when I should consider seed therapy?

If you are a candidate for external-beam therapy, then you may also be a candidate for this technique.

Are the seeds as effective as external-beam therapy?

In the short term, five to ten years, the effectiveness may be as good. The true test of this option rests with long-term results, which are not yet known. I know of one doctor who offers both radioactive seeds and external-beam therapy. He believes the seeds are not providing as good as a result as the external-beam therapy.

Radioactive Seeds

Advantages	Disadvantages
25% to 61% impotence	Possible irritation of bladder and/or rectum
Quick recovery	Lymph nodes not evaluated or treated
Short hospitalization	Unknown long-term results
No transfusions	Expensive

Do seeds ever come out on their own in the urine or semen?

Yes, frequently. These tiny seeds can work their way out into the urethra, often in the first few days or weeks.

Can the seeds cause damage to surrounding tissues?

Hopefully not. It is always possible your rectal wall could be very sensitive to the radioactive pellets that lie nearby. These pellets could cause many of the symptoms previously described with radiation proctitis.

Will I need a catheter in my bladder afterward?

Yes, you will have one for just a short time. Most men urinate without problems or a catheter the day after the seeds are inserted.

Can these seeds be used for large prostates?

In general, radioactive seeds are best for small to moderately sized prostates. If you have a very large prostate, you should consider other treatment options.

What if my doctor is concerned that the cancer may have grown outside the prostate gland itself?

Then you are not a candidate for radioactive seeds.

They are intended for those cancers confined (localized) within the prostate gland.

Can I have the seed treatment if I have had a TURP before?

Yes, but it is harder to do. The TURP is intended to reduce the blockage from an enlarged prostate by scooping out much of the tissue, leaving just a shell of tissue behind. The removal of tissue distorts and changes the normal prostate anatomy, making it more difficult to insert seeds accurately in the remaining tissue.

Can the laparoscopic lymph-node dissection be done at the same time the seeds are placed?

Both can be done together, but usually they are performed separately. If you have a lymph-node dissection, you will usually recover and go home while awaiting the final pathology evaluation and report about the lymph nodes. If there is no cancer in the lymph nodes, then you would go ahead with the seed placement.

If the cancer comes back after external-beam therapy, can I have radioactive seeds?

No. When the maximum amount of radiation has been delivered to the rectal wall just behind the prostate, no additional radiation is permitted. To insert radioactive pellets into the prostate at that stage of treatment would increase the dose to the rectal wall beyond the amount that can be safely tolerated.

Will I be radioactive after seed therapy?

No, there will be a tiny amount of radiation given off by the seeds but not enough to be a threat to anyone.

Will my urine or semen be radioactive?

No, neither will be.

Will I be a danger to my wife or kids?
No, not at all.

What if I don't like the side effects of the seeds later on?
Hopefully the side effects will gradually subside over time. There are some medications that can help control side effects if they occur. Remember, the seeds can't be removed.

When can I go back to work?
You can usually safely return to work within a few days.

When can I resume activities like golf, tennis and exercising?
You can safely resume most activities within a few days. By then, you should be feeling better.

When can I resume sexual activity after the seeds are placed?
You should abstain for about four to six weeks.

Who does seed implantation?
This is done most often by radiation therapists, but a urologist may also be involved. In some locations, the urologist may actually do the procedure and simply use the radiation therapist to help with the radiation dose calculations and preparation.

How soon will I know if the seed treatment worked?
You will have to wait several months at least, if not up to a year or more, watching the PSA test results. As long as the PSA continues to go down gradually, we feel good that cancer cells are being killed. The radiation doesn't always kill all cancer cells immediately.

20

Lymph-Node Dissection

It is common before radical prostatectomy and sometimes before radiation therapy to remove and evaluate the lymph nodes. This is done to be certain that the appropriate treatment has been chosen.

Until recently, the only way to remove the lymph nodes for analysis was through a lower abdominal incision at the time of radical prostatectomy. This method is fairly quick, safe and easy to perform. It allows the surgeon to move ahead quickly with the prostatectomy.

There is a new technique called *laparoscopic lymph-node dissection*. This allows your surgeon to evaluate the lymph nodes as a separate procedure *before* radical prostatectomy if he is highly suspicious that the cancer may have spread.

What is a laparoscopic lymph-node dissection?

Called *lap-node dissection* for short, this is a very new technique in which surgeons remove lymph nodes that drain

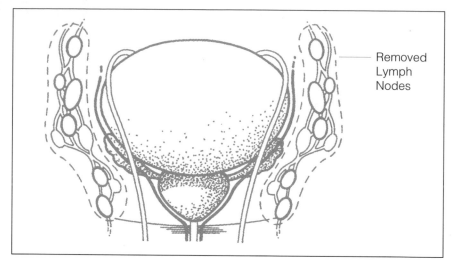

LYMPH-NODE DISSECTION: Whether by standard open surgery or laparoscopic dissection, these lymph nodes that drain from the prostate are removed and analyzed by the pathologist to see if cancer has spread.

the prostate. This is done through several tiny incisions without having to make a single large incision. Through a fiberoptic instrument called a *laparoscope*, the surgeon can see and remove lymph nodes as he views a television monitor to see what he is doing.

What is the reason to have a laparoscopic lymph-node dissection?

The laparoscopic lymph-node dissection can be done if there is reasonable suspicion that cancer has already spread to the lymph nodes from the prostate gland. This provides a minimally invasive way to evaluate the nodes without a full incision.

Should everyone have a laparoscopic lymph-node dissection before a prostatectomy?

No. In fact, many times a radical prostatectomy with a lymph-node dissection will provide the same information with less cost and risk. If your doctor explains that he will be doing a laparoscopic lymph-node dissection, ask why and how the information from this procedure will change or modify his treatment plan.

How is a laparoscopic lymph-node dissection done?

This is performed in the hospital under anesthesia. Several small incisions are made in the lower abdomen to allow placement of the laparoscopic instruments. The first one is placed into the abdominal cavity, which is then filled up with carbon-dioxide gas (CO_2). This allows easy visualization of the tissues. The lymphatic tissue and nodes are then removed and brought out through the laparoscope.

When the procedure is completed, the instruments are removed. Any remaining CO_2 is quickly reabsorbed by the body without harm. The incisions are sewn up and the patient should be ready for discharge later that day or the following morning.

The surgeon may or may not choose to proceed with a radical prostatectomy at this time. Sometimes the patient will be discharged and then brought back for the prostatectomy at a later time.

Is a laparoscopic lymph-node dissection ever done before radiation?

Yes, if there are questions that cancer may have spread into the lymph nodes. If indeed it has, then just radiating the prostate would be inadequate to control the cancer. With the information from the node dissection, your treatment can be more specific to your particular situation.

How long does the operation take?

This depends on which surgeon is doing it and how many he has done before. Assuming you are in the hands of a skilled and experienced urologist, it can take from two and a half to four hours or more, as compared to about one hour for a node dissection through an abdominal incision.

How long will I be in the hospital?

If you are having only the node dissection, you could be home that day or the next morning, assuming that all goes well.

Who does the operation?

Urologists do the majority of laparoscopic lymph-node dissections. Sometimes general surgeons or some gynecologists can play a role. Who does it depends on the experience of the local doctors.

What are the advantages of a laparoscopic lymph-node dissection over a standard operation through an incision in the abdomen?

There is a definite advantage to a laparoscopic lymph-node dissection if identification of cancer in the lymph nodes will prevent you from proceeding with a radical prostatectomy. This is because it can save you a large incision and perhaps get you out of the hospital quickly.

In other words, if there is a significant chance the cancer has spread to the lymph nodes, and you and your doctor decide this would keep you from having a prostatectomy, then a laparoscopic lymph-node dissection is probably a reasonable option.

If you are at low risk for cancer spread, meaning the PSA level is not high (10 or less) and the tumor is low or intermediate grade, then the laparoscopic lymph-node dissection probably is unnecessary. If it's not likely to show us something that will change what we do in treatment, then you probably shouldn't have this operation.

Is the laparoscopic lymph-node dissection expensive?

Yes. It can add $8,000 to $10,000 or more to the cost of a standard prostatectomy by using quite a lot of disposable and very expensive laparoscopic equipment and supplies. Plus, there are expensive operating room and anesthetic charges. If this is being done as a first stage of a two-stage operation, then there would also be the extra costs of anesthesia, the hospital, surgeon's and assistant surgeon's fees for the additional procedure.

Is there another way to take out the lymph nodes?

The routine method is to have a smaller abdominal incision with the idea that if no cancer is found in the lymph nodes, the incision could be extended and the radical prostatectomy completed. This saves the very high costs and potential complications of a laparoscopic lymph-node dissection.

Can the lymph nodes be biopsied without surgery or anesthesia?

In selected cases where we know the lymph nodes are enlarged, and if there is a high likelihood of tumor in the nodes, we can do what is called *percutaneous needle aspiration.*

This outpatient technique does not require anesthesia. A radiologist inserts a tiny needle while the patient undergoes a CT scan. He tries to *aspirate* (suck into the syringe) some of the contents of a suspicious lymph node. If it shows cancer cells, then no further surgery is necessary and you've saved yourself an operation.

However, if no cancer is seen, then it simply means no cancer cells were aspirated into the syringe. Cancer could still be present. This technique is very dependent on the skills of the interventional radiologist, a doctor who specializes in invasive procedures using X-rays.

Can the prostate be removed through laparoscopy?

No, this technique is only useful for removal of the lymph nodes at this point. Some urologists around the country are experimenting with the removal of kidneys and bladders by laparoscopy, but as yet prostates still have to be removed the old-fashioned way.

If my PSA level is low, do I still need a laparoscopic lymph-node dissection?

Probably not. If the PSA is below 10, the odds of having cancer in the lymph nodes is so incredibly small that the procedure probably is not necessary. Very low PSAs and low-grade disease have a low risk for cancer in the lymph nodes. In selected patients, the lymph nodes are not removed.

Are there certain reasons why I should not have a laparoscopic lymph-node dissection?

The most important reason not to have a laparoscopic lymph-node dissection is if the information it will provide will not change your treatment plans. If you are going to have a prostatectomy anyway, there is no reason to spend the money and assume the additional risks of a laparoscopic lymph-node dissection. Your lymph nodes can be removed at time of the prostatectomy.

From a medical point of view, if you have had multiple abdominal surgeries or infections, your risks of having a complication from the laparoscopic surgery are increased. Your doctor can discuss with you why you are a good or bad candidate for the procedure.

Is this a procedure that is routinely performed?

This depends on the approach each urologist takes toward prostate removal. Because I prefer an abdominal, also called *retropubic*, approach rather than the perineal approach, it is rare for a patient of mine to be a candidate for this procedure. I prefer to do the lymph-node dissection through a smaller abdominal incision, which is quicker than a laparoscopic lymph-node dissection. This mini-incision can be extended if I choose to proceed to the prostatectomy.

How soon after a laparoscopic lymph-node dissection before I can return to normal activity?

Usually about three to five days unless there is a problem at the time of surgery. Most men do great and feel good, ready to move ahead with whatever the next treatment involves.

Can I have a hernia or gallbladder repaired at the same time as my laparoscopic lymph-node dissection?

Yes, you can do most combination procedures together with the laparoscope, but this can dramatically increase the time of surgery.

What can go wrong with a laparoscopic lymph-node dissection?

This operation is very challenging and not easily mastered by everyone. Your surgeon operates through small incisions, using a video camera and special extended instruments. He loses the three-dimensional benefit of standard open surgery.

During this procedure, there is always a chance that one of the large nerves that passes through the pelvis can be cut or damaged. These nerves are important for certain movements of the legs.

Likewise, blood vessels can be torn. If nerve or blood-vessel damage occurs, the surgeon will have to stop the laparoscopic lymph-node dissection and make an abdominal incision to control the bleeding or repair the cut nerve.

Are there any long-term complications to a lymph-node dissection?

Yes. Rarely after open surgical lymph-node removal, a *lymphocele* can develop.

What is a lymphocele?

A lymphocele is a pocket of lymphatic fluid that builds up in the pelvis, usually following the lymph-node dissection. This fluid can put pressure on surrounding tissues and organs and cause lower abdominal pressure or pain. If it becomes infected, you can become quite ill with fever, chills and severe abdominal pain.

Why does this pocket develop?

It develops because the normal drainage of lymph fluid is interrupted when the lymph nodes are removed.

How common is this complication?

This is fairly rare, occurring in only one or two men out of every 100 operations performed. The incidence may actually be higher, but if the lymphocele is small and not causing any problem or symptoms we wouldn't know about it.

How is a lymphocele treated?

If the lymphocele isn't large or isn't causing problems, I usually leave it alone. If it is causing pain or fever, then I drain the fluid. This is usually performed by a radiologist, often with the help of a CT scan or ultrasound.

Catheters or drains can be left in temporarily to continue the drainage. Rarely, surgery is required to open the pocket of fluid. Some urologists drain the fluid through laparoscopy with good results.

Can the lymphocele come back?

It can come back at any time in the future. Most are found within a few months to a year or more after surgery.

21

Surgery ~
Radical Prostatectomy

Radical prostatectomy is a surgical operation where the entire prostate gland and adjacent glands are removed surgically for the treatment of prostate cancer. It is one of the most common operations being performed today and also one of the most controversial.

Most prostate-cancer specialists believe the radical prostatectomy offers men a better chance for long-term survival and a longer time without return of the cancer than do the more conservative treatment options, such as radiation, hormone treatment or "watchful waiting."

Why have I read that the surgery is not needed for
prostate cancer?

A small but vocal group of physicians is asking that we pull back and stop doing the surgeries until we have definite proof to support those of us who consider surgery a good choice in the right patients.

We know that prostate cancer is a disease whose response to treatment, whether or not it works, is measured in 10 to 15 years. That being true, do we doom many tens of thousands of men to an early death while we wait for new facts that may be a decade or more away? There are experts who believe early detection and treatment have resulted in definite survival advantages for men who want to live without cancer. This is my belief and position.

Is early detection important for other types of cancers in the body?

For almost all other cancers, early detection and removal is associated with better survival. I'm not really sure why these vocal few are asking the medical community to assume that prostate cancer is *different* from all others. I understand the desire to do no harm, but I believe the current information available supports continuing prostate surgery, at least as a reasonable option for some men.

Is surgery a good option for every man with prostate cancer?

Surgery is definitely not for everyone. I agree that many men who choose the surgery will *not* live long enough to see the benefits. This is why we tend to look at surgery as an *option* for younger men. As a man grows older, his risks associated with surgery go up, his recovery is slower, the rate of potential complications increases and, in general, the risks begin to outweigh the benefits.

Is this a major or minor operation?

A radical prostatectomy is considered a *major* operation. It requires a significant hospitalization and has some potentially serious risks.

Goal of Surgery

What is the goal of the surgery?

    The intent of this operation is to remove the cancer from your body before it has had a chance to spread and potentially reduce your quality of life and life span. Some specialists perform a radical prostatectomy when cancer has already spread outside the gland, with the hope of reducing the amount of cancer cells remaining in your body. They believe it is then easier for your body's immune system, assisted by medications and treatments, to work more effectively. However, there are definite and unavoidable risks with the surgery. It is a question of balancing the possible benefits with the potential risks.

Who is a candidate for this operation?

    I use three requirements to decide who is a candidate for radical prostatectomy and who should consider this as a reasonable option.

1. The patient must have prostate cancer that is believed to be *confined* to the prostate. Though there are a few experts who think otherwise, most agree the goal of the operation is to remove *all* the cancer from your body. If this can't be done, then surgery isn't the best option.
2. The patient should be able to safely undergo an operation requiring general anesthesia.
3. The patient should have a life expectancy long enough to see the benefits of surgery, usually seven to ten years or more.

Because I meet the candidate guidelines, does that mean I should have this operation?

    No. It only means this is a *reasonable option* for you to consider. I believe that if you have a long life expectancy ahead of you and it seems the cancer is potentially curable,

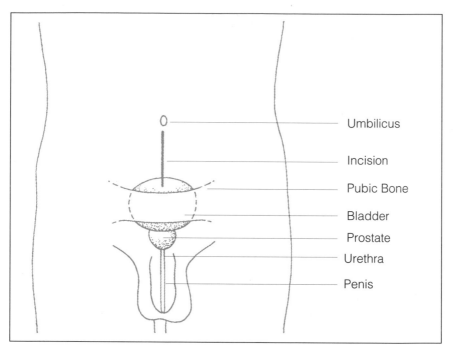

ABDOMINAL INCISION FOR RADICAL PROSTATECTOMY: *In a radical retropu-*
bic prostatectomy, the prostate is removed through a lower abdominal incision that
extends from the top of the pubic bone, just above the penis, up to the umbilicus (belly
button).

then the surgery may be your best treatment choice. But
surgery may not be right for everyone. Lifestyle, risks and family commitments may all impact on what choice is best for you.

Surgical Options: Retropubic vs. Perineal Approach

The most commonly used technique for radical prostatectomy in the U.S. is called the *retropubic approach.* This is the
approach I prefer and use. An incision is made from just
below the bellybutton to the top of the pubic bone. See diagram above. The space behind the pubic bone is opened up,
with the abdominal contents pushed up and out of the way.
The surgeon then exposes and removes the lymph nodes that
drain the prostate. If there is no cancer identified, then the
prostate gland itself is removed.

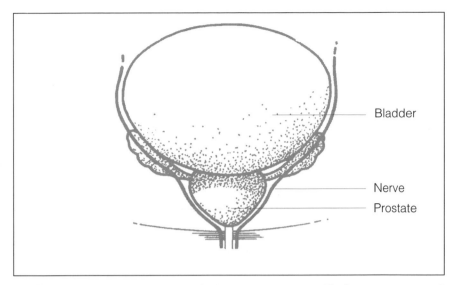

NERVES ALONGSIDE THE PROSTATE: Nerves responsible for erections travel alongside the prostate and can easily be damaged or cut during prostate removal. Nerve damage can also occur during radiation.

If the cancer has spread to the lymph nodes, removal of the prostate would not be curative. I would then stop the operation and *not* remove the prostate. Other optional treatments, such as hormone therapy, would be the next consideration for the patient.

What is the nerve-sparing technique I have heard about?

The nerve-sparing technique for prostate removal is based on a better understanding of the location of nerves that are responsible for penile erections. When these nerves are not removed or damaged during surgery, some men are later able to regain erections. It can take up to 12 to 18 months for erections to return.

If the nerves are not removed, however, our big concern is that we may be leaving cancer cells behind in addition to the nerves. My preference is to consider leaving only the nerves on the side opposite the cancer location to be certain that all the cancer *is* removed. See diagram above.

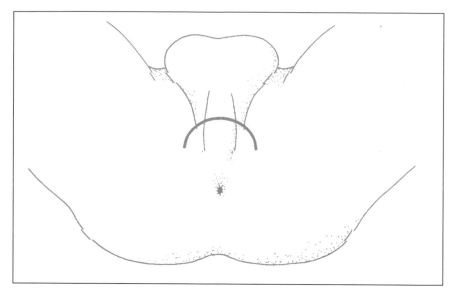

PERINEAL INCISION FOR RADICAL PROSTATECTOMY: In a radical perineal prostatectomy, the prostate is removed through an incision under the scrotum, with the legs elevated.

What is the advantage of the retropubic approach?

The main advantage of the retropubic approach is its easy access to the lymph nodes, nerves and blood vessels that are all adjacent to the prostate. The lymph nodes can be removed at the same time and through the same incision used for the prostate-gland removal. Also, nerves can be identified and preserved and blood vessels controlled.

What is the perineal approach?

The *perineal approach* to remove the prostate is made using an incision under the scrotum, in front of the rectum. The prostate is then separated from surrounding tissues and removed. (See diagram).

What are the advantages of the perineal approach?

The perineal prostatectomy has always had the reputation of being less traumatic to the body, with a quicker recovery and less pain. With advances in the retropubic approach,

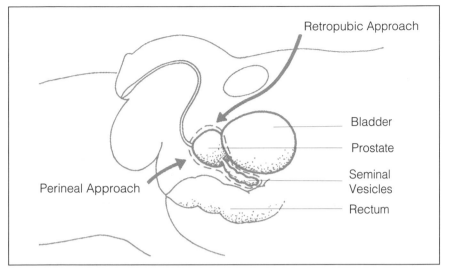

COMPARISON OF RETROPUBIC VERSUS PERINEAL PROSTATECTOMY:
Retropubic approach for radical prostatectomy is behind the pubic bone and in front of
the bladder. Perineal radical prostatectomy allows for access to the prostate through
the perineum.

these past advantages of the perineal technique are less an issue but are still being debated. The advantages of one technique over the other are less clear today.

However, the perineal approach is excellent for obese men where using the retropubic approach would be next to impossible because of the large lower abdominal wall.

What are the disadvantages of the perineal prostatectomy?

The main disadvantage is the inability to remove and evaluate the lymph nodes of the pelvis through the same incision. To assess the lymph nodes, one must first undergo a lymph-node dissection. If the PSA is low and biopsy report shows the cancer is low-grade, it may even be reasonable to simply skip the removal of the lymph nodes, because they probably will be normal anyway. Also, the perineal approach makes it difficult to do a nerve-sparing option, if appropriate.

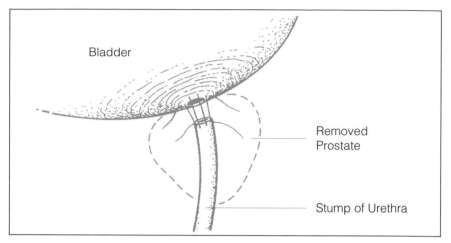

ATTACHMENT OF URETHRA TO BLADDER: After removal of prostate gland, stump of the urethra is then sewn back to the opening in the bladder neck.

Which approach is better?

It is most important for the surgeon to do whatever technique he feels is best for you, the one he can perform best and with the least complications. Each surgeon tends to have a favorite technique, one he was probably trained to do and perform most often. In competent hands, it doesn't make a difference in the long run which approach is used.

How is the urethra attached to the bladder after the prostate is removed?

A radical prostatectomy leaves a small hole at the bottom of the bladder where the prostate used to be located. The cut and unattached urethra also remains. Stitches are then placed through the urethral stump to the bladder neck, a catheter is placed into the bladder and the bladder neck and urethra are brought together. See diagram above.

How long does the operation take?

A radical prostatectomy can take two to four hours, depending on how easy it is to get to the prostate, the approach taken and the experience of the surgeon.

Is it an easy operation to perform?

No. It probably is one of the more challenging operations to learn correctly. Even when a surgeon has the skills mastered, it still can be a challenge.

What can make the operation more difficult?

Men who are quite obese and have a very wide abdominal wall or perineum force us to work in a deeper hole through a narrower opening. Some men have particularly deep and narrow pelvic bones, which can make the procedure more challenging. Occasionally the prostate can have very large blood vessels adjacent to the top of the gland. And as if these aren't enough obstacles, very large prostates or prostates in men who have had previous surgery (such as a TURP) can be difficult to remove.

Why does the operation take so long?

Because of the prostate's deep location, the surgeon may encounter problems. The care required to minimize bleeding and achieve good technical results also adds to the time.

If another surgeon is faster, does that mean he is better?

No. Quality of the results, patient satisfaction and keeping problems and complications to a minimum are the only factors that should determine how good a surgeon is.

The history of the "fast surgeon" dates back to a time when there was no anesthesia. The faster the surgeon could amputate a limb, the less pain you had. Fortunately, we now have anesthesia. We can take our time and do operations carefully and accurately.

Preparation for Surgery

What things do I have to do in preparation for surgery?

There are a number of routine preoperative tests and treatments we do to reduce the risks of surgery, to get you as ready as you can be. The reason for the following procedures is to minimize risks that cannot be eliminated from surgery.

The first risk is bleeding during surgery. To help lower the risk of bleeding, we request that you stop taking aspirin and aspirin-containing products for 10 days before your scheduled surgery. Some of the most common over-the-counter brand-name products containing aspirin are AlkaSeltzer®, Anacin®, Bayer®, Aspergum®, Empirin®, Bufferin®, Ecotrin® and Ascriptin®. If you take ibuprofen, Advil®, Motrin®, Anaprox® or similar anti-inflammatory medications, these also should be stopped for at least three to five days before your surgery date. If you are not sure about any of your medications, ask your doctor. If you were put on aspirin by your doctor because of heart or blood problems, then you need to get permission from that doctor to stop the aspirin.

Another risk, though rare, is tearing of the rectal wall adjacent to the prostate. In the "old days" the torn area would be sewn up and a colostomy would be made to divert the feces away from the healing area of the rectal wall. Three months later the colostomy would be closed, and your normal bowel function would return

The fear with this injury is the development of an abscess, or pocket of infection. To eliminate or dramatically reduce the odds for an abscess, we put you through a bowel-prep. With a bowel-prep, your intestines will be relatively cleaned out, and you will be given antibiotics to reduce the risks of infection.

We have you drink two or three liters of Go-Lytely® solution the day before surgery. This specially developed solution is something like a fancy Gatorade®. It results in a rapid onset of diarrhea that cleans out your intestines from one end to the other, while keeping the needed balance of salts and minerals. Because you can still get a little dehydrated after this, be sure to drink lots of water or clear liquids afterward.

Anti-Inflammatory Medications

Ibuprofen	Feldene	Mefenamic Acid
Advil	Flurbiprofen	Motrin
Anaprox	Indocin	Naprosyn
Ansaid	Ketorolac	Naproxen
Clinoril	Lodine	Nuprin
Daypro	Meclomen	Nalfon
Diclofenac	Meclofenamate	Oxaprozin
Etodolac		

The faster you drink the liquid, the faster the diarrhea will be over. Usually after two liters of Go-Lytely are consumed over a two-hour period, you will have diarrhea for three to four hours.

The mechanical cleansing alone will not usually protect you from infection, so we have you take antibiotics the evening before your surgery. You will be admitted to the hospital the morning of surgery, so you will do this bowel preparation and antibiotics at home the day before surgery.

Also the day before surgery, we ask you to eat no solid foods and drink only *clear liquids*. This helps your intestines stay cleaned out after the bowel-prep.

Because the complication of rectal-wall injury is so rare, many urologists don't believe it is necessary to have a bowel-prep. I would rather put you through it, and not need it, than not have it done and wish later that we had.

Clear Liquid Diet

Apple Juice	Tea
Grape Juice	Coffee
Cranberry Juice	Broth, Clear
Carbonated Soda	

When you arrive at the hospital, they will measure you and put stockings on you to reduce your risks of blood clots. Many doctors use *pneumatic sequential stockings:* special inflatable stockings that intermittently squeeze and release around your calves and legs, forcing blood to circulate to reduce the risk of clots. This is done even if you are not moving and are asleep during surgery. You will be directed to use these stockings for a few days after surgery.

Will I need to donate my own blood before surgery?

Yes, your doctor will probably ask you to donate your own blood, which is called *autologous blood.* If you should need a transfusion, your doctor can use your own blood.

When you donate your own blood, you can give up to one unit or pint of blood each week. I usually have my patients give two or three units. Because the blood is good for up to only 35 days, you must have a scheduled surgery date before they will let you start donating. You can give blood until the week of surgery. It is best if you are well-hydrated with liquids so you won't become dizzy when you give blood.

Because it is uncommon to need your blood, some surgeons don't routinely require this.

Does pretreatment with hormone shots actually cause the cancer to shrink?

There is much debate on this question. Some experts have thought that with hormone pretreatment we could *down-stage* the cancer, or convert it from a stage with cancer growing *outside* the gland to a lesser stage with the cancer confined *within* the prostate.

However, recent studies don't support this belief, so I wouldn't count on down-staging. We do know that hormone shots will cause the prostate itself to shrink in size, which can make the surgery much easier to perform.

Anesthesia

Is there significant pain with surgery?

There should not be. Most of my patients are surprised how good they feel afterward. Many tell me they never had any real pain, not even enough for a single over-the-counter pain pill.

These days, with the use of epidural anesthesia, new medications and PCA pumps, pain is not usually an issue. Not that long ago, if you had pain you would have to ring for the nurses, who would then give you a shot of morphine or Demerol®. Now, just before surgery, many men have an epidural catheter placed to control any pain or discomfort.

What is epidural anesthesia?

Epidural anesthesia is the same anesthesia that many women have during childbirth. This is a type of anesthesia in which a small amount of a potent narcotic drips directly into the fluid that surrounds the spinal cord. This results in blockage of all pain, but still allows normal sensation and muscle function. It is a rare patient who can't have an epidural placed. I almost insist on one with every case, because it makes the postoperative time so well tolerated.

There are some new methods where the epidural is used for only a day or two, and then a non-narcotic is given to control any pain. Some surgeons are using this powerful non-narcotic alone with excellent results.

What is a PCA pump?

PCA stands for *patient-controlled analgesia*. This is a device attached to the intravenous-fluid line. Whenever you feel pain, you simply push a button and a small amount of narcotic is injected into your bloodstream. The machine has internal controls to prevent an overdose and limit the maximum dose.

How is an epidural different from a spinal anesthetic?
The spinal anesthetic blocks the ability to feel and use the legs. The epidural anesthetic can block just pain.

How does an epidural work?
An epidural works by putting the anesthetic medication around the nerves that transmit the sensation of pain up from the lower abdomen and legs.

Does an epidural work on everyone?
No. There are some men who say they still feel pain. We can use other medications or the PCA pump with good control of pain.

What if I still have pain?
It may mean the epidural medication is not enough, or perhaps the catheter that provides the medication may have moved out of position.

How long is the epidural catheter left in?
It is usually left in for one to three days. I prefer to have it removed after 24 hours.

What if I've had previous back surgery?
That can be a problem if the doctor is unable to place the epidural catheter into the correct location because of scarring from the back surgery.

Does it hurt to have an epidural placed?
Not really. Your skin is numbed first so you should only feel minimal discomfort, if any.

What are some of the side effects of an epidural anesthetic?
The most common side effect is itching, which can be treated. Rare risks include breathing difficulty or infection.

What if my surgeon doesn't want to use an epidural?

Some urologists are using a powerful non-narcotic medication with very good results. Many men describe minimal discomfort and are going home in just a few days.

Will I be asleep during the surgery if I have an epidural?

Yes, every patient is put under a general anesthesia so that he is in deep sleep and totally unaware of proceedings during surgery, whatever method of pain control is used after surgery.

During the Surgery

Can I have my hernia fixed at the same time I have prostate surgery?

Yes. If you have a hernia that may need to be repaired, be sure to ask your doctor and talk to a general surgeon as well. It is important to tell your urologist so he can coordinate this with the general surgeon. Although the urologist can do the hernia repair, general surgeons do most of them.

Can I have my abdominal aneurysm fixed at the same time I have my prostatectomy?

Yes, these can be done together, although with a longer operating time and potentially increased risks.

Can you remove just the one side of the prostate that has the cancer?

No. Even if the biopsies and/or ultrasound show that the cancer appears to be on just one side of the prostate, the pathologist will often find that the cancer really is on both sides. So for this reason alone, it is not safe to consider a partial prostate removal.

In addition, technically it would be almost impossible to remove only one side completely. It is fairly easy to sew the cut end of the urethra onto the bottom end of the bladder after the prostate is removed. To leave one side of the prostate would make the operation very difficult and make the recon-nection less water-tight and more likely to leak.

Does surgery on the prostate cause cancer cells to spread?

No, there is no evidence or research indicating that cancer spreads with surgery. When we do this operation, we do it in a way to keep the gland and surrounding tissues as intact as we can.

Do you examine the prostate gland when it is removed?

Yes, the entire specimen is analyzed and cut into slices. Key pieces are reviewed under the microscope by a patholo-gist. He will determine the type, grade and extent of cancer. Information regarding the volume of the cancer as well as the status of the lymph nodes will be reported. This information allows the urologist to decide if additional treatments are needed, and which would be best.

Prostate Evaluation During Surgery

What if you are concerned during surgery that the cancer has spread?

We can always send tiny pieces of tissue to the pathol-ogists to see if cancer is present. We also send the lymph nodes, which are analyzed immediately by frozen-section analysis to be sure the cancer has not spread.

What is a frozen section?

This is how pathologists look quickly at tissue sent in during your surgery to see whether or not cancer is present. This is most commonly done with the lymph nodes to be sure there is no evidence of cancer spread before proceeding to remove the prostate itself.

Rather than routine processing and analysis, which can take a day or more, *frozen-section analysis* allows the pathologist to freeze the tissue very quickly with liquid nitrogen. Tiny, thin slices of the frozen tissue are then cut off and examined for cancer.

Although a rapid procedure, the freezing process can distort what is seen and make it less accurate than the routine analysis, called *permanent section.*

Recovery Room

Can my wife visit me in the recovery room after my prostatectomy?

No. Most recovery rooms are not set up to allow visitors. They are often very large rooms with a number of nursing stations and beds placed between these stations. It would be awkward if you walked right in among men and women in different stages of recovering from surgery. Usually the nurses will let your family know how you are doing and when you are transferred to your regular room.

How long will I be in recovery?

It is common for a patient to be in recovery for an hour or two or even more after a radical prostatectomy.

Hospitalization

Will I need to stay in the Intensive Care Unit?

Probably not. In my experience, it is a rare patient who needs more nursing care and observation than is offered on the regular urology floor. If there are medical concerns, your doctor may place you in the Intensive Care Unit (ICU) for the first night. After a radical prostatectomy, patients usually go to the ICU not because they are very ill, but because they have the potential for problems.

The ICU provides close one-on-one nursing and monitoring. These rare patients may have significant heart or lung problems, or perhaps there were some irregular heartbeats during surgery that we want to observe more closely.

If you are so ill from a nonurologic problem as to require ICU care after surgery, then perhaps you really aren't a good candidate for surgery in the first place. This is something to consider and discuss with your doctor.

In the ICU, visitation by family members is fairly limited. Friends are usually not allowed. Traffic and noise must be kept to a minimum.

How long will I be in the hospital?

You would usually spend between four and six days in the hospital, including the day of surgery. Most of my patients go home on the third postoperative day.

How soon you are discharged depends on how quickly you recuperate. When your bowels "wake up" after surgery and you begin eating a regular diet, then you usually are discharged. Unlike in the past, it is usually considered best to get out of the hospital as soon as you are able. You are better off to walk and be active than to lie in a hospital bed, waiting for nurses to come in and walk you.

Another reason to go home is to avoid infection. Despite the best hand-washing in the world, hospitals are known for harboring dangerous and difficult-to-treat infections. The sooner you get out, the better.

How long will I need intravenous fluids?

You will need to continue receiving fluids through your veins throughout most of your hospitalization. When you are able to tolerate and keep food down and are getting close to discharge, then the IV may be removed. Some hospitals require that an IV be kept in if you have an epidural catheter in place, just in case you have problems breathing and they need to give you medicine.

How long do I have to stay in bed while in the hospital?

We don't want you to stay in bed. We want you to get up and walk around. The more you are up and around, the quicker your recovery. In my practice, I ask you to walk about two times the night after surgery, and then at least four to six times every day afterward. The bed should really be the place where you go only to sleep or take a nap.

Is it better to take one long walk or several small walks?

The goal is to get you up and moving. With this in mind, more frequent short walks are much better than a long walk.

Do I have to wait for a nurse to help me?

The first few times you walk, you will need to have a nurse or assistant accompany you. You probably will have several lines and tubes attached to your body. The nurses will get these positioned so you can walk. Sometimes you can get a little dizzy or light-headed at first, so it's always better to have someone with you who can support you and help you back to bed.

What can I do to reduce dizziness?

When you get up to walk, do it *slowly* and sit on the edge of the chair or bed for a few minutes before you stand up.

How soon can I shower?

As soon as you feel like it, usually on your third day after surgery before you go home.

Should I bring my own medications to the hospital?

Yes. This is very important so we can continue your regular medications. Bring them in the original containers to help the hospital pharmacist identify each medication.

Will my primary-care doctor be at surgery?

Not usually. Some family practitioners like to assist with surgery on their own patients, but this is infrequent.

Will my primary-care doctor need to see me after surgery?

If you need to be seen for other serious medical problems or concerns, yes. Usually, however, it isn't necessary. You should at least call after you get home and let your primary-care doctor know you are home and doing well. If you don't need to be seen, then a follow-up visit with him or her can be on your routine schedule. If you do have any problems at all after surgery, you should contact your urologist and primary-care doctor right away.

Controversy: Quality of Life vs. Longevity

There is much debate on the quality of life accorded with each of the treatments for prostate cancer. We want to know if the patient is happy with his choice of treatment and the potential complications, such as urinary incontinence or impotence.

I have found that most men are indeed pleased with the treatment they have chosen. My personal philosophy and emphasis has always been to provide the necessary information so my patients can select the option they feel is best. I want them to consider the potential risks and complications from their choice.

If you are told by someone else what you are going to do, then I suspect you will be less tolerant of anything less than perfect results. On other hand, if you make your own decision with complete awareness of the risks, then in my experience you are far more likely to accept whatever happens as a result of your choice.

Isn't it easy to assess quality of life?

All individuals interpret quality of life differently. My patients' perceptions of their problems after surgery have always amazed me.

I recall one man who had a very aggressive, advanced cancer that required radiation after surgery. Subsequently, he became incontinent of urine, yet he remained positive and

optimistic about the future. He was very happy and appre-
tive of my services.

The first man's attitude contrasts with a patient who,
after much deliberation, finally decided to have a prostatectomy. He was clearly unhappy with what he felt was his only
real option, but he went ahead with surgery. Six months later,
he came in for a follow-up appointment, very disturbed and
depressed over his continued incontinence. On further ques-
tioning, it turned out that about once every few weeks, if he
lifted a heavy object when his bladder was full, he might leak a
few drops of urine. He was upset about his "horrible situation."

He was unhappy because he believed he had no choice
about treating his cancer, even though his results weren't
nearly as bad as he perceived. At the same time, the first man
was thrilled that his cancer was under control and that he was
able to live and enjoy the day-to-day joys of life, in spite of
the nuisance of leakage.

My point is, quality of life is not something you can
"standardize" for all people. Each patient has to decide if he is
happy with how things turned out. I suspect a fair number of
men are unhappy, not so much with any problem but more
with the fact that they had cancer and required a treatment
they really didn't want to have.

I try to tell my patients they need to look at the cards they
are dealt and make a decision based on those cards. At least they
have choices, although not what they might prefer. I remind
them there are men who don't have the options they have.

Controversy: Long-Term Benefits vs. Potential Risks

Most urology experts believe that radical prostatectomy offers
the potential for better long-term survival, based on this
important observation: The success rate of radical prostatectomy and radiation is roughly the same for the first 7 to 10
years. After 7 to 10 years, the success rate of prostatectomy is
higher compared to radiation.

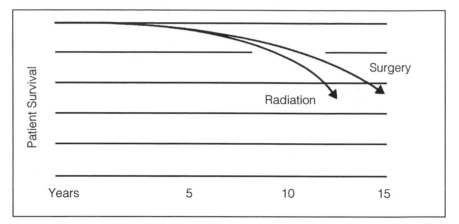

SURVIVAL AFTER SURGERY VS. RADIATION: Patients who have had surgery have survival advantages after 7-10 years.

I tell my patients, "If you don't think you're going to be around in seven to ten years, then don't take the risks of surgery. You can choose a more conservative choice, such as radiation, that can provide essentially the same results with significantly less risks."

There are those who believe that prostatectomy has not been clearly proven to offer advantages over radiation therapy or no treatment at all. Many long-term studies are underway to compare these options. Until we have conclusive data, I believe that it is important to base our decisions on current clinical experience.

The psychological benefits of surgery are also important, although difficult to describe. For some men, it is important to know that the cancer is out of their bodies and in a jar in the pathologist's back office.

Other men are willing to undergo less aggressive therapy in order to avoid the potential risks of surgery. Your personal feelings about the risks and benefits of surgery as compared to radiation therapy are very important. You must choose the treatment you are most comfortable with.

22

Risks & Complications
of Radical Prostatectomy

It is important to understand that the decision to have a radical prostatectomy carries with it a number of potential risks. The most common potential problems are *impotence*, or the lack of penile erections, and *urinary incontinence*, or the leaking of urine. These special problems are discussed in detail in later chapters.

Other risks include *bleeding* during and after surgery, the development of a *bladder-neck contracture, deep venous thrombosis, pulmonary emboli* and *urinary-tract infection.*

Bleeding

Why is there bleeding during surgery?
The prostate and adjacent structures are rich with multiple and often large blood vessels. In the process of removing the prostate, it is common to lose a lot of blood.

How can there be bleeding after surgery?

If a clot breaks off of a small artery or vein, bleeding can begin. This is quite rare. It's something urologists are aware of as a risk but rarely see. If the bleeding were significant, then you might need transfusions or possibly even a return to surgery to identify and stop whatever is bleeding.

How often is a transfusion required?

This is variable, depending again on the surgeon and the volume of blood loss. Some surgeons may need to give blood on a regular basis if the blood loss is high. In my practice over the past several years, I can recall giving only one patient transfusions in addition to his own blood, because of 17 bleeding stomach ulcers that were diagnosed after surgery. The average is about 5% of men nationally who need transfusions during and after surgery.

Can you recycle blood lost during surgery?

Yes, many urologists use a machine called a *cell saver* that takes the blood lost during the removal of the prostate and prepares and recycles the blood back to the patient.

Can I donate my own blood ahead of time to reduce the need for a transfusion if bleeding does occur?

Yes, I ask my patients to donate two to three units of their blood in advance of surgery. Called *autologous donations*, this blood is held only for you and can be given if a transfusion is required. The donation of blood ahead of time also stimulates your own body's blood-production mechanisms to move into full speed, which helps with your immediate recovery. In my practice it is uncommon to lose enough blood to justify giving you your own blood back.

How often do you have to give autologous blood to a patient?

It is only the rare patient who needs some of his own blood back. I prefer to look at the autologous blood as an insurance policy so that if there is an unexpected problem, we'll have some of your own blood available.

Should I sign the hospital consent to allow for transfusion even if I've already given autologous blood?

You should definitely sign "yes," giving your doctor permission to administer blood products as needed. This must be signed in order for you to receive your own donated blood. In case of that rare situation where there is dramatic blood loss, you will have given your doctor permission to give you transfusions if it is felt necessary to save your life.

Every doctor is aware of the unlikelihood of the patient getting hepatitis or AIDS from a regular blood transfusion. This risk is very small and should be balanced with a sudden need for blood in an emergency situation.

If you have any questions, talk to your urologist before surgery. Express your concerns. For your own safety, don't sign "no" unless your urologist knows of your intentions ahead of time.

What do they do with the autologous blood that is not used?

The blood must be thrown away. It is drawn specifically for you. If not used, it must be discarded according to Red Cross guidelines.

Why can't I just get my blood back anyway?

There is always a tiny chance of a paperwork mistake, so it is considered acceptable to have an autologous donation only if you truly need the blood.

Can I have someone donate blood for me?

Yes, you can. This is called *directed donation*. However, most often the blood types do not match closely enough to be used. Even if they do match, there is actually a higher risk for hepatitis and AIDS than from the general population of people who regularly donate blood. This is explained by the fact that there may be tremendous social and family pressure for a relative to donate blood even if he or she has had experiences in the past that may have increased the risk of picking up one of these diseases.

Bladder-Neck Contracture

What is a bladder-neck contracture?

This is scar tissue that forms at the bladder neck, where the urethra was sewn to the bladder. This can result in urination problems.

How do I know if I have developed a contracture?

Most men describe a weakened urinary stream with more and more difficulty urinating. Because the prostate is totally removed, you shouldn't have any significant problems with blockage. Any symptoms that suggest there may be a blockage should be evaluated further to be sure there is no scar tissue.

How common is bladder-neck contracture?

It is uncommon, but can occur in about one out of every 20 to 30 prostatectomies.

How are these evaluated and treated?

I identify bladder-neck contractures in my patients with an office cystoscopy. If I find a scar, I try to stretch it open in the office with metal dilators. Though uncomfortable for a few moments, it saves most men from a trip to surgery under anesthesia. There may be bleeding after the scar is opened. Some men complain of increased urinary incontinence after the stretching procedure. This can be significant but is rarely permanent.

If simple stretching hasn't worked and surgery is required for a severe or recurrent scar, I often just cut the scar open in two locations and leave a catheter in for about 24 hours. This is usually done successfully as an outpatient under anesthesia. The main concern is the return of urinary incontinence after the scar is opened up.

Can the scar tissue come back?

Yes, occasionally some men will have a return of the scar, although this is uncommon. It can come back within a few weeks or perhaps years later.

Deep Venous Thrombosis (DVT)
and Pulmonary Embolus (PE)

What is a DVT?

A *deep venous thrombosis* (DVT) is a blood clot that can develop in the veins of the legs or pelvis. Such clots can cause swelling of the leg. They are of concern because of the potential for breaking loose and floating up to the heart and lungs. If a clot breaks loose and reaches the heart and lungs, it is called a *pulmonary embolus (PE)*.

How is a pulmonary embolus dangerous?

A pulmonary embolus is a large blood clot in a vein of the leg or pelvis that breaks loose and flows with the blood up to the heart. It then passes through the right side of the heart and is pumped at high pressure into the lungs. If large, it can totally block blood flow and result in an almost-instant drop of blood pressure. This would cause death almost instantaneously. This is one of the most common causes of sudden death after surgery. Fortunately, these are quite rare. Pulmonary emboli can occur days to weeks after surgery.

How can I avoid the risk of a pulmonary embolus or venous thrombosis?

To help reduce this potential risk, during surgery I use special stockings that inflate and deflate to keep the blood flowing through the veins. I get the patient up and walking

Radical Prostatectomy Risks

Impotence	Bladder-neck Contracture
Incontinence	Blood Clots/Heart Attack
Bleeding/Transfusions	Need for Additional Treatments
Infections	

the evening after surgery and frequently thereafter. I also have him use support stockings after surgery.

Not all blood clots break loose, and many cause only minor problems. It is the rare large clot that can be fatal.

Other Complications

What are the risks of getting pneumonia?

This complication is very uncommon, especially now that we get you up and walking right away after surgery. To reduce risks for lung infections, we also have you work on deep breathing during your hospital stay. I do not recall any of my patients developing a pneumonia following radical prostatectomy.

Will I have an allergic reaction?

There is always a rare but possible chance you could have some kind of reaction to any medication you are given. If you are allergic to a medication, then we try not to give it unless the problem is felt to be life-threatening and you will need the antibiotic or you may die.

Most allergic reactions are rashes, itching, hives or blisters. You could get a fever. More serious reactions include swelling of the lips and tongue or difficulty breathing. The most dangerous reaction is *anaphylaxis*, which can include sudden heart stoppage or halted breathing without warning. Fortunately, these serious reactions are extremely rare.

What are the risks of getting an infection?

Infection is always a possibility. To minimize this risk, we have you shower the night before with an antiseptic soap such as Hibiclens® or Betadine®. In addition, you will probably receive antibiotics at the time of surgery and for a day or so afterwards.

The odds of developing a skin infection along the incision are very low. If you develop redness and tenderness or drainage of fluid, you should see your doctor and point out these changes.

Urinary-tract infections are always possible but unlikely. In my practice, I give antibiotics just at and after the time of surgery, then again around the time the catheter comes out. It is very rare to have a patient who develops an infection with this regimen.

Can I get stomach ulcers after the surgery?

Over the years I can recall only one patient who developed stomach ulcers from the stress of surgery and the hospitalization. If you have a history of stomach ulcers, it is important to tell your surgeon so he can consider giving you preventive medications.

What is the risk of a rectal injury requiring a colostomy?

As discussed in the previous chapter, this is a very rare complication that can occur when the back wall of the prostate is stuck to the front wall of the rectum.

Consent Form

Every surgery patient is asked to sign a *consent form*. See the Appendix for a copy of the radical prostatectomy consent form that I use. Every doctor's consent form is different, but this is one that points out many of the most serious problems that can occur during surgery. Always read a consent form carefully and make sure you understand it before you sign it.

23

After Surgery ~ Home from the Hospital

The main goal after surgery is to get you back to your normal lifestyle as quickly as we can. There are some limitations during your initial recovery, but they shouldn't slow down your ability to resume normal activities and regain your strength. How quickly you recover is a direct reflection of your motivation to bounce back.

It is important not to let surgery or recovery get in the way of your life. You may be slowed down temporarily, but you shouldn't be stopped. As good as you feel after surgery, your body still is recovering from the stresses of an operation. You must be aware of this and allow yourself the flexibility to tolerate the limitations and changes you feel.

What can I expect regarding my short-term recovery?
You will notice a lack of the energy level and endurance you had before surgery. When you have been up and around, you will find that you tire easily. At first, you might get up from a nap, shower and then need to lie down

again. When the tiredness comes on, it hits you like a wall. You might feel weak, lightheaded and possibly dizzy or even nauseated.

How long is the recovery after a radical prostatectomy?

Most working men take off several weeks before returning to work. If you have a desk job, you might be ready to work three to four weeks after surgery. If you do heavy lifting or straining, it may take four to six weeks. We urge you to stay as active as possible. Strength doesn't return to the man who sits and watches TV, waiting to get better. You have to go out and earn it.

Catheter

Your doctor will send you home from the hospital with a *Foley catheter* in place. A Foley catheter is a hollow tube that is placed into the bladder during surgery to provide continuous urine

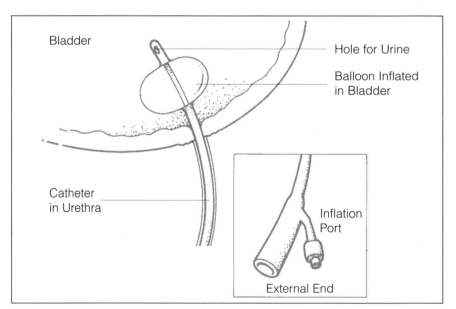

FOLEY CATHETER: Rubber or silicone catheter placed through the urethra into the blad-der to allow constant urine drainage. Catheter is held in place by a balloon filled with water through an inflation port off to the side of the external end of the catheter. External end drains into a collection bag.

drainage. It is held in place with an inflated balloon and connected to a drainage bag which should be emptied regularly.

How long does the catheter need to stay in?

The average time for the catheter to remain is about 21 days. This allows the area of the urethra sewn to the bladder neck to heal. If we took it out too soon, it would increase the risk of urinary incontinence. There's not much reason to leave it in longer than three weeks from the day of surgery.

Will the catheter bother me?

As the three weeks go by, the catheter will become an increasing nuisance. It is perfectly normal to have occasional leakage of urine around the catheter, often without warning. You may have occasional bladder spasms, which usually go away over time.

What are bladder spasms?

They are a "squeezing down" of the bladder with a cramping, lower abdominal pain that usually goes away in a few minutes. It can come on suddenly or gradually build up. Your bladder does not tolerate the irritation of the catheter and balloon. Therefore, your bladder is trying to rid itself of the irritation by squeezing it out. I usually consider this a good sign of quick return of bladder function.

How can I stop the spasms?

Your doctor can help reduce the frequency and intensity of spasms by prescribing medications such as Levsinex, Ditropan or Urispas. If you are on such medication, ask your doctor when it is to be stopped. I usually stop the medication about 24 to 48 hours before the catheter is removed. The good news is that most often the spasms may reduce and even go away within a few days.

What can I do to reduce problems with the catheter?

First, it's important to keep the area clean at the end of your penis where the catheter comes out. Wash the area with soap and water at least once or twice each day. You can also put a small dab of over-the-counter antibiotic ointment just at the opening. This not only will reduce the risk of developing an infection but also will reduce discomfort from the catheter sticking to the skin.

To keep the catheter from tugging on your penis, I recommend you attach the drainage bag with a safety pin to the elastic on your underwear.

Will I get an infection with the catheter in so long?

Probably not. You may get what is called *colonization*, where germs are present (they "colonize") on the catheter and in the urine. But they have not progressed enough to cause an infection or symptoms. Just having germs on the catheter is not bad and does not require treatment.

Exercise

What can I do to speed up my recovery?

To overcome this reduced strength, you need to really push yourself. As I tell my patients, you can't just lie in bed and wait for your strength to return. You need to be up and active.

The more walking you do, the better and more quickly you'll recover. Frequent short walks are better than one long walk. If your house or apartment is too small for exercise, or if the weather outside is not good for a walk, then go to an indoor shopping mall. There you don't have to worry about the weather. You'll find plenty of places to sit if you get tired or need a drink or something to eat.

No other exercise is as good for your recovery as walking. Treadmills are also fine to use, but keep it fairly flat and slow and just try to put in the time.

How will I know if I've pushed myself too far?

During a walk, you may find yourself suddenly weak and tired, perhaps even nauseated and flushed. This is your body's way of letting you know you pushed yourself a little too far. You will notice that your strength and endurance is not what it was before surgery. But with work and patience, you'll be surprised how quickly you will recover. Often a midday nap or two is all you need for a while.

When can I walk after surgery?

You should be walking regularly even before you leave the hospital. When you go home, you should continue to walk about as much as you feel you can. Walking builds up your endurance, reduces risks for fatal blood clots and brings back that feeling of well-being and health. You should gradually build up the intensity, walking longer distances each day.

How often should I walk?

I tell my patients to walk four to six times each day. Each time they walk, they should always walk a little farther than they feel comfortable doing. Keep pushing just a little more each time. Those men who follow this guideline are very surprised how good they feel in just a few weeks.

Realistically, it may be four to eight weeks before you are 100% back to your presurgical stamina and strength.

How soon can I get back into my regular exercise?

If you are an active person, you will need to gauge what you do by how your recovery progresses. Let your doctor guide you. We don't want you to strain or hurt yourself during the initial recovery phase, when your tissues aren't very strong. Whatever you do, move into it gradually. Don't sit back and avoid any activity and then suddenly jump in full speed. Rather, work into it slowly. Gradually build up your strength and skills.

How soon can I walk my dog?

This depends on the type of dog you have. If you are taking a docile toy poodle out, any time you feel up to it is fine with me. On the other hand, if you want to walk—or be walked—by your Rottweiler or Great Dane, I suggest you wait three to four weeks.

How soon after surgery will I be able to resume golf?

I usually encourage my golfing patients to keep active, and when they feel up to it, go out with the guys and just walk the course. Initially you may only want to do a few short walking bursts and then ride a cart the rest of the way.

I don't want you to take full driving swings off the tee too soon. But when you're feeling stronger, I think it's reasonable to practice your chipping and putting. At about five to six weeks after surgery you should be able to play without restrictions.

How soon can I start playing tennis or racquetball?

Tennis and racquetball require certain straining, so I ask that you hold off playing full speed until about four to six weeks from the day of your surgery. But until then, you should be able to go out and gently hit a few balls at about "half speed." But remember, plain walking is your best exercise after surgery to get your strength and endurance back.

How quickly can I resume bicycle riding?

Bicycle riding is something you need to avoid until you really have recovered at six weeks or later after surgery. You should avoid putting pressure on your perineum during the initial recovery phase. This is the general area where your bladder and urethra have been surgically connected, and of course this is also what you sit on for bicycling.

When you do resume biking, do it slowly. You might find it more comfortable if you don't sit on a narrow, firm seat. Perhaps a wider seat with more padding would make your transition back to cycling more pleasant.

What about using stair-steppers and the treadmill?

These activities you can start doing right away. Just be aware that you won't have the endurance you did before surgery.

What about weightlifting?

You should avoid weightlifting for a full six weeks from the time of surgery. Light arm exercises are okay until then.

How soon can I start bowling again?

Wait four to six weeks, depending on how good you feel. The bowling ball weighs more than I want you to carry until the incision is fully healed.

How soon can I paint my house?

I usually suggest waiting three to four weeks before doing moderate work around the house, especially if much straining is involved. If you plan to stand on a ladder, then you should wait a full six weeks.

Can I work in my garden?

Yes, as long as you don't do any heavy lifting or straining. It is okay to bend over and do light gardening activities. Just take it easy and start slowly.

Travel

How soon after surgery will I be able to drive a car?

You should not drive a car for at least two weeks after surgery, for two reasons.

One, your incision is healing and may be tender. If you were driving and an emergency occurred or sudden braking was required, you may hesitate or be unable to perform at 100% because of pain or discomfort. You would be putting yourself and others at risk. It is generally accepted that after a major abdominal operation, you need a few weeks to recover enough to drive safely.

Second, if you are involved in an accident and you just had a radical prostatectomy, even if it's not your fault, your legal position might look questionable.

How soon can I be driven around town?

You can go out as soon as you are discharged from the hospital, as long as someone else drives you. The sooner you are up and around, the quicker your recovery will be.

Can I go as a passenger on a long trip?

Yes, if you must. Ideally you should refrain from long trips for a few weeks. Long travel is okay only if at least every hour you get up out of your seat (or out of a car) and walk around to keep the blood moving through your veins. I also recommend that you wear support stockings.

How long after surgery can I travel?

If you're planning an elective vacation, I usually ask that you wait about four to six weeks to be sure you are well on your way to recovery. You can travel any time if you need to, but don't do any heavy lifting or straining. This means you can't carry your own luggage and should use all the help you can get.

Bathing

Can I shower or bathe after I go home?

Yes, there are no limits on showering or bathing. I prefer that you not take tub baths for a week or two. Avoid the potential strain of climbing in and out of a tub. Most men find it easier to shower for the first few weeks.

How soon can I swim after surgery?

I ask that you wait until the catheter comes out. By then, the incision will be fairly well healed, and you should be able to do light swimming. You should avoid strenuous swimming for about four to six weeks.

Can I use a hot tub, Jacuzzi or sauna after I get home?

  You probably should avoid these for a few weeks until the incision has had a chance to heal and the catheter is out.

Support Stockings

Why do I need to wear the support stockings?

  After surgery, the reduced blood flow through the veins and the reduced walking puts you at increased risk for developing blood clots for up to six to eight weeks after surgery. Blood clots in the legs can be painful, and they can also be quite dangerous if they break loose and move up to the lungs. Large blood clots can cause sudden death if they block large blood vessels. This is why we encourage you not only to walk frequently after surgery but also to wear support stockings when you're just lying around. The stockings work by compressing the veins and reducing the odds of blood pooling in the veins.

How long should I wear support stockings after I go home?

  Technically you are at risk for developing blood clots in the veins of the legs and pelvis for as long as six to eight weeks. With this in mind, I usually recommend that whenever you are going to be inactive for an extended period, like being a passenger on a long car or airplane trip, it is a good idea to wear support stockings. If you are active and walking quite a lot, then you do not have to wear them. If they don't drive you crazy, then I suggest wearing them for about six to eight weeks after surgery.

  Some nurses and doctors wear them regularly if they are on their feet for extended periods. Wearing them can increase your comfort, so keep them on even after the eight-week time if you feel you need to.

Diet

When will I be able to eat after surgery?

You should be able to eat anything you want after you get home. You may have a tendency toward constipation, so get plenty of fiber and bulk in your diet, and drink plenty of water and fluids.

Are there any dietary restrictions after I go home?

There are no limits on what you can eat. You may be a little anemic, with a low blood count, but a balanced diet with some foods high in iron should be adequate.

Should I take iron supplements?

This is probably a good idea, at least for the first few weeks after you leave the hospital. This will provide plenty of iron to rebuild your blood counts back up. Iron can be constipating, so drink plenty of fluids and increase the fiber in your diet.

What if I get constipated after I get home?

I usually recommend that you take some milk of magnesia as a gentle laxative. If your constipation is severe, talk with your doctor about medications such as Colace® or Surfak®, which can work to prevent constipation before it develops.

Incision

How long will it take the incision to heal?

Most of the healing occurs within six weeks, but the incision will continue to heal for six to twelve months.

Why does the incision feel thick and hard?

This is your body's way of healing normally. As the tissues slowly heal, the thickening and firmness will gradually go away.

*How will I know if I'm developing a skin infection
in the incision?*

Usually there will be increased tenderness, possibly redness and maybe even drainage of pus from the incision.

What can be done for an infection in the incision?

Usually opening up the incision where the infection is located will allow drainage and normal healing. Sometimes I'll start my patient on antibiotics if I'm really concerned. I may even pack some sterile gauze into the incision opening to help with drainage of infection. The open incision will heal together naturally over time.

Is there anything I can do to help the incision heal?

Keep the incision out of the sun. Sun exposure can cause the delicate new skin tissues to become permanently tanned. After surgery, the incision will first be red. Then over a few months, it will gradually fade into normal skin color.

How are my insides different now after surgery?

You are missing your prostate gland and the adjacent seminal vesicles, as well as the lymph nodes that drain the prostate. The bladder is now attached directly to the urethra, rather than to the prostate gland as it was before surgery. There are no other changes internally.

*What if there continues to be pain where the intravenous line
went into the skin?*

This pain is common, but occasionally it can represent an infection or blockage of veins in the arm. Unless the infection spreads, it is easily treated with heat, ideally warm compresses. If it has quite a lot of redness and tenderness, then it may be an infection. You will probably need to be put on antibiotics and to watch the area closely.

How often do I have to be seen by my urologist for follow-up after surgery?

In my practice, I usually would see you about seven to ten days after surgery to do a quick check of the incision and to remove the skin stitch. About 21 days after surgery, I would remove the catheter. I would see you again about four to six weeks later just to see how you are doing, review the pathology report and discuss long-term follow-up.

Do I need to see my primary-care doctor right away after surgery?

Not usually, unless you are having medical problems unrelated to the surgery that need attention. I suggest that you call and talk to your doctor or the nurse just to let them know you are home and doing well.

Depending on your health insurance, when your immediate recovery is over you may need to be seen by your primary-care doctor. For example, certain HMOs may require you to see your primary-care doctor some time after the immediate postoperative period.

24

Hormone Therapy

Hormone therapy is one of the standard options for treating prostate cancer. Like each of the other treatment choices, hormone therapy is best suited for specific situations and patients.

What is hormone therapy?

This is a treatment where the male hormones (called *androgens*) are eliminated from the body. The most common male hormone is called *testosterone*.

Why do you remove testosterone from the body?

We remove the hormone from the body during treatment because prostate cancer is *hormone-sensitive*. Testosterone stimulates the cancer's growth.

When the hormone is eliminated from the body, the cancer generally stops growing and may actually go into a dormant phase, like going into hibernation. Similar to treatment of breast cancer, where women are given the opposite-sex hormone, men can be treated with female hormones or

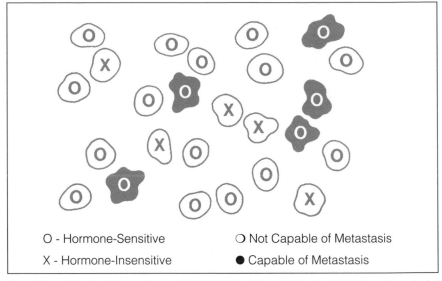

O - Hormone-Sensitive   ◯ Not Capable of Metastasis

X - Hormone-Insensitive   ● Capable of Metastasis

CANCER CELLS: HORMONE SENSITIVITY AND RISK OF SPREAD: Though the specific percentages vary from person to person and cancer to cancer, some of the prostate cancer cells are considered sensitive, while other cancer cells are referred to as hormone-insensitive and will not be affected by any change in testosterone levels. Likewise, some of the cancer cells are capable of spread, while others are thought to be incapable of spread, independent of their hormone sensitivity. This explains why cancers behave so variably and may not follow any set patterns or responses to treatment.

with other options that eliminate testosterone from the man's body.

Who is a candidate for hormone treatment?

Ideally, hormone therapy should be used for those men whose disease has shown signs of progression after radiation and/or surgery. Because so many men get good results from hormone therapy for several years, it is often used as the *primary treatment* in older men when we want to do something more than just follow the cancer but radiation or surgery is too much or inappropriate.

What are other reasons to use hormone therapy?

One of the main reasons to use hormone therapy is for the treatment of widespread metastatic disease. If the cancer has gone to the lymph nodes or to the bones, hormone therapy is considered the correct treatment option. Hormone therapy may be used *before* surgery and *before* or *during* radiation to reduce prostate size or keep the cancer in check.

Does hormone therapy work well for everyone?

When this treatment works, it works very well. But as with all treatments, everyone responds differently. Some men can go many years after hormone therapy with no evidence of any cancer growth. Some will experience substantial cancer regression and shrinkage. For some, the cancer may remain dormant for many years, perhaps 10 years or more. Others may have good results for only a short period of time.

How can the cancer cells start to grow again?

Some cancers can learn to grow without the usual hormone stimulation. These cancers are called *hormone-insensitive.*

In what situation is hormone therapy least likely to work?

The worst scenario is where the hormone treatment only seems to slow down the cancer growth for a while, perhaps just a few months or years. This is seen with men who have a very aggressive cancer, often at an early age and with a very high PSA level. For these men, we're not sure hormone therapy will impact much on the cancer's growth. For these few, it appears the most aggressive cancers are harder to treat and control.

How can we tell which cancers will respond to hormone therapy and which won't?

At present we do not have any reliable way of testing to see who will and who won't benefit. It is thought that if you are a candidate for hormone therapy, you should be given a trial. If it works, and it usually does, then you have your answer.

Does hormone therapy actually cure the cancer?

No, not like radiation or surgery. Rather, the elimination of testosterone removes a major stimulant of the cancer's growth. Hormone therapy is an effective *control*, not a *cure*.

Will hormone therapy prolong my life span?

We hope so and think so, but this is *not* guaranteed. For many men, hormone therapy offers many years of quality, comfortable life. For others, the cancer may be so aggressive that it may not respond to hormone treatments. If the cancer does respond, hormone therapy may only work for a few months rather than the expected years.

Will hormone treatment improve my quality of life?

For most men, we hope hormones will keep the cancer from growing. There are side effects, however, that can possibly reduce the quality of your life.

What are the possible side effects of hormone therapy?

The most common side effect men complain of is hot flashes. These occur in 10% to 15% of men receiving hormone injections and a bit less after orchiectomy. (Injections and orchiectomy are explained later in this chapter.)

For most men, hot flashes seem to come and go. Then they may gradually become less frequent and less bothersome. For a few men, however, they can be quite overwhelming and disabling. Flashes can come on without warning and result in waves of heat and sweats. Fortunately for many men, the flashes tend to be self-limiting. Most men just put up with them.

What causes hot flashes?

No one really understands how eliminating testosterone from your body brings on hot flashes.

Treatments for Hot Flashes

DES (Risks!)
Flutamide
Megace®
Progesterone
Clonidine® Patch
Estrogen Patch
Stop Injections

What can be done to treat hot flashes?
Different men respond to different treatments. We have seen success with Clonidine® patches, the hormone Megace® every other day, Provera® twice a day, estrogen patches once or twice a week and even low-dose estrogens (DES). DES and estrogens are explained later in this chapter.

I heard that some men have breast problems with hormones. Is this true?
Yes, breast tenderness and/or fullness does occur in a small percentage of men after starting hormone therapy. In many, the tenderness will eventually go away. Rarely, patients may require low-dose radiation or surgery to remove the enlarged and tender breast tissues.

Will hormone therapy affect my voice or behavior?
Hormone therapy will not affect your voice, outward appearance or behavior.

Will hormone therapy make me impotent?
Yes, it may very well remove your ability to have an erection. Or, it may possibly reduce the *quality* of the erections you have. It may eliminate your desire and interest in sexual activity.

Potential Side Effects of Hormone Therapy

Hot Flashes
Breast Tenderness
Breast Enlargement
Reduced Sex Drive
Impotence

How will the effectiveness of hormone therapy be monitored?

As with other prostate-cancer treatments, the PSA blood test is the best way to know if and how effectively the hormone treatment is working. Ideally, the PSA should drop to very low levels, in the range of 0.0 or 0.1. But it may possibly go to 0.4 or 0.5. The faster the level drops and the longer it stays down the better.

Hormone therapy's effectiveness will depend quite a bit on how much cancer is in your body and how high the PSA level was before the treatment was started. The more cancer that is present, the less effective the treatment may be.

I usually check the PSA level six to eight weeks after starting hormone injections or performing the orchiectomy. Then I would probably follow the PSA every three or four months for the next year or two, then every four to six months. How closely we follow depends on when the treatment is initiated, the tumor volume, the cancer aggressiveness and the long-term outlook.

Should I start the hormone treatments immediately?

There are those who believe urologists should wait as long as possible until there are definite symptoms of the cancer spreading before hormone treatment is started. I disagree with this delaying approach. I lean toward early treatment— as soon as the advanced disease is identified. I think this provides the best long-term results.

Options for Hormone Therapy

Estrogen (DES)
LHRH Analog (Lupron or Zoladex)
Orchiectomy (Removal of Testicles)

How is this done?

There are several ways of undergoing hormone therapy today. For years, men were simply given the female hormone estrogen (DES) as a once-a-day pill. This worked well to stop the cancer's growth. Unfortunately, estrogen has serious potential side effects in men that are discussed below.

Because of these life-threatening side effects, the use of estrogen has fallen out of favor. Instead, we now tend to remove the testicles (source of testosterone) surgically. Or we may give a monthly injection of an artificial hormone that "tricks" the body into stopping testosterone production. Both treatments are equally effective in dropping male hormone levels in the body.

DES (Diethylstilbestrol)

What is DES?

Diethylstilbestrol, called *DES* for short, is a type of estrogen or female hormone.

Why isn't DES used anymore?

Most doctors stopped using DES several years ago when safer alternative treatments became available. We now know that DES can cause heart attacks, strokes and fatal blood clots. In lower doses, it may still be used to help control hot flashes. In general, though, it doesn't make sense to treat with a therapy such as DES that is more dangerous than the cancer being treated.

How long does it take for DES to drop the testosterone levels?

It can take 30 to 60 days after starting DES therapy for testosterone levels to reach the bottom level.

What if I'm already on DES and have had no problems?

If you've been on DES for a few years, you'll probably continue to do well. There is a risk of developing heart problems, strokes or blood clots. I recently had an elderly patient who had been maintained on DES for over 10 years, doing well without any side effects. I explained my concerns and his options, and he chose to continue with DES therapy.

What is the advantage of DES therapy?

DES is fairly inexpensive ($10 to $20 per month) and easy to take, just one pill each day.

Orchiectomy

What is an orchiectomy?

Surgical removal of the testicles.

Is removal of the testicles an effective treatment?

Yes, this results in a very rapid and effective drop in the testosterone level to almost zero. This treatment is *permanent*. You don't have to worry about testosterone levels sneaking back up, and you don't have to worry about daily pills or monthly injections.

Orchiectomy is the standard against which all other hormone treatments are measured. Some claim to be as good. None are better.

Why would a man care about keeping his testicles if this is the best treatment?

Some men simply don't want or like the idea of having their testicles removed. It is an emotional issue. It has something to do with one's self-image. In talking with patients about this option, I explain that they get to keep their scrotum intact and that we only remove the testicles from within the scrotum. Based on this knowledge, some men then decide to go ahead.

Is having an orchiectomy the same as castration?

Yes, they both mean removal of the testicles.

How quickly does the operation lower my testosterone levels?

The testosterone level drops rapidly down to zero, within three to 12 hours. Men with pain from cancer in the bone may experience disappearance of the pain within a few days or less! I even had one patient who was riddled with cancer. He noted a dramatic improvement and almost total elimination of bone pain the next day.

How is an orchiectomy done?

This is performed as an outpatient procedure where you go into a hospital or outpatient facility, have the operation and go home a few hours later.

Under anesthesia, the testicles are removed from the scrotum through a small incision. This incision, about one to two inches long, is made in the front of your scrotum. Each testicle is separated from surrounding attachments. The blood vessels are then clamped and tied off with suture material.

The testicles are removed and sent to pathology to be analyzed for cancer, even though cancer in the testicles is extremely rare.

Who actually does the surgery?

Usually done by a urologist, the procedure can easily be done by a general surgeon if no urologist is available. It is considered a relatively easy operation to do.

What are the main risks of this surgery?

The biggest problems following this operation are infection and bleeding. Each of the following problems is quite rare. These risks definitely shouldn't keep you from having the operation. You should not be alarmed if you have a little swelling or some bruising, which *is* common.

If you notice increased redness, swelling or pain, or if the incision starts to ooze pus-like drainage, you need to inform your doctor and be seen right away. You may have developed an infection of the incision. Your doctor will most likely start you on antibiotics, or he might open the incision slightly to allow drainage. Infections are quite rare because of the good blood supply to the scrotal skin.

The other problem is potentially more serious but quite rare—serious bleeding. If a small blood vessel starts to bleed after the surgery, the scrotum can swell up rapidly, turn purple and look like a large eggplant. This is a *true emergency*. It requires immediate surgical exploration under anesthesia to identify and tie off the bleeding blood vessels and to drain out the blood built up in the scrotum.

What type of anesthesia will I need?

There are two basic types of anesthesia that can be used for this operation. The most common is general anesthesia where you are put to sleep for the entire operation. The second most common is called a MAC (*monitored anesthesia care*) where the anesthesiologist gives you a sedative through your veins. The sedative puts you out long enough to allow the surgeon to inject a long-acting numbing anesthetic solution into the tissues. You would then return to a partially sedated state. You won't feel anything during the rest of the operation.

In a few men, I have even performed the orchiectomy under a local anesthetic with no sedation at all. The choice is up to you. Sometimes your general health may suggest that one anesthesia may be safer than another for you. Talk with the anesthesiologist. On rare occasions, I have done this surgery using a spinal anesthetic, but this may delay your quick discharge home somewhat.

Does it hurt afterwards?

There is usually no pain, but some men complain of an ache or soreness for a few days. Most are surprised how easy it is and how good they feel afterward. There can be some swelling of tissues or even a little bruising, but this isn't usually a problem.

Will I need to have stitches removed?

Most doctors use absorbable stitches, so you should not need to have any removed. They dissolve on their own. Occasionally the skin edges may open up. This is quite common and will usually heal quickly on its own. I recommend that you keep the incision clean and dry, washing with a diluted hydrogen-peroxide solution once or twice a day. You may want to use an antibiotic ointment such as Neosporin® or the equivalent once or twice a day.

What does it cost to have an orchiectomy?

The total cost for the surgeon, anesthesiologist, the facility and all of the equipment and supplies comes to about $2,000, but it can be higher in large cities. This obviously varies widely depending on where you are having the surgery done. Big cities tend to be the most expensive. The cost can be thousands more.

Is orchiectomy covered by insurance?

Yes, it is a covered expense, because it is for the treatment of an illness and is not considered "cosmetic." You might encounter a problem if you have private insurance and the prostate cancer was a pre-existing condition. If you are not sure, check with your insurance company. Medicare does cover an orchiectomy for the treatment of prostate cancer.

For insurance purposes, do I need a second opinion because this is surgery?

No, orchiectomy coverage is most often approved by insurance companies without a second opinion. If you are not

Author's Note: *Shortly after I opened my practice, I treated an elderly man with advancing prostate cancer. Following a rather lengthy discussion with him about the options, he wanted to proceed with the orchiectomy. At his first follow-up visit, he was visibly upset. He explained he was doing fine, but he was surprised to find that not only had we removed his testicles but we also took his "eggs." After a few moments I realized he had no idea what his testicles were. He was surprised to find out exactly what we had done during his procedure.*

sure, call and ask your company. Don't assume anything, or you might find yourself stuck with all the costs. You may simply need preauthorization. In my practice, most insurance plans don't require permission for an outpatient procedure such as this.

What happens after I go home?

To make your recovery easier, I ask you to avoid heavy lifting and straining for the first week or two. You should apply ice packs to the scrotum every hour or so for the first 48 hours to keep the swelling down. Be careful to apply the ice over a layer of clothing and not directly to the skin, as this can cause injury.

When can I shower?

Any time you wish is okay. I recommend not taking a tub bath until the incision is totally healed, usually about a week or two after surgery.

When can I drive?

If you are not taking any pain medications you should be able to drive within a few days. Ask your doctor.

How soon can I resume normal activities such as golf, tennis, swimming or bowling?

It would probably be best if you avoided strenuous activity for about two weeks, but it is important to stay active by walking as much as you can.

How soon can I ride a bike, exercycle or horse?

I advise not sitting on a bicycle, exercycle or horse for a few weeks.

Monthly Injections

What kind of medication is given during monthly injections?

The medication is called an *LHRH analog.* It basically is a "copy" of a naturally occurring hormone in the body that stimulates the production of testosterone.

How do the monthly shots work?

The shots stimulate a short burst of testosterone for about two weeks. Your body interprets this burst as having *too much* testosterone. Then your body essentially *shuts down* the hormone production. This results in the same low level of hormone in the body as if the testicles had been removed. To maintain the benefits of these injections, you should continue them every month for the rest of your life.

Could the flareup of the hormone right after the start of the shots cause any problems?

This is a rare but potentially serious problem if the cancer has spread alongside the spinal cord in the backbone. If there is prostate cancer in the spine, then a bone scan may show the location. Only a CT scan or MRI would show that it may be squeezing the spinal cord. It is not standard procedure to order these tests in most circumstances.

The cancer may possibly increase in size during the flareup of testosterone levels, which can squeeze and damage the spinal cord. Though rare, this could cause you to become paralyzed.

What are the advantages of LHRH shots?

You get to keep your testicles and still receive an effective treatment to drop your testosterone level. Later, if you have side effects, such as the hot flashes mentioned earlier, and you are intolerant of the treatments, then you could choose to have the orchiectomy.

Are the various types of hormone shots the same?

They effectively do the same thing but are slightly different variations on the same theme. From a medical point of view, they are equally effective and are as effective as removal of the testicles in decreasing testosterone.

What are the hormone medications?

There are two kinds of LHRH analog medications available: Lupron® and Zoladex.™ Both are similar and work the same way to cause a drop in testosterone.

How are the injections given?

Lupron is given as a once-a-month injection into the muscle of one of the buttocks. Many doctors will alternate from one side to the other, month to month.

Zoladex is a pellet that is injected into the tissue just under the surface of the skin, usually given somewhere on the lower abdominal wall. This is considered a good location, because this area has fewer nerves and a good blood supply. This injection usually first requires administration of a tiny amount of local anesthetic to numb the skin before the pellet is inserted. Then the pellet is inserted through a tiny nick in the skin made with the injection needle. Some doctors prefer to give the injection without first numbing the skin.

Pharmaceutical companies are developing long-acting versions of these medications which may allow injections that will last several months.

How long does the treatment last?

If you choose hormone shots, you take them every month for the rest of your life. You can always switch from shots to the surgery, and then of course the shots would no longer be necessary. Occasionally with very advanced disease, we stop the shots when we try other treatments.

What do the shots cost?

The monthly injections cost about $500 per shot for Lupron and $400 for Zoladex. A variable amount is charged by the doctor for preparing and giving you the shot. These costs are usually covered by insurance, HMOs and Medicare. You may be responsible for a small portion for your co-pay.

What if I'm late getting a treatment?

The benefits of injections only last about 28 days. Being a few days early or late shouldn't really make a difference. If you are more than a few days late, then you will just have to accept that there will be period of time where there is no hormone reduction. On an occasional basis, this probably won't cause any problems. I ask patients to stick to the 28-day schedule as much as possible.

What if I miss a treatment?

Then you will have some return of male hormone to your system. This shouldn't cause a problem. It's not a good idea to miss entire treatments regularly.

What if I'm planning to be out of town when my injection is due?

I usually give my patients two options. First, I can

e a written note or prescription that you can present to a doctor in the community you are traveling to. I have had several visiting patients come to me for an injection. I have been told by a few patients that it may take a call or two to find a urologist willing to do this for you.

The other option is for you to buy the Lupron or Zoladex and take it with you. You would then have to find a doctor willing to give you the injection. Just to be sure there are no problems, I also provide a prescription or letter asking that you be given the shot on or about the due date.

Total Androgen Blockade

Do these hormone therapies eliminate all of the male hormone?

No, a small amount of the male hormones *(androgens)* are secreted by the *adrenal glands,* located on top of the kidneys. There is much debate whether or not this remaining male hormone plays a role in cancer-treatment failures. Some experts believe that in addition to the injections of Lupron or Zoladex, or removal of the testicles, you should also take another medicine daily called *flutamide*, whose brand name is Eulexin®.

How does flutamide work?

Flutamide blocks the cells' ability to absorb any hormone, producing what is called *total androgen blockade.* There is evidence that suggests it may work to keep the cancer in check longer than orchiectomy or monthly injections alone and could add seven to twelve months or more to your life span. Flutamide must be taken three times a day.

Can I take flutamide at a later time if there's a concern the cancer is growing?

If you choose not to take flutamide and at some point your PSA level starts to go up, then flutamide can always be added to your treatment, usually with good results. No one really knows if this approach will work as well as starting the medication in the beginning of initial hormone therapy. In fact, there are some physicians who prefer to add it only if you need it.

How long do I have to take flutamide?

It is intended to be taken for the rest of your life. If you're taking flutamide and the cancer starts to come back, when the flutamide is stopped you may see a drop in your PSA levels. Why this occurs no one really knows.

Does flutamide work?

Probably. Only time will tell if it is of significant benefit. I recommend my patients take flutamide if they can afford it.

What does flutamide cost?

It costs $300 per month, which can be a financial burden for some men. If you shop around, you can usually find it for a little less. Some patients have traveled to Mexico to buy it, thinking they will be able to purchase it for substantially less. For years it was available in Canada before patients could buy it in the U.S.

Most border pharmacies, however, charge almost as much as those in the U.S. That is, assuming you are really being sold flutamide and not something else. I had one patient who was sold a potassium supplement, thinking it was flutamide. No wonder it was so much cheaper.

What are flutamide's side effects?

The only significant side effect is diarrhea. This can be quite significant and very upsetting if it is severe or prolonged. If you start flutamide and get diarrhea, we usually reduce the dose from two pills, three times each day, to one pill, three times each day.

If diarrhea is still a problem, we will stop the flutamide altogether to see if flutamide is really the culprit or if you just have a touch of intestinal flu. Even if the diarrhea goes away, we will restart the flutamide slowly and gradually build back up to a full dose, three times each day.

Intermittent Therapy

What is intermittent therapy?

This is starting hormone therapy, then stopping it when your PSA drops down to its lowest level and stabilizes. Hormone therapy would be restarted when the PSA level starts to climb again. Therapy would be continued until the PSA again drops back down.

This experimental pattern of on-and-off hormone therapy would be less expensive than continuous therapy. If you are bothered by hot flashes or impotence, intermittent therapy might give you occasional breaks with a return to "normal life," perhaps though only for a short time.

Could this intermittent hormone therapy be dangerous?

Animal studies trying intermittent therapy suggest it may not cause any problems and might even be better than continuous hormone therapy. No good studies with humans are available yet to help determine any dangers. For now, intermittent therapy is not the main treatment of choice.

Use of Hormones Before Surgery or Radiation

Why does my doctor want me to take hormone shots before I have surgery?

The hope is that by using hormone shots for two to four months before surgery, the size of the prostate may be reduced and make the surgery easier to perform. Though it doesn't work for everyone, many men with large prostates can have a significant reduction in prostate size with a few months of hormone therapy. There is still debate about whether or not it really makes a difference.

Flutamide Side Effects

Diarrhea
Hot Flashes
Decreased Sex Drive
Impotence
Nausea/Vomiting
Breast Enlargement and/or Tenderness
Liver Damage (rare)

Can taking hormone shots make the cancer shrink?

This was originally the idea when hormone therapy was given before surgery. There are a large number of studies comparing men who had hormone shots before surgery and men who didn't. Most researchers feel that if it does shrink the cancer, it is only in a small percentage of those men having prostate surgery. In my experience, the hormone pretreatment, called *neoadjuvant therapy*, really hasn't made much of a difference.

What is the reason not to try the hormone shots before surgery?

The main concern expressed by my patients is the fear of unpleasant side effects, such as impotence and hot flashes.

Can hormone shots be used to keep the cancer from spreading if I can't have surgery or radiation for several months?

Yes, hormone therapy may work to prevent continued cancer growth. If the cancer has already grown outside the prostate, hormone therapy will probably not change this.

If my PSA level falls dramatically after hormone shots, do I have to go ahead with surgery?

Yes. Hormone therapy isn't a long-term cure. It's a short-term control. Under the influence of hormone therapy, it is common to see the PSA level drop dramatically. This does not mean the cancer has gone away, but rather that the ability to secrete the PSA substance is reduced. In other words, the cancer is still there.

Would it help to take hormone shots before radiation?

In selected men with very large prostates, it may be reasonable to try several months of hormone therapy to reduce the gland size and therefore make it easier to treat.

Is there ever a reason to stay on hormone shots even after radiation?

Yes, if the cancer is high-grade or large and is thought to be potentially very aggressive, then staying on hormone therapy may provide better long-term cure rates than radiation alone.

Option	Cost	Type of Treatment	Side Effects	Benefits
DES	$30/Month Lifetime	Daily Pill	High Dose Risks: Heart Attack Strokes Blood Clots	Inexpensive, Effective
Orchiectomy	$2500+ One-Time	Outpatient Surgery	Hot Flashes, Breast Tenderness	Quick, Single Treatment Rapid Drop in Hormones Overall Less Expensive
Lupron/ Zoladex	$400-$500/Month Lifetime	Monthly Injections	Hot flashes Breast Tenderness	Avoid Surgery
Flutamide	$250-$300/Month Lifetime	Pill 3 Times a Day	Diarrhea	May Prolong Survival

25

Cryotherapy, Microwave & Lasers

As doctors explore new ways to treat prostate cancer, three techniques stand out as possible options. They include cryotherapy, microwave therapy and laser therapy. Of these, *cryotherapy* is the most promising.

Cryotherapy

What is cryotherapy?

This is the controlled freezing of the prostate gland for cancer treatment, intended to serve as a cure.

Is cryotherapy the same as cryosurgery?

Yes, they refer to the same treatment. *Cryosurgical ablation* means the same thing.

What is the role for cryosurgery?

This is a new and still relatively experimental technique where the prostate tissue is *frozen*. The purpose is to

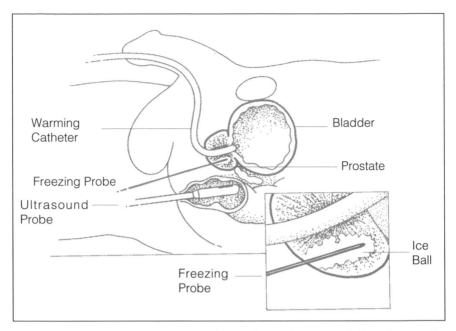

CRYOSURGERY: Prostate tissue is frozen by probes inserted directly into the prostate. This creates an ice ball of prostate tissue, killing the cancer cells. A catheter placed in the urethra circulates a solution to keep it warm during the procedure. An ultrasound probe is used to be sure that the rectal wall is not frozen.

kill the cancer cells. The relative simplicity, reduced costs, ease and quickness of cryosurgery make it potentially a better treatment than the prostatectomy or lengthy radiation treatments. At this point, we don't know if cryotherapy will be effective as a long-term treatment for prostate cancer.

How is cryosurgery performed?

Cryosurgery is performed under anesthesia. Special probes are placed throughout the prostate. Their positions are confirmed with rectal ultrasound. Liquid nitrogen is circulated through the probes, freezing the tissue of the prostate. A rectal ultrasound probe is used to monitor the freezing and to let the surgeon know when enough tissue has been treated.

The goal is to create an "ice ball" big enough to kill the cancer. According to supporters of this technique, there is no damage to the adjacent bladder or to the rectal wall, which lies just behind the prostate.

Cryosurgery is still considered experimental. There are no long-term results yet, so we really don't know whether this will be as good as radiation. The experts presently are hesitant to get very excited. There are concerns that some cancer cells may escape being frozen, and other cells may be outside the prostate and would not be treated.

How cold does the prostate get with cryosurgery?

The temperature can get to -195F (-126C). The point of killing cells is -20F (-29C).

Does cryotherapy also freeze the urethra?

A catheter is placed in the urethra to circulate a warming solution that protects the urethra from freezing during treatment.

When is cryotherapy best?

If there is a role, it may be as an option *after* or *instead* of radiation treatment. As with all new techniques, the final answer is still not yet known. Even experts who are regularly doing this procedure are not sure of the role for cryosurgery in the future. In time, cryotherapy may be used on a large number of men with prostate cancer. Then perhaps we'll know if this is another great idea that just didn't work or if it is the great answer we've been waiting for.

Does cryosurgery work with big prostates?

Not really. It works best when the prostate gland is measured with ultrasound to be about 40 grams or less in size.

What can be done if I've been told that I have a large prostate, but I want cryotherapy?

You could try to shrink the gland with three to four months of total hormone blockade, using both the monthly shots and the drug flutamide. You would then need ultrasound re-evaluation to confirm that the prostate is small enough to be effectively treated by cryotherapy.

Can I have cryotherapy if I've already had a TURP?

Yes, but it is harder to perform with less precise freezing. Cryosurgery is best done in prostates that have not had previous surgery.

What are the most common side effects of cryotherapy?

The treatment can cause quite a lot of irritation to the bladder or urethra, resulting in many symptoms such as frequent urination with little warning, burning, blood, pain with urination and similar symptoms of irritation to the rectal wall. Almost half of men who have cryotherapy complain of some degree of penile or scrotal swelling. This is usually temporary.

What else can cause problems after cryotherapy?

Some men develop scars in the urethra, while others can have trouble urinating, requiring a catheter. Fortunately, these risks are relatively uncommon.

Can cryotherapy make me impotent?

Yes. Up to 80% of men who undergo cryotherapy complain of impotence afterward. The risk of impotence depends on how aggressively the surgeon freezes the prostate tissues.

Can I become incontinent after cryosurgery?

This is relatively rare and shouldn't be a problem after cryosurgery.

Are there any other serious complications from cryotherapy?

In addition to the irritation symptoms, the two main risks are the potential formation of an abnormal connection between the urethra and rectum, called a *fistula*, and possible incomplete treatment of the cancer.

Microwave Therapy

What about microwave therapy for prostate cancer?

Microwave therapy still is considered experimental for noncancerous enlargement of the prostate. It is not being used for treatment of cancer. Whether or not it is an effective treatment for simple enlargement of the prostate still is unknown. No long-term studies have been completed to address this mode of therapy with prostate cancer.

Laser Therapy & Electrovaporization

What about laser therapy for prostate cancer?

There are no uses of laser therapy for prostate cancer, at least at this point. The laser is being used to open up the prostate when it causes blockage. But because the laser blindly destroys tissue, it hasn't been used routinely for treatment of cancer. Removing the prostate requires that the entire gland be taken out. The laser would simply destroy tissue without letting you know if any residual cancer remained.

The only role that I'm aware of for lasers in prostate-cancer cases is when a patient has chosen radiation and needs to have a significant blockage relieved. In this situation, the laser may be a reasonable option to discuss.

What is electrovaporization?

Electrovaporization is a new technique that uses heat to destroy prostate tissue.

26

Incontinence

Urinary incontinence is the *involuntary* loss of urine. In simpler terms, it is leaking urine when you don't know that you are or when you are trying not to. This condition can be a temporary or permanent side effect of treatment for prostate cancer.

Under normal conditions, what keeps a man from leaking urine?
    The key to bladder control is a combination of the circular muscle fibers at the bladder neck and the sphincter muscles located beneath the bladder, surrounding the urethra. This muscle combination works to close off the urethra and prevent leakage of urine from the bladder.

Why do some men become incontinent of urine after a radical prostatectomy?
    When the prostate is removed from the base of the bladder, damage can occur to the urinary sphincter that gives the man a mechanism for holding in urine naturally. This

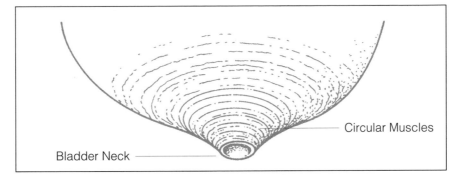

BLADDER NECK: Circular muscles of the bladder neck squeeze together to keep urine from leaking. These can be damaged during surgery or radiation, resulting in urinary incontinence.

damage can result in incontinence. There are various surgical techniques for operating on this anatomy during a prostatectomy, but the danger of tissue and muscle damage is ever-present.

What can I do to reduce the time I will leak after the catheter comes out?

In time, many men can relearn how to use the muscles damaged during surgery. I strongly encourage all my patients to begin *Kegel exercises* even before surgery.

What is a Kegel exercise?

It is simply an exercise to strengthen the pelvic muscles. As a group of muscles, it can be exercised and trained to be stronger. This is the reason we encourage Kegel exercise for men who will undergo radical prostatectomy. After surgery, while the catheter is in place, it's important for you to continue working the pelvic muscles. I have had patients tell me that when they stop the exercises, they notice a dramatic increase in the amount of incontinence they have.

How do I do Kegel exercises?

You probably already do this exercise unknowingly.

When you are urinating and suddenly stop midstream—that's the Kegel exercise! If you are standing in a public place and suddenly feel the urge to pass gas, and you "snug up" the muscles to hold it in, that too is a Kegel exercise. I would best describe it as a *tightening of the pelvic muscles.*

Or—imagine that you are standing on top of a hill, naked, with a $1,000 bill tucked between the cheeks of your buttocks. You are not able to use your hands, but you need to hold onto the bill during high gusty winds. That squeezing of your buttocks, pulling up internally and tightening down with your pelvic muscles, is a Kegel exercise.

Will people around me know I am doing the exercises?
If you are doing them correctly, no.

How often should I do the Kegel exercises?
You need to do them regularly, not just when you think of it. I suggest at least every hour for five minutes. When the catheter is removed, you should be doing the exercises at least 20 times a day. It is important that you don't just tighten up and then let go. Rather, tighten up and then hold it, then let go and repeat. Don't just do it as an exercise. Before surgery and after the catheter comes out, practice stopping midstream when you urinate. Hold it and then restart forcefully. This should help build up and restore the muscle tone.

How long should I continue to do the Kegel exercises?
You should continue to do these exercises as long as you have a problem with urinary leakage. This could be a few days to a few months. Rarely, some men may have to do them forever.

How long can I expect to leak urine after surgery?
There is no way to predict who will leak and who will not, or for how long. Some men claim they never leaked after

the catheter came out, while most describe a few weeks to a few months or more of continued leakage. A few patients have complained of continued leakage for more than a year before it stopped. A small percentage of men will have continued leaking *permanently.*

If the leakage goes on for a very long time, does that mean it will never stop?

No. Some of my patients have reported continued leakage to some degree for many months before everything "dried up." I recall one patient who continued with some incontinence for 18 months before he no longer leaked. It is important that you don't become discouraged after a few weeks. But be aware that there are no guarantees as to whether or not you will leak.

If I leak, does that mean something was done wrong in surgery?

No. It is simply a reflection of how your body healed. I recall some patients who had everything put back together perfectly during surgery but still ended up with some incontinence. Then there have been others who had problems in surgery that left us with expectations of leakage, and they were as dry as a man can be after the catheter came out.

What if I am not leaking?

If you don't leak, consider yourself fortunate. I have had patients who had absolutely no incontinence after the Foley catheter was removed. One patient wasn't worried until he went out to play golf with three other men who also had prostate cancer surgery. In sharing their experiences and problems, he was made to feel that he was supposed to leak, as they did. He felt sure something must be wrong. I had to reassure him during his postoperative checkup that all was well and that he was one of the fortunate ones who had a quick recovery with no leakage.

Are there any medications that can help?

Certain medications and decongestants such as Entex LA® and Ornade® help to snug up the urethral muscles and may reduce urine leakage. Because these medications possibly can increase your blood pressure, it is a good idea to have your blood pressure checked twice a week.

What about the penile clamp?

This is a device that snaps onto the penis and prevents urine leakage. If used at all, it should be used only for short periods of time. If left on the penis too long, damage to the skin and underlying tissues can occur.

I discourage men from using a clamp in the first few months after surgery. I have seen a few patients who have become totally dependent on the clamp. These men stop trying to regain control. They no longer do the Kegel exercises and remain incontinent.

How does it work?

The penile clamp applies direct physical pressure to the urethra, forcing it shut so there is no leakage of urine.

How long can I leave it on?

It is important to take it off about every 30 minutes to let your bladder empty and then reapply as needed. This will also allow the blood flow to keep tissues healthy. I ask patients to use the clamp only for special occasions, such as going out to dinner, to a movie or to church.

Are there any problems with the clamp?

If you use a clamp too early after surgery and too often, you will not be motivated to work on controlling leakage with Kegel exercises. This excessive reliance can result in permanent problems in controlling your urine.

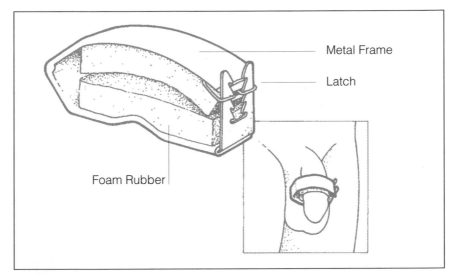

PENILE CLAMP: Penile clamp squeezes the urethra shut to prevent urine from leaking.

How soon after surgery can I start using a clamp?

I usually ask that you wait at least six to eight weeks.

What about adult male undergarments?

These are simply large *absorbent underpants*, often with a hole cut out in which the man places his penis. These work by absorbing any urine that leaks. These are usually used in the early phases of recovery after surgery.

Are there any operations to correct incontinence?

Yes. If the leakage is severe and prolonged, the urologist can operate to place a device called an *artificial sphincter*.

What is an artificial sphincter?

This is a device made from silicone-based materials. It is surgically placed around the urethra, just at the bladder neck. When activated by a pump in the scrotum, this device tightens around the urethra and prevents urine from leaking.

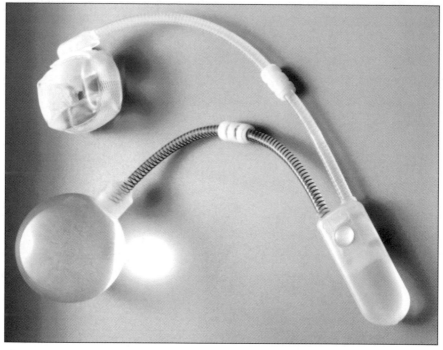

ARTIFICIAL SPHINCTER: *Placed surgically, the artificial sphincter provides relief from severe urinary incontinence. Cuff surrounds bladder neck and urethra and squeezes shut, compressing and blocking any urine leakage. Device is activated and deactivated by a pump placed in scrotum. Photo courtesy of American Medical Systems, Inc.*

How long does the operation take to place the artificial sphincter?

This procedure usually takes several hours under anesthesia. Usually there is at least one overnight stay in the hospital.

What is done before a sphincter can be put in?

It is important to have a complete evaluation before surgery to be sure there is normal bladder function and no scarring or other irregularities that may compromise the results. A detailed study of bladder function, called a *urodynamics evaluation*, may be performed. A cystoscopy is usually done to evaluate the bladder neck visually.

What problems can occur with an artificial sphincter?

Because this is an operation with implantation of a

mechanical device, be aware that there are risks for failure or problems. These problems include bleeding, infection around the device, urinary retention, continued incontinence and malfunction or breakage of the artificial sphincter.

Though rare, these problems can occur. Only a small percentage of men need additional surgery to adjust the device or repair any malfunction. It's important for you to be aware of how this device works so you will have realistic expectations. Because it is a mechanical device, a low percentage of malfunction is expected, which can require additional surgery.

Are there any other operations for incontinence?

Yes. Many men are having injections of collagen into the bladder neck to try to reduce leakage.

How do collagen injections work?

The collagen is injected through a flexible needle into the tissues at the bladder neck. When successful, this causes the tissues to enlarge and squeeze together to prevent leakage.

What is collagen?

Collagen is the protein extract of connective tissue from cattle. It is injected elsewhere in the body by plastic surgeons as a filler to add shape or fullness.

How many collagen treatments are needed?

Five to seven sessions of collagen injections may be required to achieve control of urine. There is no way to know in advance how many times a person will need treatment.

Do I need anesthesia?

Yes. Most injections are performed under general anesthesia, but it is also done under local anesthesia.

How long will the collagen last?

If it works, it should be effective for at least a few years. Some men will notice that it gradually becomes less effective over several years. Each individual may have different results. Some may have great urinary control for several months and then notice increased leaking. Others may go many years without problems.

Does collagen injection work for everyone?

No. In fact, as a treatment for urine leakage after a radical prostatectomy, perhaps only a third of patients may notice some improvement. The nice thing is that collagen injections are easy to do as an outpatient procedure, and can be repeated.

Do I need to have any tests before collagen-injection treatment?

Yes. One of the side effects to the collagen is an allergic reaction. You must have a skin test at least three to four weeks before the collagen treatment to make sure you are not allergic to collagen.

The skin test involves an injection of a tiny amount of collagen just under the surface of the skin of your arm. If you are allergic to collagen, you will get a reaction in your arm, including redness and firmness, with possible fevers or aches.

What are the chances I might have an allergic reaction to collagen injections?

This is very rare, but because it can be serious, special precautions are performed, such as the skin test.

What else can be injected instead of collagen?

Some researchers are working with fat injections, but so far this hasn't worked as well as we would like.

How much does the collagen cost?

Each syringe costs several hundred dollars. Considering that it can take several syringes of collagen for each treatment, this could cost thousands of dollars.

How long should I wait after my prostatectomy to try collagen injections to control urinary leakage?

You should wait at least one year.

Can I have collagen injected if I've also had radiation?

Because of scarring of the tissues, it usually will not work to try to inject collagen if you have had radiation following a radical prostatectomy.

What else can be done if I leak urine?

A device called a *condom catheter* is sometimes used, but I don't recommend it. Placed over the penis, this device catches leaked urine and drains it into a bag. Condom catheters can be associated with many problems, including urinary-tract infections. Because of this, I strongly discourage the use of condom catheters.

Is biofeedback a treatment option?

Yes, some men who can learn to control their pelvic muscles through biofeedback can have improvement with less urine leakage.

Treatments for Incontinence

Biofeedback
Kegel Exercises
Medications
Condom Catheter
Penile Clamp
Collagen Injection
Artificial Sphincter

27

Impotence

Impotence and problems with erections are potential side effects that can result from various treatments for prostate cancer.

With few exceptions, if you develop prostate cancer, you will have to consider the impact of the treatments on your ability to have an erection. For those men who already have lost the ability to obtain an erection, there is a lot of interest in regaining their potency.

This chapter will explain some of the options that are available to bring back this part of your sexual life.

What exactly is impotence?

Impotence is the inability to achieve and sustain an adequate erection for sexual intercourse.

What is erectile dysfunction?

Erectile dysfunction is the ability to achieve an erection that may not be as adequate as you might prefer. Your penis might be erect, but the erection may not last long enough before it fades away. *Erectile dysfunction* is a broader term than *impotence*.

How does prostate cancer affect erections?

All aspects of prostate cancer and treatments can somehow impact on erections. Surgery and radiation can damage the nerves and blood vessels that allow men to achieve and maintain an erection. Hormone therapy can often eliminate erections through unknown mechanisms. In addition, a lack of interest can sometimes accompany the loss of testosterone.

The good news is that with all the new and exciting nonsurgical methods of restoring erections, almost everyone can be happy with the final outcome.

Can I become impotent if I choose to do nothing for my prostate cancer?

Yes. Many men describe problems with erections even without any of the dramatic curative treatments that are available. It may be that as the cancer grows and spreads, it can grow through the outside of the prostate and damage the nerves that are just outside the gland. Or perhaps it is a result of fears, concerns, anxiety and stress that can go along with prostate cancer. As I tell many of my patients, even ignoring the cancer and trying to forget about it can still lead to erectile problems.

Can I become impotent if I choose radiation?

Yes. 25% to 50% of men who undergo radiation therapy will become impotent. Unlike after surgery, where impotence is immediate, radiation may cause problems slowly. Even if you have great erections before, during and after the radiation treatments, many men describe a slow loss of erections over about one year's time. It is believed to be a result of radiation injury to the small blood vessels and nerves.

Can I develop erectile problems after interstitial seed therapy?

Yes. Up to 80% of men who have good erections before treatment will have significant problems with erections afterward. Like external-beam therapy, seed therapy can take quite a while to cause loss of erections.

How does radical surgery actually make a man impotent?

Many times the tiny nerves that transmit messages to get an erection can be cut or damaged when removing the prostate. If the message can't get to the penis to allow blood in, there will be no erections. In addition, there may be injury to the blood supply that helps with erections.

Author's Note: *John D. came back to see me about four weeks after his prostatectomy, quite concerned that I must have done something wrong at his surgery. He went on to tell me that when he compared notes with his three best golf buddies, all had significant problems with erections, even years after treatment. I explained to him, "Well, you're only four weeks out from surgery, and it can take a while for things to return to normal, if they do at all."*

"No, that's not the point," he explained. "Something must be wrong. I've already had several good erections since I've been home." Then why the concern, I asked.

He then hit me with the question, "Are you sure you took my prostate out?" I showed him his pathology report confirming that indeed his prostate was in a jar. I then reassured him he was just going to have to live with his normal erections.

Why am I still impotent if I had the nerve-sparing
radical prostatectomy?

Even if you had the nerves saved, it can still take many
months and occasionally up to a year or two for men to gradually regain the ability to have an adequate erection. If only
one side of the nerves was saved, then your odds of regaining
potency are not great, but it can still happen. This delay may
be as a result of injury to the nerves during their preservation.
Nerves are very slow to heal.

Does cryosurgery cause the same damage to nerves?

Yes. It appears that nerves can often be damaged when
the prostate is frozen, resulting in erectile dysfunction in up
to 80% of men. As with surgery, there is a fine line between
trying to kill all the cancer with freezing and possibly performing an incomplete treatment by attempting to preserve
nerve function. The procedure is not precise enough to tell
exactly where to stop the freezing process so that all the cancer is killed, yet leaving the nerves undamaged.

Why does hormone therapy eliminate my interest in sex?

The male hormone testosterone is responsible for much
of the male sex drive, called *libido*. In addition, testosterone
plays an important role in the ability to get an erection. When
testosterone is eliminated from the body, it is common for men
to become impotent, which is not such a problem because they
are no longer interested in sex. This doesn't happen to everyone
though. There are some men who are still quite interested in
sex and claim they continue to have normal erections.

How does blocking testosterone make me impotent?

No one really knows. We know that the brain and hormones work together with nerves and blood vessels to bring
on an erection. The disruption of that fine balance may be
enough to keep an erection from developing.

Author's Note: *Tony was an otherwise healthy 47-year-old patient who was found to have widespread prostate cancer during an evaluation for back pain. We went ahead with total removal of all male hormones from his body through an orchiectomy to remove his testicles and daily doses of flutamide.*

Despite his total hormone blockade, he continued to have normal erections and an interest in sex right up until he died suddenly almost two years after his cancer was detected. This should serve to remind us that medicine is still an art more than a science. There's always someone who responds to treatment in a way that isn't supposed to happen.

Does the quality of my erection before treatment affect whether or not I have erections after treatment?

Definitely, yes. Younger, healthier men with good erections are far more likely to have the return of their erections after surgery or radiation than older men who already had erection problems.

What can I do to regain erections if I am impotent after treatment?

There are several excellent options that you have to choose from to bring back erections like those you used to have when you were younger. These include *vacuum erection devices, penile self-injections* and *penile implants*.

Options for Treatment of Impotence

Do Nothing
Vacuum Devices
Penile Self-Injection
Penile Implants
> Bendable (Malleable)
> Mechanical
> Inflatable, No Separate Pump
> (Self-Contained)
> Inflatable, Separate Pump
> (Multi-Component)

Vacuum Erection Device

How does the vacuum device work?

The first and perhaps easiest option is the *vacuum erection device*. This is a large plastic tube with a pump attached. Placed over your lubricated penis, the pump is activated, creating a vacuum inside the tube. Blood flows into the penis because of the vacuum, giving you a great erection. Then you pull an elastic ring off the tube onto the base of the penis. The ring holds all the blood in the penis, which gives you a good erection until the ring is taken off, up to 30 minutes later.

Will the vacuum device work even if the nerves are cut or damaged?

It works in almost everyone, whether or not the nerves are intact or functional. It doesn't rely on the body's ability to pump in blood. It is an external mechanism to achieve the same results.

Why can I leave the ring on for only 30 minutes?

The blood being held inside the penis by the ring is not able to circulate. If the blood is kept in your penis too long, serious problems could develop. Therefore, you need to

VACUUM ERECTION DEVICE: A vacuum erection device uses a pump attached to a plastic cylinder. The cylinder is placed over the lubricated penis, and a vacuum is created by the pump. This results in blood flowing into the two chambers in the penis that create an erection. An elastic ring is then slipped off of the cylinder onto the base of the penis to keep the blood in place and the erection intact. Photo courtesy of Osbon.

take the ring off after no more than 30 minutes, but you can always put it back on several minutes later if you need to.

How often can I use the device?

There are no limits as long as you follow the instructions and take off the ring every 30 minutes.

Does the rubber ring hurt?

It can be tight for some men. There are a number of different-size rings so that over time you'll be able to decide which one works best for you. The ideal ring is one that is not too tight, is not uncomfortable and squeezes enough to maintain an erection to your satisfaction.

Can I still ejaculate with the ring on?

Maybe. If you have had a prostatectomy, there will be no ejaculate as the glands that make the semen have all been removed. If you have had radiation or hormone therapy, then many times you can still ejaculate. Some of the rings are modified to allow for ejaculation. Don't confuse *orgasm* with *ejac-*

ulation. Ejaculate is the fluid that comes out of the penis during orgasm. Orgasm is a generalized feeling of well-being that occurs at the same time as ejaculation would normally occur.

What if I have problems or questions regarding the vacuum device?

Some companies offer excellent support services with the product. Some have toll-free telephone numbers to call anytime with questions. Others provide trained representatives who can meet you and work to overcome any problems or concerns. They can also teach you some of the fine points that can't be taught in a video or booklet.

What are the biggest complaints about the vacuum device?

Couples who are unhappy usually have only a few complaints. First, the penis will be *cooler* to the touch because fresh blood is not recirculating through it. This can bother some couples. One couple didn't like the fact that with the ring the penis appeared unnatural. Some men don't like the feeling of the tight ring. Others just don't like the idea of going through the motions of putting on "that darn contraption."

I try to explain that a couple's unreasonable expectations can get in the way of satisfaction with the device, especially if they think erections will be like they were at age 18.

Often the man will think that in the middle of foreplay, he has to stop, get up and go into the bathroom and put on the device. But if used as *part* of foreplay, with both partners putting on the pump and ring, the vacuum device can be quite satisfying to both man and woman.

What percentage of couples are happy with the device?

The literature says that more than 90% of couples are happy using the device. My own clinical experience supports that finding.

What if I'm not happy?

Many companies that sell these devices offer a 90-day money-back guarantee. Before you buy a vacuum device, ask if you can return it for a full refund if you are not happy.

Will using the device bring back my natural erections any faster?

Although there is no proof, patients who use the device sometimes describe a quicker return of their own natural erections over time.

Where do I get a vacuum device?

These can be purchased from many pharmacies, doctor's offices and directly from manufacturers. Many companies advertise in senior-citizen magazines. Shop around. Be wary of a hard sell from a mail-order company. Talk to your urologist.

How much do these vacuum devices cost?

They run about $300 to $500. In general, the more that you pay, the better the device and the more support services are available to you.

Do I need to have a prescription?

Yes. This can be from your urologist, radiation therapist or primary-care physician.

Is the device covered by Medicare?

Yes, but usually you have to buy it yourself and then submit to Medicare for reimbursement for the "approved amount." The portion of cost you are responsible for should be less than $100. Government rules change frequently, so ask your doctor.

Do most HMOs and private health plans pay for the device?

This depends on the plan. In my community, one of the big HMOs does not cover the expense of the device. The majority of plans do pay for the vacuum device, however. I strongly encourage you to read what the covered benefits are before you buy any health insurance or sign up with an HMO.

Penile Self-Injections

Self-injection of certain medications into the penis to cause an erection is one way to compensate for the erectile dysfunction that can result from prostate-cancer treatments.

How do self-injections work?

Certain substances allow blood to flow into the penis, resulting in an erection. Researchers developed a technique for a man to inject a tiny amount of these very active substances into one of the two chambers of the penis called the *corpora cavernosa*. Over the next 10 to 20 minutes, both chambers fill with blood, causing the penis to become erect.

What medications are injected?

Urologists use any one or a combination of papaverine, phentolamine or PGE (prostaglandin E). Each doctor has his own preferred medication that he feels works best with the least problems. I prefer PGE, because it seems to cause fewer problems with fairly good results.

Doesn't the needle hurt?

No. Most men are surprised when they realize that injecting this medication through a tiny needle into the penis isn't painful at all. Occasionally a patient will complain that his penis ached or was sore, probably from the medication.

How good are the erections?

When it works, it works great.

How long do the erections last?

Erections from penile injection can last from 30 minutes to two hours.

How often can I do a penile self-injection?

You should limit yourself to about twice a week. Doing this more often increases the risks of scars and penile damage.

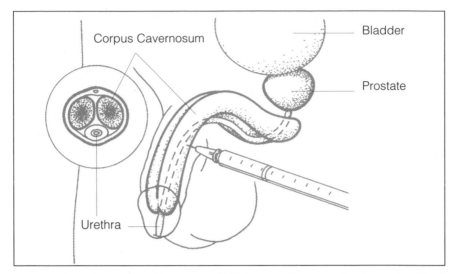

Corpus Cavernosum

Bladder

Prostate

Urethra

PENILE ANATOMY AND SELF-INJECTION: Normal erection develops when blood flows into both corpora cavernosa within the penis. Penile self-injection is an effective technique to produce an erection by stimulating blood flow with medication injected directly into one of the corpora. After the medication is injected through a tiny needle, blood flow increases and an erection develops.

How difficult is it to learn how to give myself an injection?

For most men, it is very easy. I teach my patients over three separate visits how to prepare the medication, draw up the syringe to the correct dose and then to inject the medication into the corpora safely.

What does it cost?

The medication can run from $50 to $150 or more for a vial that has about 20 injections, depending on the type of medication, the pharmacy and your location.

Is the medicine covered by insurance plans and HMOs?

Usually, yes. However, it is very important that you understand the specific coverage points of your insurance plan. Some may not cover the visits or the medication costs.

What can go wrong with a penile injection?

It is possible to develop scarring at the injection site if you use the same place every time. Some men can get a bruise or swelling of the penis if there is bleeding from the injection. The most serious complication is called *priapism*. This is a condition when the erection persists and won't go away. Though this may not sound like a problem, a persistent erection can be very painful and become a true emergency, requiring immediate treatment.

How often does this happen?

Priapism is quite rare, but it is something you should be aware of.

What should I do if the erection won't fade away?

First, apply an ice pack to your penis. Sometimes this is enough to get the erection to fade away. Never apply the ice directly to your skin. Apply it over a cloth or underwear. If the ice doesn't cause the erection to subside, call your urologist *immediately*, even in the middle of the night. Do not wait until the next day! He may send you to the nearest emergency room for evaluation and treatment.

How long should I wait before calling if the erection persists?

If the erection is still present after several hours, call your urologist. Some doctors want to be called sooner. Others will direct you to call later. You should not wait all night or call after 18 hours to tell your doctor about this problem. The

Author's Note: *I had one young man in his 50s who, in anticipation of his prostatectomy, started on the PGE injections before surgery. He was so surprised to see just how good an erection he could have that he commented he wished he had known about these injections years ago.*

longer you wait, the more difficult it will be to get your erection to go away. It may even require drainage of the blood, with the possible risk of additional problems.

Why is priapism a problem?

If the blood remains in your penis too long, it begins to *lose oxygen* and starts to *thicken*. The blood may turn into a dark sludge if you wait too long. This is harder to circulate and may damage the delicate tissues inside the penis.

What if I inject into the wrong place on the penis?

This is possible but usually doesn't cause much effect except failure to give you an erection. Occasionally, you can get penile pain. You could damage the nerves or blood vessels if you totally miss the mark, which is hard to do.

How long will the medication supply remain usable?

I ask my patients to keep their PGE solution in the refrigerator until it is needed. I have been told that if refrigerated, it will be good for up to one year.

Can my wife participate in the injections?

Yes, this is encouraged. This doubles the number of people learning the technique, making for fewer mistakes. The wife's participation adds to the ritual foreplay, which can result in better erections.

Can I keep adding more medication if I want to?

No. You must stay on the same dose that you worked out with your urologist, unless otherwise directed.

Other Injections

What about testosterone injections?

No. I strongly discourage the use of testosterone injections for impotence after treatment for prostate cancer. Even though there may be no cancer left in your body, there is no way we can be absolutely sure. If there is a small speck of tumor remaining, then testosterone stimulation may activate the cancer.

Penile Implants

Surgically placed *penile implants*, also called *prostheses*, offer an alternative to the more conservative options discussed for overcoming erectile dysfunction.

Implants are permanent. They are inserted into the corpora under anesthesia. There can be pain after surgery, and there is always a risk that the device will break or malfunction. The fancier and more complicated the device, the more likely it will have a problem that could require surgery to replace the broken component.

With penile implants, regardless of type, the head of the penis does not swell as it would in a normal erection.

There are four main categories of implants. You can choose between a *bendable*, a *mechanical,* an *inflatable (self-contained)* and the deluxe *multi-component inflatable implant.*

Bendable (Malleable) Implant The bendable or "malleable" prosthesis is usually a collection of silver wires braided inside a silicone sheath. It is the simplest type of implant and least likely to break. The problem is that the penis is permanently rigid. It can be bent to aid with urination and concealment. This is the least expensive product and quickest to put in. It is one of my favorites because of its reliability. This implant slightly increases the diameter of the penis.

Mechanical Implant This type is essentially a wire inside a series of small cups. These can be bent. They are easier to work with than the bendable implant, especially if you have bad arthritis in your hands. Mechanical implants are more likely to stay as you position them. This implant slightly increases penis diameter.

Inflatable (No Pump) This category includes a large number of different devices. Each one has chambers of fluid. When the tip of the prosthesis is repeatedly squeezed, a pump inside the cylinder is activated and the fluid shifts within the device. This results in an increase in rigidity within the prosthesis. This implant slightly increases penis diameter. The penis is relaxed by bending the implant and activating the release valve.

Inflatable (Multi-Component with Pump) This type of device provides an erection that is the most like a natural erection. It uses a separate pump placed in the scrotum between the testicles. Some devices even use reservoirs to hold more fluid under pressure. This extra fluid allows the device to become larger. The pump is repeatedly squeezed, which transfers fluid from the reservoir into the pump cylinder. This implant slightly increases penis diameter and length. The penis is relaxed by squeezing a release valve.

Because these are so much more complicated than the other types of devices, the odds of having a failure, leak or malfunction are increased. If you choose one of these, be prepared for a technical problem requiring additional surgery. These are complex mechanical devices, with no guarantees.

How are the devices inserted?

These products can be put inside the corpora cavernosa through an incision between the penis and scrotum. The inside of each chamber in the penis is stretched open to allow placement of the device. The chambers are then closed and the skin stitched closed.

How long will I be in the hospital to have an implant?

These are often done as outpatient procedures or perhaps with a brief overnight stay.

How soon can I use the implant after surgery?

It is best if you wait about four to six weeks to allow the incision to heal before having sexual intercourse. There is

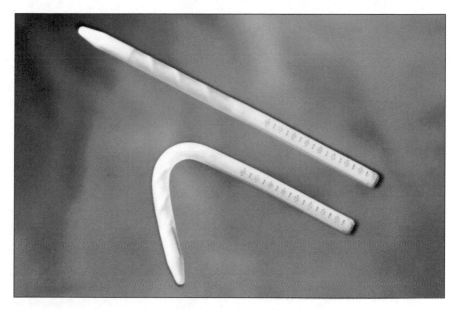

MALLEABLE PENILE IMPLANT: A bendable prosthesis placed into both of the corpora can be bent in any direction. There are no moving parts, so problems with malfunction or breakage are rare. Photo courtesy Mentor Urology, Inc.

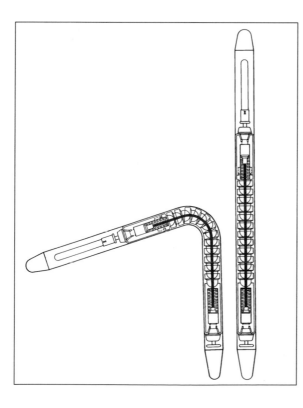

MECHANICAL PENILE IMPLANT: This movable device, also placed into the corpora, is easier to bend and stays in position better than the malleable penile implant. Drawing courtesy Dacomed, Inc.

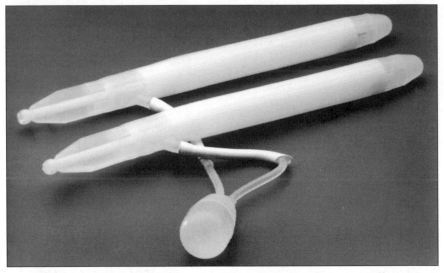

INFLATABLE PENILE IMPLANT: *Inflatable penile implant with scrotal pump which is also the reservoir. This is squeezed to pump fluid into the device and results in increased rigidity.*

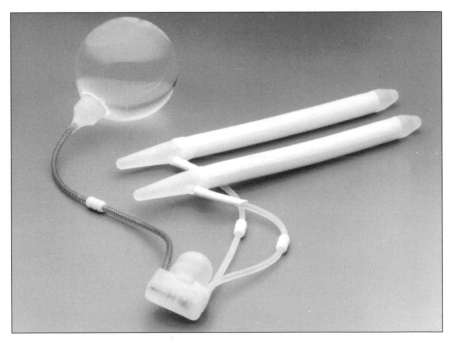

MULTI-COMPONENT INFLATABLE PENILE IMPLANT: *Inflatable penile implant uses separate pump placed in the scrotum to inflate and deflate separate cylinders in the corpora. A separate reservoir may be used to hold fluid. This device allows for the most natural results. Photos courtesy American Medical Systems, Inc.*

Penile Implant Comparison

Malleable   Bendable
                                    Slight increase in penis diameter
                                    Always rigid (can be bent)
                                    Least likely to malfunction
Mechanical   Easier to bend
                                    Slight increase in penis diameter
                                    Always rigid
                                    Rare malfunction
Inflatable (Self-Contained) Increase/decrease rigidity
                                    Pump at end of penis
                                    Slight increase in penis diameter
                                    More risk of malfunction
Inflatable (Multi-Component)
                                    Most like normal
                                    Increase/decrease rigidity
                                    Slight increase in length and diameter
                                    Most likely to malfunction

---

some variability depending on which implant model and style you have chosen.

Is there a lot of pain after surgery?

A patient will often be quite sore for a while, but it shouldn't be too painful. The pain will gradually subside over time and should easily be handled with pain medications.

How often can the device break or malfunction?

Though uncommon, any of the devices can break or fail. This is an unavoidable possibility with any mechanical device.

Are there any devices that will not malfunction?

No. Even the most basic malleable device with no moving parts can still develop cracks in the silver wires. Nothing is 100% free of risk from malfunction.

What are other possible complications that can occur with penile implants?

Erosion Erosion is the protrusion of the implant through the end of the penis or urethra. This can occur if your body rejects the device, if it is put in incorrectly or if there is a weakness or breakdown of the surrounding tissue or urethra.

Infection This is unlikely with all of the antibiotics, sterile techniques and close follow-up that are ordinarily done.

Torque This occurs when the wires of the prostheses twist on each other. In other words, a twisted penis results.

Pain Patients may complain of pain as a result of the device putting pressure on surrounding tissues, but this is rare.

Unsatisfactory results The results are never as good as you might remember from your own natural erections. Some men are unhappy with the device because of high and unrealistic expectations. Although most men are happy, there are others who, for a variety of reasons, regret having the device implanted. The implant can be removed, but erections will no longer be possible, even with the other treatment options.

How much do these devices cost?

Including surgical and anesthesia fees, hospitalization and the device itself, charges can range from $3,000 to $15,000 or more. The more elaborate the implant, the more expensive it is. Charges are usually much higher in big cities and on either coast.

What is covered by Medicare?

All penile implants are covered, except for the usual deductible.

What options are covered by private insurance or HMOs?

Assuming the surgery has been preauthorized, most plans do pay for these operations.

Costs of Treating Impotence

Option	Cost
Nothing	$0
Vacuum device	$300-$500
Penile self-injection	Medication: $60-$150 / 20 injections
	Initial office visit: $300-$500
Implants	Bendable: $3,000-$8,000
	Mechanical: $4,000-$10,000
	Inflatable: $5,000-$15,000

Should I be concerned about a silicone reaction or other problems from the implant material?

No. In the many thousands of men who have had implants placed, there has never been a scientifically documented reaction to the solid silicone material used to make the implants.

Everyone realizes that these implants are placed in an aging population where naturally occurring health problems and diseases increase in frequency. The health problems are not caused by the implant devices. Rather, the problems are just coincidental to the implants because both are present in older men.

28

What is the Right Treatment for Me?

When prostate cancer is diagnosed, deciding on the type of treatment for each patient is the bottom-line question. If we could know what each patient's future holds, and what is really going on in his prostate, then the answers would be easy. But no one knows what tomorrow holds for any of us.

I had a 62-year-old patient who had a flawless prostatectomy with excellent final pathology results. For all intents and purposes, he should have lived a long time.

But two years later, without warning, he had a massive heart attack and died. He had no personal or family history of heart disease. Yet this was "his time to go." Had we known this was going to happen, we probably would have told him not to do anything for the cancer.

On the other extreme, I had a very ill 79-year-old patient who was diagnosed with prostate cancer. Because of his poor health and limited anticipated life span, the patient, his primary-care doctor and I all agreed we would simply follow him without treatment. After all, we didn't want to do any harm.

Well, this gentleman surprised everyone and lived for several years, long enough to have continued growth and progression of his cancer until it became significant. He hasn't yet died of the cancer, but he may very well have problems from it because we were so conservative.

How can I know what treatment is right or wrong for me?

I find it interesting that with prostate cancer, everyone expects that we will have all the answers and know for an individual what the "right" course of treatment will be. Yet with every other aspect of health, men and women are accustomed to not knowing these answers.

Questions like, "Should I choose a heart-bypass operation or not?" or "Should I have my hernia fixed before it becomes an emergency?" or "Should I have my abdominal aneurysm corrected before it can burst and kill me?" are common. Patients and physicians generally understand that it is essentially impossible to make "right" or "wrong" answers to these questions, because the answers must be qualified by the *possible benefits* and *potential risks*.

But with prostate cancer, there is a general expectation that unless we have proof beyond a reasonable doubt that treatments will give you better results, many men should consider just ignoring that they have a potentially lethal disease.

What if I change my mind about treatment?

It depends on what you've chosen to do for your prostate cancer. If you've chosen to do nothing and there is evidence that the cancer has spread, then you may still be able to opt for the choices previously presented to you.

If you've chosen surgery as a treatment, you have the option of changing your mind right up until the day of surgery. If you are having second thoughts, then you should talk with your doctor right away.

When you have started radiation, you should finish all the treatments.

If you are having hormone shots, you could choose to change over and have the surgical removal of the testicles. It is not safe or wise to stop the hormone therapy unless told to do so by your doctor.

How long can I take to choose a treatment?

There really isn't a time limit. You should take the time to gather the information you need to make an intelligent decision. Try to avoid snap decisions. Most of my patients decide within a few weeks what treatment they wish to pursue. Remember that if you choose surgery, there will be delay of several weeks while you donate your autologous blood to the Red Cross.

I have had patients who chose to postpone treatment until after a wedding, a cruise that was already planned, a military reunion and things of that nature. If it is a delay of a few months, then it probably won't make any difference as far as whether or not the cancer will progress during that time. Of course, there's no way to know for certain and there are no guarantees.

If you are going to postpone treatment for several months or more, as a few of my patients have done, then you may want to consider going on the hormone shots once a month just to keep the cancer in check. Although controversial, some would encourage pretreatment with three months of the hormone shots to shrink the prostate gland and make the surgery easier or the radiation more effective.

The point to remember is that there are *no guarantees* the cancer won't spread during a significant delay of treatment.

Is there any way to know when the cancer will spread so I can hold off treatment until that time?

It would be nice if we could tell if and when the cancer was going to spread. At the present time, this is not possible with any certainty. We know that the higher the PSA levels, the more aggressive the cancer. We also know that the more volume of cancer seen, the more likely the cancer is going to or has already started to grow through the capsule or spread to distant sites.

29

Costs of Treatments

It would be ideal if cost were not important in your decision-making, but in reality it can be. Often, the fear of unknown costs and an incomplete understanding of your own insurance coverage can interfere with your judgment. A few men gamble with time and find themselves very ill, with no insurance, and not yet eligible for Medicare.

Are treatment costs standardized, or do they vary a lot?

Actual costs vary quite a bit from one location to another. Costs tend to be a lot higher in big cities and on the coasts. Perhaps more importantly, the doctors' and hospitals' own costs to provide the medical services tend to be quite a bit more with higher overhead and expenses.

Ask your urologist about the expected costs in your community for the services you are considering. You should also talk with the hospital and with radiation therapists regarding their charges.

In general, radiation will cost less than surgery, because it avoids the hospitalization. The "retail asking price" for external-beam radiation therapy can be about $5,000. Radioactive seed-implant therapy can cost up to $10,000. Radical prostatectomy, with hospital and doctors' fees (including the anesthesiologist, pathologist and assistant surgeon) will run $15,000 to $20,000 or more. Therefore, you need to ask your insurance about your particular plan's coverage of various services and treatments.

How much of the cost will I be responsible for?

If you belong to an HMO, you may owe nothing, as long as the treatment is done by the HMO-designated doctor at a contracted facility. The entire workup and procedure will require HMO approval before it can be done.

Medicare will pay 80% of their approved amount for eligible patients. This is what they declare to be reasonable and customary, even though it may be neither. If you have a supplemental or secondary insurance, it will usually pick up the majority of the 20% balance owed, after you have paid your deductible. Medicare tends to pay about 60% of the actual community standard payment.

Whatever the cost, you should choose the treatment that is best for you. It is always sad to hear patients make a decision based on their finances and expenses. Talk openly to your doctor about possible financial concerns or problems. We may be able to work as your advocate to get you a special rate at the hospital or with other doctors, but if we don't know there is a financial problem, we can't help you.

30

Second Opinions

If you have questions or concerns about your disease and your treatment options, it is always a good idea to get a second medical opinion before you make a final decision. With prostate cancer, you have time to think about treatments and to seek additional opinions. Many insurance companies *require* a second opinion, although this is often waived for cancer treatment and surgery.

This book provides some basic information and background to assist you in making a decision, but it cannot and should not be used to take the place of a qualified physician who can individualize your specific situation and develop recommendations based on the facts.

Will I insult or upset my doctor if I ask for a second opinion?

Be aware that some doctors may feel insulted or hurt if, after spending an hour going over all the details and options, you say you want a second opinion. It is important to tell your doctor that you appreciate the time and effort given and that you respect and trust his or her opinion. But make it clear that before you finalize your decision, you would like to speak with another urologist and/or radiation therapist. Most doctors will encourage you to talk to as many other specialists as you need to feel good about making a decision. In my practice, I also try to encourage my patients to talk with their primary-care physician as well.

What if my urologist doesn't want to me to get a second opinion?

You have a right to understand why your doctor is trying to limit your access to another opinion. He may think that what he's telling you is true, and so there's no reason to get another opinion. He may be concerned that another clinic or institution may try to do the surgery and not send you back to him. Whatever the reason, talk with your doctor and reassure him that you intend to return if you choose surgery.

How do I find names of other urologists or doctors for second opinions?

You should not see another urologist in the same group of doctors. If the second doctor disagrees with the recommendations of his partner, he may be reluctant to tell you. Talk with other urologists who do a large number of radical prostatectomies and who are well respected. Be aware that not all urologists do many of these operations, and some don't do them at all. Some will do a few operations a week, while others may do only a few each year. Often, your urologist will be able to provide names of other urologists in the community who he respects. You can also ask your primary-care doctor, the local medical society or the local chapter of the American Cancer Society.

What kind of doctor should I talk to for a second opinion?

Ideally you should talk with physicians who are familiar with prostate cancer and have a good working relationship with specialists from all fields. I prefer to send my patients to another urologist if radical surgery is an option. If you are considering radiation therapy, then definitely you need to talk with a *radiation therapist*. If the cancer is advanced, you may want to meet with a *medical oncologist*, a specialist who treats many cancers with medications, chemotherapy and hormones.

Each doctor will be looking at your situation from his own personal and professional biases. Take everything with a grain of salt. If every doctor advises you to have surgery, then you should strongly consider surgery. If they can't agree, then go back to your urologist and ask him why. Perhaps it will be necessary for the specialists and your primary-care doctor to get together and discuss your case so they can come to an agreement about what is best for you.

Should I talk with my primary-care doctor for his or her recommendations?

Yes, this is always important. He or she should be able to tell you whether or not you are a good candidate for surgery and whether or not your expected life span is long enough to make surgery worthwhile. I always try to refer patients back to their primary-care doctor for a general medical evaluation and medical clearance before surgery. If they don't have a primary-care doctor, then I will provide names of several doctors with whom I work and whose opinions and clinical judgment I respect.

Don't most insurance companies require second opinions for surgery?

Many private insurance plans require a second opinion for *elective noncancer procedures*. Surgery for cancer usually does not need a second opinion. If you are uncertain, call your insurance company and ask. Record the name of the person you speak to and the date and time that you called. Occasionally, insurance companies change their requirements.

What should I do to prepare for a second opinion?

To get the most from a second opinion, take with you all the necessary records so the doctor can know what has

> **Author's Note:** *Not long ago, a gentleman came from Hawaii to see me for a radical prostatectomy. He had gone through all the necessary exams and consultations and was ready to schedule his surgery. As is my preference, I asked him to see an excellent internist for preoperative clearance. During the evaluation, he was found to have several medical problems that could have caused problems with surgery or anesthesia. After talking with the patient and his internist, we agreed that surgery wasn't the best answer in this man's case. The man proceeded with radiation therapy instead.*

happened to you. These records should include 1) the pathology report, 2) PSA test results (old ones as well as the most recent), 3) copies of reports on the bone scan and/or CT scan, if performed, 4) your past medical history and 5) a list of medications you are currently taking.

If you ask your original doctor to forward your records to the doctor providing the second opinion, call the office of the second-opinion doctor a few days before your appointment and confirm that the records have indeed arrived. The best way to ensure that your records are there is to bring them with you. Give your original doctor plenty of time to copy the records for you.

Should I bring just the reports or do I need the X-rays?

Bring the actual X-ray films with the reports, not just the reports. You should also bring the actual glass pathology slides, which you can get from the pathology office that read the slides. Although it usually isn't necessary, some urologists (especially at teaching institutions) prefer to have their own pathologists and residents look at the slides. They will usually return the slides and films for you, after your appointment.

How do I obtain the X-ray films and pathology slides?

Well in advance, you will need to go to the facilities where the X-rays or scans were taken and sign a release. Sometimes the films will be at your original doctor's office, but he won't be able to give them to you. The general rule is, he will have to return them to the X-ray facility, which can then check them out to you. You should also contact the pathology lab to pick up the slides or to have them sent to you, if the lab is located out of town.

Will the doctor providing the second opinion write to my original doctors?

If you want your second-opinion report sent to your doctors, give the doctor the names and addresses of those doctors so that a full report of the second opinion can be sent to them.

Should I travel to a well-known institution for my surgery or radiation?

Probably not. If you are in a relatively rural area, or if you have a limited choice of urologists, then you may want to travel to a big-name facility. Otherwise, it is unlikely that the care in a far-off medical center is really any better than what's available in your own community. I spent two years of my training at a well-known medical center with an international reputation. We often wondered why some patients would travel long distances to see us, when some of the best doctors were in their own hometowns.

In other words, you shouldn't have to travel to get good care. Many of the country's leading urology residents often move to smaller communities or even rural areas to avoid the politics or fast pace of the big cities. Whether or not you need to go elsewhere should be dictated by whether or not the quality of care you need is available at home. You will often be wrong if you assume the level of care elsewhere is better.

What if my children want me to have my surgery where they live?

This happens a lot. Children decide the urologist in their community is better than the one you are seeing. Obviously they can't really know anything about your doctor, but still they may try to pressure you to travel to their home-town for your surgery or radiation. They may explain they need to be around during your recovery.

My advice is for you to make your own decision about who will be your physician. Your recovery shouldn't require any special care or assistance. In other words, you decide where you will have your treatment and thank your children for their concern.

Can I bring my wife or other family members with me to my second-opinion appointment?

Absolutely yes. I strongly encourage my patients to bring anyone whose opinion will be important in making a decision about treatment options. In fact, I am somewhat disappointed when the patient shows up alone for his consultation. I once had such a large family show up to participate that we had to use the office lobby to handle everyone.

What if the doctor can't see me for a second opinion for several weeks?

This is usually the case. A few weeks won't hurt anything. It is better to get a regular appointment than to try to squeeze in a "quickie" opinion that may be inadequate to discuss your situation.

What if the doctor providing the second opinion wants to do the surgery?

Although there are no laws regarding this, it is considered by many to be *unethical* for the doctor providing the second opinion to try to "steal" you as a patient. Sometimes, they can be subtle by suggesting they can do a better job. Sometimes they don't even ask—they just tell you that you have been scheduled for surgery or radiation. Be wary of this.

Some referral centers depend on doing the surgery following second opinions. Watch out for the "factory approach." Before you realize it, the treatment is finished and you're leaving the hospital. Unfortunately, this happens all too often.

If you believe the services in your area are not good enough, talk to your doctors honestly for a referral to a regional center or a urologist in a larger community.

If you truly feel more confident with the physician providing the second opinion, then you should tell both the original doctor and the second doctor how you feel. Explain why you have decided to change doctors. Some doctors will not take over your care unless the first doctor resigns as your treating physician, even if you *want* the second doctor to assume your care.

If I'm giving a second opinion, I always try to send the patient back to his urologist unless the patient has very personal and legitimate reasons for wanting me to assume his care. It is extremely important that you choose a physician you trust and feel good about.

31

How to Find a Good Urologist

Obviously you want to have the best urologist available taking care of you if you have prostate cancer. Unfortunately, there really isn't an easy way to find one of the best. You will usually have to depend on your primary-care doctor for a referral.

Sometimes the best urologist may not be the most personable. Also, the best doctors will not be the easiest to see on short notice. Take the time to make an appointment to see the doctor when he can spend the necessary time with you. Occasionally patients will "sneak" in more quickly than they should by claiming to have some urgent problem that needs attention immediately. Don't use this as an excuse to get an appointment.

The potential problem in my office is that I set aside about 60 to 90 minutes to talk with someone about prostate cancer and the treatment options available. If another patient squeezes in because he wants urgent attention, there is no way I can give the first patient all the time and attention he needs. Such schedule interruptions can ruin the day for the next 15 patients who did wait weeks for their appointment that day.

Don't be alarmed or surprised if you have to wait. Actually, it is a good sign if the doctor has a waiting list of several weeks or more. In my practice, nonurgent patients can sometimes wait several weeks or more for an appointment. If you have a truly urgent problem or if your primary-care doctor calls over to get you in sooner, then my office has a policy of trying to find a time slot somewhere.

Be patient with your doctor. It may be worth the extra wait to see a doctor who will be honest and straightforward and won't try to push you in a direction that isn't right.

Who will my primary-care doctor refer me to for urology treatment?

Your primary-care doctor will usually give you the names of several urologists to whom he refers his patients. But be aware that a doctor on this list may or may not be the best one for you.

In the real world, doctors get set in their referral patterns and usually don't refer to another specialist even if the other doctor may be better. In fact, the quality of the care provided is not usually a factor in the referral. Often doctors will refer to others of a similar age group. Young doctors tend to refer to other young doctors, while older doctors tend to keep referring to the other doctors of similar age and training.

Your HMO or insurance plan may have contracted urology specialists for referral. If the urologist in the HMO isn't the best or if you don't get along, you are essentially stuck unless there are several to choose from.

Does it matter if my urologist is younger or older?

Some patients like doctors recently out of training, thinking they will be up-to-date on new techniques and treatments. Other patients prefer older physicians with experience and wisdom.

The truth is that it is the quality of the individual

physician that counts. His age is irrelevant. There are some young physicians with experience, wisdom and common sense, while there may be older physicians who are very current on the newest procedures and techniques. Don't prejudge a urologist solely on his age.

So how do I find the best urologist in my area?

To find the best urologist in your community, talk to your friends and ask for names. This is how I ultimately developed the list of specialists to whom I refer my friends and family. I just ask many fellow doctors who they like, and slowly a few names rise to the top.

Find out who is liked, and just as important, who isn't liked. Ask why. Does the doctor explain everything, or does he just tell you that you need an operation and turn you over to a nurse to set it up?

Talk to nurses, especially those who work in the operating rooms, in the recovery rooms or on the surgical floors. Call your county medical society. Call the local chapter of the American Cancer Society.

When you have a name, you can contact your state board of medical examiners to see if there have been a large number of lawsuits against him. Most urologists will have had a few lawsuits in their careers, which does not necessarily suggest wrongdoing. Instead, the lawsuits often indicate bitter patients who are unhappy with outcomes of treatment that the urologist had no control over.

Are there specific qualities that I should look for in a doctor?

Be concerned about any doctor who won't answer your questions or seems bothered or annoyed that you are interested in a conversation rather than a lecture. This could mean he is insecure with his own knowledge or skills. It may also mean he is insulted that you don't trust him to make all your decisions.

I have many patients who left their original doctor because he refused to answer questions or became upset when they demonstrated they had done some reading on the subject of prostate cancer.

Watch out for any doctor who tries to corner you into making a snap decision about your care or insists that he is the only one capable of caring for you.

What if my doctor is not listed as a board-certified specialist?

When you check on the credentials of a doctor, make sure you are using an up-to-date information resource.

I recently had a patient who was concerned that I was not board-certified. He had checked into my credentials through a friend who had a book of surgical specialists. As I sat and looked at my Certificate of Board Certification, I confirmed to myself that I was indeed board-certified and then asked my patient how old the reference book was. Obviously, it was several years older than my certification was.

What does being "board-certified" actually mean?

This is a *voluntary* examination to maintain and promote a basic level of knowledge in the specialty. In urology in the United States, this is monitored by the American Board of Urology. In Canada it is the Royal College of Physicians and Surgeons, located in Ontario. Each country has its own certification process.

What does a doctor have to do to be board-certified?

The certification process is a very intense experience in which the urologist first must provide a detailed log of every surgery performed for at least 12 months. If this list is deemed adequate, then the doctor is required to take a two-day written and oral exam. If the doctor passes all parts of the exams, he will be certified by the board.

How can I find out if my doctor is board-certified?

In the U.S. you can call the American Board of Urology at 1-810-646-9720. In Canada you can call the Royal College of Physicians and Surgeons at 1-613-730-8177.

If he is board-certified, does that mean he is a good urologist?

It means he has a good fund of knowledge and was able to pass written and oral exams about different aspects of urology and urologic surgery. However, good judgment and operating skill are two things that cannot be measured by this certification process.

I know of excellent doctors who had problems, not with their skills and knowledge, but with the examination process. In general, board certification does assure the community that the urologist at least has a good fund of knowledge. There's more to being a good doctor than being board-certified.

Are doctors board-certified for life?

This depends on the specialty and when they took the exam. Urologists who became board-certified *before* the mid-1980s are board-certified forever. They are not required to retake the certification test ever again. Urologists who were first board-certified in the mid-1980s or later are required to retake the exam every 10 years to maintain board-certification status.

Should I go to a urologist at a university hospital?

You shouldn't select a physician just because he or she is affiliated with a university teaching or research setting. You may have heard that you should get your care only in a university system. It's been said that university doctors are well-published, authors of many articles and books and therefore must know more about surgery.

As far as the publishing of articles and books is concerned, there is no correlation between surgical skill and how

well a doctor speaks or how many articles and books he may
have written. The doctor should be judged on his or her own
merits. Whether or not he or she practices in a community
setting or at a powerful university teaching center has nothing
to do with the doctor's skills.

What you really want is a caring and compassionate
urologist, technically excellent, with a good track record, outstanding judgment, a history of minimal complications and
happy patients and referring doctors.

32

Questions to Ask Your Doctor

When you are being treated for prostate cancer, it is a good idea to ask a lot of questions and keep a record of your progress. Here are some key questions to ask your urologist or primary-care doctor.

1. What is my PSA level?
    a. Does it fall within the "normal" range?
    b. What were the levels of my past PSA tests?

2. Has my PSA level changed significantly over time?

3. Is there a reason to recheck the PSA in six to eight weeks? (A recent infection or catheter might be a reason.)

4. What is the grade of cancer in the biopsies and how significant is that?

5. What did the bone scan show, if one was done?

6.   What were the results of the CT scan? (If one was done.)

7.   What is the clinical stage of cancer and how significant
     is that?

8.   Do you think the cancer is curable?
     a. What are the chances that the cancer has spread to
        the lymph nodes?

9.   What are the treatment options available for me?

10.   What are the chances the cancer will progress if it is left
      untreated?

11.   If radical prostatectomy is an option, who will do it?
      (If your doctor is a urologist, he probably will do it.)

12.   How many of these operations do you do in a year?
      (Twenty-five or more is good.)

13.   Are resident physicians involved in the surgery or
      postoperative care?
      a. If yes, what exactly do they do in the surgery?
      b. What year of training after medical school are they in?
         (In other words, how many years of postgraduate
         training have they had?)
      c. What specialty training are these residents in?
         (Sometimes, residents may rotate their training
         among various specialties.)

14.   Do you use autologous blood transfusions during
      prostate surgery? (Because autologous blood—donated
      by the patient for his own use—is so infrequently
      needed for transfusions, some doctors don't even ask
      for the donation.)

15. How often do you have to use Red Cross blood for transfusions during surgery? (Should be used very rarely.)

16. After surgery, do your patients go to the Intensive Care Unit (ICU)? (Ideally, this should be almost never.)

17. How many days do your patients usually stay in the hospital, not counting the surgical day? (This should be from two to five days.)

18. What percentage of your patients have severe, permanent incontinence after treatment? (This should be around 1% to 3%.)

19. Are you board-certified? When did you take the exam? (Remember, some older urologists were "grandfathered" in so they automatically have certification for life. More recently trained urologists have to take recertification tests every 10 years).

20. Do you use an epidural anesthetic during surgery? For how long?

21. How long do you leave the Foley catheter in after surgery? (I leave it in for about 21 days.)

22. How often should I expect to see you for follow-up visits after I go home?

23. Who will do the long-term follow-up after my treatment? (This is an important question, especially if you belong to an HMO where the primary-care doctor may actually follow your treatment, hopefully at the direction of the urologist.)

24. How soon can I go back to work or resume normal activities, such as golf, tennis, gardening or bike riding? (The answers will vary depending on what you do.)

25. Will I be admitted to the hospital the day before or the day of surgery?

26. What kind of preparation for surgery will I need? (This might include bowel-prep enemas or antibiotics.)

27. How soon should I have the surgery after learning I have cancer? (It is never an emergency. Be wary if a doctor tries to push you through quickly before you have a chance to think about treatment options.)

28. If radiation is recommended, how soon should I start the radiation?

29. After surgery or radiation, how long should I wait to see if I can still get a normal erection before I seek treatment for impotence?

30. After radiation or surgery, how long should I wait to consider treatment options for urinary incontinence?

31. Do you believe in early or late treatment of advanced prostate cancer? (I prefer early. Some doctors like to wait until the cancer is causing problems.)

32. Which type of hormone treatment do you prefer and why?

33. Do you believe in the use of flutamide (Eulixin)?

33

Follow-up After Treatment

Follow-up care will be necessary for the rest of your life after you've been treated for prostate cancer.

Today, the PSA blood test is the best and least expensive way of making sure that the cancer hasn't come back after treatment. As long as the PSA level remains stable, you are doing fine. How often you need to be seen depends on your particular medical situation, the treatment you received and how likely it is that the cancer was cured.

Initially after radiation or surgery, you will probably need to get the PSA rechecked every three to four months for the first year, then every four to six months the next year or two, then every six to twelve months thereafter. The longer you go after treatment without signs of cancer recurrence, the longer you can go between PSA checks.

What happens if the PSA goes up?

The answer will depend on how much change there has been in the PSA, to what level and over how much time. You should remember there is some fluctuation in lab testing.

Minor changes probably don't mean anything. But if the PSA continues to rise with each recheck, then it means the cancer has come back. The faster the climb, the more concerned we are. A rapid increase suggests that the cancer not only is back but is growing vigorously. Sometimes the PSA elevation is so small and so slow, we choose to just watch it over time.

What should the PSA be after a radical prostatectomy?

The PSA level should be 0.0. We hope there is no more cancer or prostate tissue left behind. No other tissues can produce a significant amount of PSA. Sometimes the PSA is reported as less than 0.3 or 0.5. These basically mean the same thing. It's just the lab's way of reporting the result.

Some lab machines don't try to determine the exact amount if it is at a very low, almost undetectable level. Occasionally the report will come back at 0.1 or 0.2. Lab tests are not perfect. There are some minor variations in lab testing that are always present and unavoidable.

Should I worry if the PSA level starts to go up after surgery?

Not initially. Before I become worried, I would want to get a repeat test result. If the PSA continues to rise, then it usually means that there is some recurrent prostate cancer.

No one really knows when and if additional treatments should be started. In my practice, if the PSA goes up rapidly, then I'm more inclined to recommend radiation treatment to the pelvis or hormone therapy. At a PSA of 1 or 2, I usually recommend treatment.

It's not good that the surgery wasn't curative. If your prostate contained high-grade disease (Gleason sum 8, 9 or 10) then you are at a higher risk of recurrence.

What should the PSA level be after radiation?

Unlike surgery where the PSA should be 0.0, after radiation the PSA usually slowly drops down to a level ideally *below* 1.0. The longer it stays below 1.0, the better the long-term prognosis. If the PSA doesn't drop to below 1.0, then statistically you are more likely to have a recurrence of cancer. This is why monitoring the PSA plays an important role. If there is a question about return of the cancer, then you can be followed more closely.

If the PSA starts to go up after radiation therapy, when should I worry?

If I knew this answer, I would be able to tell the future. Much depends on how fast the PSA is going up, how high it is and how long it stayed down after the radiation treatments. The longer the time it stayed low, the better it is. The slower that it is going up, the better. If it begins to move up rapidly and consistently, then I would be more inclined to start hormone therapy.

In my practice, if the PSA keeps going up (and I check it every four months or so), then I would recommend hormone therapy when the PSA goes above 3 or 4. I realize that some experts will say that this is early, but I believe it is easier to control a small amount of cancer early on than wait until there is a large volume of cancer. That's when it may be more difficult to stop.

If your PSA is climbing after radiation therapy, stay close to your urologist and follow the PSA level regularly.

If left untreated, how long until the cancer causes problems?

If we had that answer, we would know who should and shouldn't be treated and which treatment to use. That is the dilemma of prostate cancer. Many men will not live long enough for the cancer to be a threat to them, while others may have rapid growth and live long enough to have problems because of the cancer.

In general, the less aggressive the cancer, the better your long-term outlook.

What are the options after radiation therapy?

The main option is the addition of hormone therapy. If the PSA starts to rise, then it means that some of the cancer wasn't killed by the radiation. It also may mean there was a small bit of cancer outside the field of radiation.

Surgical removal of the prostate after radiation is very difficult and has dramatically increased risks. This operation is called a *salvage prostatectomy*. Because all the tissues have been radiated, the normal layers between the tissues are usually gone, leaving the tissues all stuck together. This can make it very difficult to remove the prostate gland. Therefore, there is a significant chance of injury to the rectal wall, with a 50% chance of needing a permanent colostomy.

A colostomy is a diversion of the feces out to the skin, to be caught in a bag. This is needed because if the previously radiated rectal wall is damaged, it may not heal well, if at all. The chances of permanent total urinary incontinence are increased following a salvage prostatectomy. So the risks are high, with unknown potential benefits.

What should the PSA be after hormone therapy?

The lower the PSA goes, the better the result. And the longer it stays low, the more likely it will continue to be low. Hopefully, the PSA will drop down to well below 1.0, and maybe as low as 0.1 or even 0.0.

If the PSA goes up after hormone therapy, when should I worry and what are my options?

As with the PSA levels after radiation therapy, much depends on the actual number, how fast it is going up and how long it stayed down on hormone therapy. When it starts to climb above 2 to 5, the disease has progressed to a stage that may be better managed by a urologist or a medical oncologist. I usually ask the patient to at least talk with an oncologist about the options available. You may simply choose to follow the PSA and manage any physical symptoms you experience, or you may choose to try something experimental. Your urologist will either continue caring for you or refer you to the appropriate specialist.

If the PSA begins to go up after surgery or radiation, where are the cancer cells that are causing this increase?

Cancer of the prostate spreads to the lymph nodes and to the bone, but it can also grow into surrounding tissues. The bone scan and CT scan show abnormalities only when they are large enough to produce changes in the bones or to cause fairly significant enlargement or distortion of normal tissues on CT scan. If the PSA is going up, then we know that the cancer is growing somewhere.

Is there a role for Proscar if the PSA is going up after treatment?

Some doctors have used Proscar, occasionally with a drop in the PSA level. No one knows if this actually affects the cancer growth.

34

Will I Need Additional Treatment After Radical Prostatectomy?

The need for additional treatment must be addressed if the *surgical margins* are found positive for cancer or if there is cancer in the lymph nodes. The surgical margins are the edges of the tissue where the prostate was removed.

Let's address the surgical margins first. Having cancer at the edges of the tissue suggests there may be cancer cells left in the body. When the pathologist looks under the microscope at the tissue, he can see if cancer cells touch the edges of the specimen. If it does, it is labeled as a *positive margin*.

In the past, we sent all of these men with cancer at the margins for a course of additional radiation treatments. Though less radiation may be given after surgery than with regular radiation, it still increases the risks for urinary incontinence and impotence, as well as the standard risks that go along with radiation, including radiation injury to the bladder or rectum.

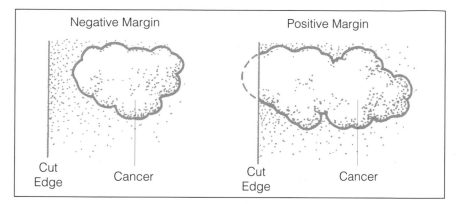

SURGICAL MARGINS: *Margins are identified by the pathologist as he studies a speci-men removed by surgery. A negative margin is when cancer is not seen at the cut edge and is presumed to be contained within the specimen. A positive margin is when can-cer cells are seen at the cut edge. This raises the question as to whether or not cancer cells may remain in the body.*

I recommend checking the PSA level every three months after surgery. If the level of the PSA begins to increase, then I refer to a radiation therapist for his opinion and possible radiation.

Will I ever need surgery again?

Radical prostatectomy is intended to be the only surgery you should need. You might, however, need to deal with a possible complication such as a lymphatic fluid collection in the abdomen or a scar that might grow at the bladder neck where the urethra was attached to the bladder. Fortunately, these complications tend to be fairly rare and are usually treated in minor outpatient procedures.

What are the options after surgery if additional treatment is needed?

After you've had surgery, the options remaining are radiation and hormone therapy. Radiation will only work if the cancer thought to remain is in the field to be radiated—in other words, *in the pelvis.*

Because of the previous surgery, the dose and length of radiation may be less than if radiation had been used initially.

Author's Note: *Many years ago, a patient who was a retired professor researched the pros and cons of adding radiation for tumor at the margins. He decided to follow his PSA regularly. If the PSA levels were to start to climb, then he would go ahead with radiation. Since then, his PSA levels have remained at 0.0.*

This will depend on your specific situation.

The risks of adding on radiation treatment include increased urinary incontinence and impotence, as well as irritation and injury to the bladder or rectal wall.

What about hormone therapy?

Hormone therapy is used when it is believed that additional treatment is needed and radiation either won't take care of the problem (if the cancer is *outside* the pelvis) or if a more conservative, less risky treatment is believed best.

35

Role of Chemotherapy

Although chemotherapy is routinely used for the treatment of most cancers it is not a main treatment choice for prostate cancer. The other treatments already discussed are more effective. However, when the cancer continues to grow and other treatments have been tried, we often turn to chemotherapy to try to slow the cancer growth.

I don't think any chemotherapy doctors, or *oncologists*, will tell you they hope for a cure. Rather, the goal with chemotherapy is to stop or at least slow the cancer growth. Even in the best of hands, chemotherapy may work in 20% to 40% of the men who receive it. How long it works is variable. And how well it works is unpredictable.

The big question with chemotherapy is whether its possible benefit outweighs its probable side effects. The treatment may add only a few months to your life span, and you may spend those months weak and nauseated. You must decide if it is worth the effort and expense, both financially and emotionally.

I know of one patient who died as a result of chemotherapy. On the other hand, there are patients who seem to tolerate chemotherapy without difficulty and appear to benefit.

There are different types of chemotherapy. A number of them may hold some promise for treating prostate cancer. Each type of cancer is treated with different chemical agents at different doses. The goal is to kill fast-growing cancer cells with the medication.

Are there experimental chemotherapy drugs available?

In many communities, you may be eligible for experimental agents as part of research treatment plans, or *protocols*, where a medication is being tried. Sometimes these experimental drugs don't work. Occasionally they provide good results.

Chemotherapy Drugs

Following are two of the common chemotherapy drugs and their uses.

Suramin

Suramin is a very old drug that is now being used to treat prostate cancer. Originally developed 100 years ago to fight parasites in Africa, its primary role now is to stop prostate-cancer growth following unsuccessful hormone therapy.

How does Suramin work?

Suramin was found to block a substance that stimulates cell growth, including cancer cells, in the body.

How well does Suramin work and with what side effects?

Early trials showed tremendous promise but were often associated with frequent side effects, such as swelling of the ankles and kidney changes. Improvement was seen in many men on Suramin, often with decrease in pain. Newer methods of giving Suramin include smaller doses for shorter times, giving better results and fewer side effects.

Ketaconozole

This medication has been used to treat fungal infections. It was always known to block the body's ability to produce male hormones. Urologists have started using ketaconozole to treat prostate cancer that has failed standard hormone therapy. Although it doesn't work for everyone, many men have a positive response.

The main side effect is possible serious liver damage, so it is important to check blood tests of liver function on a regular basis.

Side Effects

Potential side effects vary from drug to drug. Some are minimal, while others can be quite severe or even fatal.

Your oncologist can tell you specifically which chemotherapy options are best for you, whether or not you are a candidate for any experimental drugs and what possible side effects you might expect.

36

Research Studies

Patients with prostate cancer may be able to benefit from experimental research at a university or community hospital. But it is important to be aware of the risks as well as the possible benefits of subjecting yourself to medical research studies.

Don't university hospitals have research studies that I might want to join or participate in?

Yes, many advancements in cancer research and treatment do come out of academic teaching centers. This occurs because researchers are able to try new, untested procedures and medication programs. Many of the procedures and medications will not work, but some will.

Some patients will get an otherwise unavailable treatment that may work beneficially, while other patients get an ineffective treatment. Some may suffer because of the treatment, but it will be helpful for the good of society and future patients with a similar problem. This system is how researchers learn what will and will not work in medicine.

How will they decide which treatments are best for me?

In the university teaching-center environment, doctors have a number of treatment plans, called *research protocols*, that are available. The doctors look at your medical situation and try to decide which protocol you would best fit in.

What are some questions to ask before becoming a patient in a research study?

Talk with the doctors and ask questions about the treatments to be studied. What specifically is trying to be proved? Find out how long the study has been underway and if any preliminary results are available.

Ask how long you will be on the treatment plan. What kind of follow-up, tests and procedures will be needed? Who will do these tests and who will pay for them? Who will pay for the medications, surgery, radiation and other procedures?

If there's a complication, who will pay for those costs and provide the care? Can you leave anytime if you're not happy? What are the risks of entering this trial as compared to standard therapy? Who is sponsoring (paying for) the study? How will you be monitored?

Can I be involved in these same experimental studies in the private sector, outside of a university setting?

Yes, you should be able to. Most communities have a number of private-practice doctors who are participants in the same research trials.

In a research study, can I decide what treatment I want for me?

No, you usually have to agree to be randomized, which means you will be assigned randomly to one treatment or another. Using this methodology, the research results will more accurately reflect the benefits or disadvantages of a specific treatment, rather than the patient's choices.

o decides what treatment I will be assigned to in a research trial?

This is often done by a computer or a predetermined plan.

What if I'm not happy with the treatment choice that I'm assigned to?

You may have the option to quit, depending on the study. You shouldn't enter into a research study unless you are willing to accept any of the treatments being analyzed. It's not fair to the people trying to run the study to invest the time and effort only to have people drop out because they don't like their assigned treatment.

Could I be assigned to a treatment that is dangerous?

This is always possible. You should clearly understand what the study is trying to prove and the pros and cons of each of the treatment options.

How do I find out about research studies on prostate cancer?

Contact a regional cancer-research center.

What is this new project called the "PIVOT study"?

The PIVOT study includes healthy men with prostate cancer that is confined to the prostate. These men are being randomly divided between 1) radical prostatectomy, and 2) no treatment with regular monitoring. This study is being done to help decide once and for all if prostate cancer is better left untreated or if the surgery truly does offer better survival results.

Quite a lot of debate is going on for each point of view. Those who believe that cancer of the prostate is best left alone without treatment are unhappy about some men being assigned to undergo surgery. Those who believe that surgery does prolong the life span are concerned about telling otherwise curable men that they can't have treatment.

Future Areas of Research

Some new areas of research are immune stimulation, vaccines, early detection, understanding early cancer growth and spread, and genetic factors.

Immune Stimulation & Vaccines

The ideal treatment for a cancer would be to stimulate your own body's immune system to fight off and kill the cancer. This is being done in bladder-cancer treatment, but as yet still hasn't been done for prostate cancer. Studies are underway.

Some research may identify a vaccine that can locate and kill prostate-cancer cells. This may be most useful after radical surgery to find and kill any cells that remain.

Early Detection

The ideal time to detect a prostate cancer is when it is still confined to the prostate gland and easy to cure. While the PSA blood test is good, it still is far from perfect.

Research is underway on new modifications to the PSA test that may pick up advanced cancer that has spread. Accurate detection of cancer outside the prostate helps us select the most appropriate treatment and avoid unnecessary procedures. Some studies are investigating PSA bound to proteins in the blood or PSA in the urine to see if this can help identify prostate cancer at a more curable stage.

A number of experimental tests are being evaluated to identify cancer in tissues outside the prostate. One test, called *CYT 356*, is being evaluated for its ability to pick up cancer cells in soft tissues and the bones. In present tests, it is less sensitive than the bone scan for identifying abnormalities in the bones. Its use in the future is still uncertain and remains to be defined.

Early Cancer Growth and Spread

Research is underway to look at what stimulates the growth of new blood vessels to supply tiny cancers with nutrients, allowing them to grow larger. If a chemical could be identified that stimulates this blood-vessel growth, perhaps that chemical could be blocked so no cancer could ever grow beyond just a few cells in size.

Scientists are looking at why cancer cells can penetrate into blood vessels and then break loose and spread. If the blood vessels could become more resistant to cancer-cell penetration with a treatment, maybe the cancers could be prevented from spreading.

There are studies trying to identify which substances encourage cancer cells to grow elsewhere in the body. This, too, could lead to a treatment to keep cancers from spreading.

Genetic Research

Genetics, the study of heredity and how our genes and diseases are related, is a promising field where researchers are trying to identify which genes are responsible for development of cancer.

Other Questions

Are there some genes that somehow allow environmental factors to stimulate prostate cancer to grow? Could this be how a high-fat diet encourages prostate cancer to develop? Do some men have certain genes that suppress the development of prostate cancer? Can these protective genes be inactivated by diet or the environment, allowing prostate cancer to grow? Are there certain enzymes in the body that, when blocked by a genetic change, allow cancers to grow?

We don't know the answers to these questions. But research is underway around the world to try to solve these puzzles about the origin of not only prostate cancer but all cancers.

37

When All Treatments Fail

There are times when the cancer continues to grow, despite all the standard treatments and therapies. This leads to questions that most doctors and health-care providers don't feel comfortable answering.

The following questions and answers are very matter-of-fact. You should read this chapter only if you *really* want to know the answers. I have found that some men and their wives would rather not know this information.

It is provided here because I believe it is important for you to have access to this information if you want to know the worst-case scenarios. At some point, it may become clear what is inevitably coming. As a friend of mine once said, "No one gets out of here alive." We all have to go sometime.

For the patient whose cancer defies treatment and continues to grow, I hope we can help make this transition more tolerable for him and his family.

How do we know that the cancer has come back?

Usually the PSA level will continue to rise. Sometimes an irregularity can be felt on rectal examination. Some men complain of vague aches or pains, or weakness and fatigue.

Do I need additional X-rays or tests?

A repeat bone scan, CT scan or X-ray may be performed to learn if and where the cancer has returned.

Do I need to have a repeat biopsy?

Not usually. Your doctors usually will have a fairly accurate idea what the abnormality is. If there are any questions, a repeat biopsy may be necessary.

If the cancer continues to grow, how long will I live?

This depends on how advanced the cancer is. In the worst situations, it may be just a few months, or it could take a year or more. There is no possible way to predict for an individual how long he will survive with the cancer growing. There are occasions when a patient will have rapid growth of the cancer despite anything that we do.

At the other extreme, it is quite common for many men to live years longer than was predicted.

How fast can the cancer grow?

This is highly variable and can even fluctuate within a single person. For many men the cancer can take many

Author's Note: *I recall a 47-year-old man who had widespread prostate cancer. Even though the cancer started to grow after we began hormone therapy, he lived comfortably for almost two years before he became ill and died.*

years to become significant. Even then, it can grow so slowly that for selected patients, treatment may be indefinitely postponed.

For other men, however, the cancer can grow rapidly, sometimes killing the person in several months from the point of diagnosis. Most often, even in advanced cancers, the growth may take many months or even a few years.

What are the expected symptoms as the cancer grows?

In advanced cases, when all standard treatments fail, you might notice increasing fatigue, gradual weight loss, weakness, depression, changing aches and pain and loss of appetite.

Can anything be done to help my appetite?

Sometimes treatment with steroids, such as oral prednisone, can improve your appetite and give you a feeling of well-being.

How will the cancer actually kill me if we can't control it?

Most cancers kill by growing and spreading to vital organs in the body, overloading and preventing normal organ function. Prostate cancer doesn't seem to work this way. Prostate cancer will continue to grow and increase in volume in your lymph nodes and in the bone marrow.

It appears that prostate cancer in large volumes releases toxic substances into the bloodstream. These substances account for many of the symptoms seen with advanced prostate cancer. These toxic substances were originally part of normal prostatic secretions. However, in the bloodstream they can cause loss of appetite, fatigue and gradual wasting, ultimately leading to death.

What else can happen as the cancer grows?

Your blood counts may go down, making you anemic, as the blood-producing tissues of the bone marrow are replaced by cancer. You may feel weak and fatigued. The bones may become weakened, and it is possible that you could experience sudden fractures. This is most common in weight-bearing bones, such as in the top of the legs.

Sometimes a tumor in the spine can enlarge and squeeze the spinal cord, causing numbness or weakness in the legs. This is a true emergency and needs immediate attention to prevent you from becoming paralyzed!

Will I be in pain?

Many times, yes. Pain depends on *exactly where* the cancer has spread and *how much cancer* you have in your body. If the cancer has spread to the bones, this often can result in quite a lot of pain. If the cancer is growing in the lymph nodes, this usually does not cause pain unless the enlarged nodes are compressing and squeezing critical areas, such as nerves or the ureters that drain urine from the kidneys.

Can the pain be controlled?

For most men, usually. Doctors have access to a large number of pain medications that each have more powerful narcotics to help control severe pain. I often use a combination of medications to allow for the most accurate control of pain.

If the pain becomes very severe, then radiation treatments to the painful bone will sometimes block any pain. This also serves to strengthen the bone and prevent any break. I sometimes ask pain specialists (usually an anesthesiologist who specializes in pain management) to see if they can block the pain with specialized pain medications and long-acting injections.

Are there any treatments to reduce pain from cancer that has spread to the bone?

Yes. A new radioactive substance can be injected into the veins to kill cancer cells in the bone. An example of this new type of medication is strontium 89, available under the brand name Metastron®. The medication costs $1500 or more per treatment.

How effective is this type of treatment?

The results vary from person to person, but in general up to 70% of men with severe pain in the bones not helped by routine pain medication will describe some improvement, often within a few weeks. Although the degree of pain control is unpredictable, some men may even have total relief from bone pain. How long the benefits last is also quite variable.

Are there any side effects to this new medication?

Occasionally the medication can interfere with the normal production of blood. To watch for this, you will need to have blood counts checked on a regular basis after the treatment.

If the bone pain goes away, can the treatment be repeated if the pain comes back?

Yes. If you have good results with your first treatment, you can have an additional treatment or two, no sooner than every six months.

Are there any ways of controlling pain without medications?

Yes. Methods include *biofeedback, relaxation techniques, meditation, mental imagery, distraction, skin stimulation* and *massage*. Some men find relief with acupuncture and acupressure, hypnosis and electrical nerve stimulators. Before you start any of these procedures, check with your doctor, because some may cause problems.

How can I learn more about these options?

One of the best sources is the pamphlet *Questions and Answers about Pain Control*, published by and available from the American Cancer Society. Pain clinics often have literature and books.

How does kidney failure kill a person?

The kidneys filter the blood and remove toxic wastes, which are then excreted in the urine. If the kidneys are blocked by the cancer as it squeezes the ureters shut, then the waste products will slowly build up in your system. At some point, you may experience increasing fatigue, weakness, a loss of appetite and occasionally itching. The itching is from the accumulation of waste products in the tissues. Left untreated, you would gradually become weaker and weaker. Then you would quietly slip into a coma and die.

How long does it take to die from kidney failure?

This is highly variable and can take weeks, many months or longer. Sometimes there can be severe but not total obstruction, with the kidneys still filtering toxic wastes just enough to keep you alive but still with significant kidney failure. This can last indefinitely.

What can be done if I have kidney failure?

The big question is not how we address kidney failure but rather should we even try to solve this problem. If the cancer is so significant as to cause kidney failure from blockage, then relieving the blockage of the kidneys may just keep you alive long enough to die of something else later on.

If you do decide to treat the kidney obstruction, the main approach is to place a small catheter, called a *nephrostomy tube*, into the kidney through the skin on your side. This tube drains into a small bag, which has to be periodically emptied. Nephrostomy tubes are usually placed by radiologists or urologists in an outpatient procedure using just a local anesthesia.

Another way to place these drainage tubes is to pass small catheters, called *ureteral stents*, up the ureter, through the penis, usually under anesthesia. With this technique, it is sometimes impossible to pass the tube up to the kidney. Then you must have the tubes placed by a radiologist through the skin.

Is kidney failure a bad way to die?

No. Death in this manner is considered one of the least unpleasant ways to die. Most men with kidney failure complain that they have lost their appetite, or they feel weak or fatigued or itchy. Gradually, you become weaker and weaker, simply fading into a coma, followed by death.

What's the advisability of trying an alternative "last-ditch" treatment?

There will always be those who prey on desperate men and women who are willing to try anything at any price to stop the cancer from growing.

In my practice, I don't believe I should deny patients the option to seek out alternative choices. I try to encourage patients to pursue alternative treatments *in addition to* known and accepted options, not *instead of* those standard treatments. I do ask patients to be as critical and challenging to the alternative health-care provider as they were of their regular doctor.

I have had several patients who accept as fact the claims and recommendations made by an acquaintance who recommends unheard-of herbal therapy or teaches a bizarre diet for cancer. Yet these same accepting patients routinely challenge me to prove with extensive facts, research studies and documentation the benefits of any treatment that I suggest.

What should I watch out for if I'm considering alternative treatments?

Some basic guidelines apply to looking for a doctor or a treatment, no matter who the provider is. First and foremost, what kind of training did that person receive? I knew of one provider who had only taken a few weekend courses, yet claimed he had extensive training and experience in the field.

Beware of claims of "special treatments" that have been "ignored" or "shunned" by the world of organized medicine. I have yet to meet a doctor who would ignore any proven treatment that would help his patient.

Beware of testimonial-style marketing, where a small number of men and women claim to have had a miraculous recovery with a treatment.

If it looks *easy*, with results almost *too good to be true*, it usually is. If it is very expensive, watch out. Many of these treatments require cash up front. This should make you very suspicious.

Watch out if this elaborate and expensive treatment is completed in just a weekend, especially if it is in any country with few limitations on unproved treatments.

What should I find out before starting an alternative therapy?

First, see what your regular doctor thinks of it. Second, ask to have the new doctor's credentials mailed to you with reference articles showing what research has resulted in the doctor's treatment. Check with the Better Business Bureau or any state licensing organizations that may impact on those providers.

What is a hospice?

This is a facility where terminally ill patients can go near the end of their lives for care while they die. It is a place where nurses, doctors and support staff are all specially trained to attend to the special needs of the dying patient.

What about hospice as the cancer progresses?

Hospice care may be reasonable for advanced stages of cancer. Hospice nurses can provide more pain control, nutritional care and attention to the problems that can develop with a dying patient. Some communities and facilities have home hospice services where a trained nurse or aide comes to the home to help care for a terminally ill person.

How do I prepare for my death?

Though this is difficult to think about, it is best to look at what aspects of your life you have control over. Make needed arrangements so that your wife or family won't be burdened with those changes after your death. Make sure the house, the cars, any investments, business accounts and credit cards are all in good legal order so that your wife or family will not face difficult legal obstacles.

Talk to your friends. Visit family. Spend time with those you care about. As difficult as this transition is for you, it is probably much harder for your wife and children. Be supportive and comforting.

What about my legal concerns?

The American Cancer Society has an excellent pamphlet on what should be addressed by you regarding legal questions, business, taxes and loans. A brief list of things to organize includes:

> Life insurance
> Retirement plan
> Title to any assets that you have
> Property
> Bank accounts
> Collections
> Safe deposit boxes
> Vehicle deeds
> Will

For each of these items you should record account numbers, addresses, phone numbers, contact people and the locations of important keys and papers.

What about a "living will?"

This is very important to guarantee that no measures are taken *against your wishes* simply to sustain your life. You should talk to your doctor or lawyer about a living will, and you should sign a general "durable power of attorney" and a "medical durable power of attorney" to give your family or friends the necessary authority to make decisions for you. You may want to establish a possible guardian or conservator or put together a "living trust."

What should I do with my living will and medical power of attorney forms?

It is very important that you make copies and deliver them to your doctors to file with your records. Keep the original with you at home. If you go to the hospital, bring a copy with you *every time*. Even if you brought one with you to the hospital previously, it may be "lost" somewhere in medical records. It may not be readily accessible when you need it in an emergency, so bring your own copy.

Author's Note: *One of the most rewarding moments of my professional life happened when a patient's wife called and asked me if I would come to the hospice and visit her dying husband. She said it was his "last wish" to see me. We had a nice chat about a variety of topics. We talked about how much we had enjoyed seeing each other over the years. He was accepting of his imminent death, surrounded by family and friends. He died the next day.*

38

Support Groups & Resources for Help & Information

Support groups can play an important role in helping you decide which treatments to consider, which doctors to see, perhaps even which ones to avoid. Groups can provide a comfortable environment where you can share your deepest fears or concerns with men who have experienced what you are going through.

Support groups provide strategies for coping with your cancer and any hurdles that may come up.

A recent study suggested that women who attended breast-cancer support groups survived longer than those women who didn't. This raises the point of just how important your mental and emotional health is in dealing with cancer. Perhaps there's more to the cure than surgery or radiation.

Support groups give a camaraderie and bonding with other men who understand what no one else can. I strongly suggest that patients seek out a support group in the community. Even if you don't want to talk, just listening will help.

What do they do at support group meetings?

There are different types of groups. Their meetings may vary widely in focus and purpose. Some groups are purely informational, with visiting speakers on new advances and treatment options, dietary recommendations, new medications and how to cope with the changes in your life. Other meetings may consist of simply sharing thoughts, fears and concerns. Some groups have formal leaders, while others may just have a freestyle format. The goal is to increase your level of knowledge and to give you back that feeling of control that is lost with the unknown of cancer disease.

Why should I go to a group and remind myself of what I've got and what may happen to me in the future?

These groups aren't intended to overwhelm you and occupy all your waking thoughts. In fact, you might come to realize it's okay to have cancer but that it shouldn't be the focus of your life. Even in the worst-case scenarios, most men will have years ahead of them before they even have to address their mortality. You should at least go and give it a try.

Is it true that most men who go to support groups are the ones who are really sick and are looking for some new treatment?

There's some truth to this. Men who are having continued problems are probably more likely to go to support-group meetings to share experiences and learn what's new. But quite often there will be a few men who were just recently diagnosed with prostate cancer. They are looking for some advice and guidance. It is quite helpful to be there to tell someone what it's like, that the surgery really isn't so scary or that the radiation is well-tolerated.

How do I find a support group in my area?

First ask your urologist. He may know of some in or near your community. If you are unable to locate one, call your local chapter of the American Cancer Society. You also can call the number for the international support group US-TOO (see the next section on Resources) to see if there is a group nearby. Talk to your friends. If there is a group in your community, you should be able to locate it by following these suggestions.

Resources

Following is a list of some of the resources that are available to you and your family. Most are unbiased, although a few may have their own preferences for therapy. Some are established by pharmaceutical or manufacturing companies to help promote their own products. I have had a few patients who made important decisions regarding their care because of information they received from some of these sources.

Information from these sources, like this book, should serve as a foundation of knowledge for you to talk with your doctors about your care. It is not intended to make a "cookbook decision" for you. Each person is different from everyone else. What may look good on paper may actually not be best for you.

American Cancer Society

The American Cancer Society is a voluntary health organization that offers a wide variety of services and literature to patients and their families at no charge. Literature is available on all cancers, nutrition, dealing with stress and anxiety, plus legal and financial planning. Some chapters provide transportation (or can refer you) if needed, information regarding support groups and a range of other helpful services locally. The society is also involved in funding scientific research and community education.

You can check with your local chapter (look in the white pages), or contact the national office at:

Call: 1-800-227-2345

Write: *American Cancer Society*
               1599 Clifton Road NE
               Atlanta, GA 30329-4251

Canadian Cancer Society

This is the sister organization of the American Cancer Society, providing the same resources, information, literature and community support services for individuals with cancer.

Call: 1-416-961-7223

Write: *Canadian Cancer Society*
               10 Alcorn Ave., Ste. 200
               Toronto, Ontario, Canada
               M4V 3B1

National Cancer Institute (NCI)

The NCI provides written material and information on a variety of cancer-related topics, and it makes referrals to local and regional cancer-treatment centers.

Call: *The Cancer Information Service*
               1-800-4-CANCER (1-800-422-6237)

Write: *Office of Cancer Communications*
               National Cancer Institute
               Building 31, Room 10A16
               Bethesda, MD 20892

Prostate Cancer Support Network

This is one of the leading nationwide prostate-cancer support networks, focusing on increasing public awareness of prostate cancer.

Call: 1-800-828-7866

Write: *Prostate Cancer Support Group*
300 W. Pratt St., Ste. 401
Baltimore, MD 21201

US-TOO

Focuses on survivor support and offers fellowship and counseling.

Call: 1-708-323-1002

Write: *US-TOO*
930 N. York Rd., Ste. 50
Hinsdale, IL 60521-2993

Patient Advocates for Advanced Cancer Treatments (PAACT)

This is a clearinghouse for information, especially non-surgical, on cancer treatments. Some literature on cryotherapy may overstate current known benefits.

Call: 1-616-453-1477
FAX: 1-616-453-1846

Write: *PAACT*
P.O. Box 141695
Grand Rapids, MI 49514-1695

Cancer Care, Inc.

Part of the National Cancer Foundation, the Prostate Cancer Education Council will provide information and counseling to patients and families, as well as assistance for non-medical expenses. Many services are for the greater New York area, but information is available nationwide.

Call: *1-212-221-3300*

Write: *Cancer Care, Inc.*
                  1180 Avenue of the Americas
                  New York, NY 10036

American Foundation for Urologic Disease (AFUD)

The latest information on prostate cancer, new research and clinical applications is available.

Call: *1-800-242-2383*

Write: *AFUD*
                  300 W. Pratt St., Ste. 401
                  Baltimore, MD 21201

American Red Cross

Resources available to train relatives in home nursing care and first aid.

Call: *Your local chapter (see white*
                  pages) or 1-202-737-8300

Write: *American Red Cross*
                  430 17th St. NW
                  Washington, DC 20006

Board Certification

To find out if your doctor is board-certified, you can call this number or check in the *Directory of Medical Specialists*, which should be available at most libraries. Check to make sure the volume you are looking at is current.

Call: 1-800-776-2378

National Coalition for Cancer Survivorship

This is a network of survivors and related organizations that can provide information regarding local and regional support groups. The coalition works for cancer survivors as an advocate in the workplace, especially regarding discrimination.

Call: 1-301-650-8868

Write: *National Coalition for*
Cancer Survivorship
1010 Wayne Ave., 5th Floor
Silver Springs, MD 20910

The Simon Foundation

An educational service providing information on urinary incontinence and treatment options.

Call: *1-800-23-SIMON (1-800-237-4666)*

Write: *The Simon Foundation*
P.O. Box 835
Wilmette, IL 60091

Geddings Osbon Foundation

Information and a booklet on impotence, primarily focusing on vacuum erection devices, but reviewing all options.

Call: *1-800-433-4215*

Write: *Geddings Osbon Foundation*
                P.O. Box 1593
                Augusta, GA 30903-1593

Sex Information and Education Council of the U.S.

Provides literature on sexuality and illness.

Call: *1-212-819-9770*

Write: *Sex Information and Education*
                Council of the U.S.
                130 W. 42nd St.
                New York, NY 10036

Glossary

Terms used in this glossary may not be used elsewhere in the book, but they may be used by your doctor or in other literature that you read regarding prostate disease.

A

Abdomen—Lower part of the torso which contains the intestines, liver, stomach and spleen.

Abdominal Aortic Aneurysm—Abnormal swelling and weakening of the large artery that takes blood from the heart to the rest of the body.

Acid Phosphatase—Substance made in the prostate.

Adenocarcinoma—Cancer made of abnormal gland cells from the lining of an organ. Most prostate cancers are adenocarcinomas.

Adjuvant Treatment—Treatment added onto the main surgical treatment.

Adjuvant Therapy—Addition of radiation, hormone therapy or chemotherapy after surgery.

Adrenal Glands—Glands located above each kidney. They produce several kinds of hormones, including sex hormones.

Age-adjusted—Looking at a lab result as it relates to a person's age.

Alkaline Phosphatase—Enzyme produced in the liver and bones that is used to help determine if a prostate cancer has spread to the bones.

Anaphylactic Reaction—Sudden and life-threatening reaction to a substance or medication.

Androgen Blockade—Blockage of the male hormones called *androgens*.

Androgens—A hormonal substance necessary for the development and functioning of the male sex organs and male sexual characteristics such as deep voice and facial hair.

Anesthesia—Using a medication or substance to eliminate or block pain, such as during a surgical procedure.

Anterior—Front of an organ or structure.

Antibiotic—A medication used to kill germs that can cause infection.

Anti-androgen—Medication that reduces or eliminates the presence or activity of androgens in the body.

Anti-inflammatory—Medication that reduces pain, swelling, redness and irritation from injury, surgery or infection.

Anus—The opening of the rectum.

Apex—Tip of the prostate, farthest away from the bladder.

Artificial Urinary Sphincter—Surgically implanted prosthetic device that compresses the urethra and reduces urine leakage.

Aspiration—Removal of fluid or tissue by using suction, usually through a fine needle.

Autologous Transfusions—Using a person's own blood for transfusion during surgery.

B

Bacteria—One-celled microscopic organisms that can cause infection under certain conditions.

Balloon Dilation—An abandoned technique used in the past to stretch open the prostate, with the goal of improving urine flow.

Base—Wide part of the prostate adjacent to the bladder.

Benign—A growth that is not cancerous.

Beta Carotene—A nutrient found in vegetables; important for normal health.

Biopsy—Removal of small samples of tissue for microscopic examination to see if cancer is present.

Bladder—Organ in which urine is stored before it is discharged from the body.

Bladder Neck—Circular muscle fibers that come together like a funnel where the bladder opens into the prostate.

Bladder Spasms—Painful squeezing of the bladder in response to irritation or injury.

Blood Clot—Thickening of blood to form a solid mass similar to a scab but inside a blood vessel.

Blood Count—Measurement of the number of red cells in the body. Red cells carry oxygen to the tissues.

Bone Marrow—Spongy inside of the bones of the body. Produces the blood cells.

Bone Scan—A type of nuclear-medicine scan that allows a sensitive look at the entire skeleton for any changes that might suggest metastatic prostate cancer.

Bowel-Prep—Cleansing of the intestines before abdominal surgery.

BPH (Benign Prostatic Hyperplasia)—Noncancerous enlargement of the prostate.

Brachytherapy—Type of radiation treatment in which radioactive pellets are inserted into the prostate.

C

Cancer—Abnormal and uncontrolled growth of cells in the body. Cancer can spread and ultimately injure and kill.

Capsule—Fibrous outer lining of the prostate.

Castration—Removal of the testicles. *See* Orchiectomy.

Catheter—A hollow tube used to drain fliuds from or inject fluids into body cavities.

Cell Saver—Machine used to recycle blood lost during surgery and give it back to the patient during the procedure.

Cell—Smallest unit of the body. Cells make up tissues.

Chemoprevention—Use of a substance to prevent the development and growth of cancer.

Chemotherapy—Cancer treatment utilizing various powerful drugs to attack and destroy certain kinds of cancer.

Clinical Trials—Use of a new medication or treatment, under strict controls, to see if the new therapy is safe and effective.

Colostomy—Surgical opening of the large intestine to the skin, with drainage of the bowel contents into a bag.

Complication—An undesirable result of a treatment, procedure or medication.

Contracture—Scarring at the bladder neck after surgery, causing narrowing of the passage.

Cryotherapy or Cryosurgery—Freezing of the prostate for cancer therapy.

CT Scan or CAT Scan—A computerized X-ray of the body that shows the internal organs in cross-section view to visualize abnormalities. CT stands for *computerized tomography*. CAT stands for *computerized axial tomography*. The terms are synonymous.

Cystoscope—Fiberoptic instrument used to look inside the bladder and urethra.

Cystoscopy—Looking into the bladder or urethra under direct vision through a cystoscope.

D

Debulk—To reduce the volume of cancer, by surgery, hormone therapy or chemotherapy.

Deep Venous Thrombosis—Formation of a clot in the large, deep veins, usually of the pelvis or legs.

Deferred Therapy—Delaying treatment until cancer becomes a definite threat to the patient.

DHT (Dihydrotestosterone)—Active breakdown product of testosterone. DHT is more powerful than testosterone.

Diagnosis—Determination of the cause or existence of a medical problem or disease.

Diet—Regular eating and drinking habits. Specifically, what a person eats.

Digital Rectal Exam—Finger examination of the prostate gland through the rectum.

Directed Donations—Blood donated by friends or family for a patient with the hope that it can be used if a transfusion is needed.

Dissection—Surgical removal of tissue.

Double-Blind—Research study where neither doctor nor patient knows what medication or treatment is being used.

Doubling Time—Length of time for a set amount of cancer to double in size.

Downsize—To shrink or reduce size of the cancerous tumor.

Down-Stage—To reduce the initial stage of a cancer to a lower and presumably better stage.

E

Epidural Anesthesia—Specific type of anesthesia in which a potent narcotic drips directly into the fluid that surrounds the spinal cord. This results in blockage of pain while allowing normal sensation and muscle function..

Erectile Dysfunction—Any abnormality in achieving or maintaining a penile erection.

Estrogen—Female hormone.

Estrogen Therapy—Use of estrogen pills to block the male hormones as a treatment for advanced prostate cancer.

Eulexin®—Brand name for flutamide, used to provide total androgen blockade.

Experimental—Untested or unproven treatment or approach.

External Vacuum Device—A plastic tube used with suction to produce an erection. Used as a treatment for impotence.

F

Family Physician—Primary-care doctor who treats all members of a family.

Fiber Optics—New technology that allows looking at internal structures through fine fibers inside of an instrument.

Flutamide—A pill taken three times a day to provide total androgen blockade, blocking any remaining adrenal androgens from the cells. *See* Eulexin®.

Foley Catheter—Latex or silicone tube that drains urine from the bladder to an outside collecting bag.

Frequency—Term to describe the need to urinate often.

Frozen Section—Preliminary rapid analysis of tissue by a pathologist who freezes the sample so a thin slice can be shaved off to use in microscopic examination. *See also* Permanent Section.

G

Gatekeeper—Primary-care doctor, usually in an HMO, who controls referrals of patients to specialists for tests and evaluation.

General Anesthesia—Total loss of consciousness or awareness prior to surgery because of medications.

Genetics—Branch of science that studies heredity.

Genitourinary Tract—The urinary system (kidneys, ureters, bladder and urethra) and the genital system (testicles, vas deferens, prostate and penis.)

Gland—Structure or organ that produces a substance to be used in another part of the body.

Grade—In cancer, the descriptive designation of the degree of malignancy based on the microscopic appearance of the cells.

Groin—Part of the body where the legs attach to the torso on the lower abdomen.

Gynecomastia—Enlargement of the male breast, often tender. Can occur on one side or both.

H
Hematospermia—Blood in the semen.
Hematuria—Blood in the urine.
Heparin Lock—A plug placed into an intravenous site that is periodically flushed.
Heredity—Passing of characteristics from parents to children through genetic material.
Hernia—Bulging of abdominal contents through a weakness in the abdominal wall,
    often in the groin.
Hesitancy—Inability to start the urinary stream immediately.
High-Grade—Very advanced cancer cells.
High-Risk—More likely to have a complication or side effect.
HMO—Health Maintenance Organization.
Hormones—Substances responsible for secondary sex characteristics.
Hot Flashes—Sudden feelings of heat, often with sweating and flushing of the skin,
    following hormone therapy.
Hyperthermia—Heating of the prostate to destroy prostate tissue.

I
ICU—Intensive care unit. Section of hospital where critically ill patients or those
    requiring intensive observation and care are placed.
Imaging—Seeing, through normal vision or X-rays.
Immune System—Complicated system of organs, tissues, blood cells and substances to
    fight off infections, cancers or foreign proteins that can make you ill.
Impotence—Inability to achieve and maintain an erection.
Incision—Cutting of the skin at the beginning of a surgical operation.
Incontinence—Leaking of a substance. With urine, this is called *urinary incontinence*.
Indications—Reasons for doing something.
Inflammation—Swelling, pain, redness and irritation as a result of injury, surgery
    or infection.
Informed Consent—Permission given for a treatment by a person who is aware of the
    possible benefits as well as potential risks and complications.
Inpatient—A person admitted to the hospital overnight.
Internist—A type of primary-care physician who specializes in the nonsurgical
    management of disease and disease prevention.
Interstitial—Within an organ, such as interstitial radiation, where radioactive seeds are
    inserted into the prostate.
Intravenous—Into the veins.
Invasive—Moving beyond the organ of origin and into other tissues.
Investigator—Doctor or scientist involved with an experimental study of a treatment or
    medication.
IVP (Intravenous Pyelogram)—X-ray test using intravenous material that allows for
    visualization of the urinary tract.

K
Kegel Exercises—Pelvic exercises that help to strengthen the muscles used with urination.

L
Laser—Very powerful concentrated beam of high-energy light used in surgery.
LHRH Analogue—Type of medication that causes the brain to stop stimulating
    testosterone production.

Libido—Sex drive.

Lifestyle—How a person chooses to live.

Lobe—Either side of an organ, such as the prostate.

Local Anesthesia—Anesthesia or numbing of a specific area of the body.

Local Recurrence—Return of a cancer to the area where it was first located. *See also* Regional Recurrence.

Localized—Contained or limited to the area described.

Low-Grade—Early stage of cancer-cell development.

Lupron®—LHRH medication given as an injection every 28 days to drop testosterone levels for the treatment of advanced prostate cancer.

Lycopene—Substance found in tomatoes that has powerful anticancer effects.

Lymph—Clear fluid that bathes the cells of the body.

Lymph-Node Dissection—Surgical removal of the lymph nodes that drain the prostate in the pelvis. Nodes are examined microscopically to see if cancer is present before the prostate gland is removed.

Lymph Nodes—Small bean-sized glands throughout the body that filter lymphatic fluid.

Lymphadenectomy—Technical term for lymph-node dissection.

Lymphangiography—An X-ray evaluation of the lymphatic vessels using a dye.

Lymphocele—Collection or pocket of lymph fluid that has accumulated in the body.

M

Malignancy—Uncontrolled growth of cells that can spread to other organs and cause death.

Malignant—Cancerous, with the potential for uncontrolled growth and spread.

Metastatic Cancer—Cancer that has spread to other organs or tissues through the lymphatic or blood systems. (We say the cancer has "metastasized.")

Metastatic Recurrence—The return of cancer in areas distant from the original cancer site.

Microscopic—Small enough that a microscope is needed to see.

Moderately Differentiated—Intermediate grade of cancer as determined by pathologic analysis of tissue.

MRI (Magnetic Resonance Imaging)—Tube-shaped device into which a person is placed for visualizing internal body structures. The device does not use X-rays.

N

Negative—A test result that does not show what was being looked for.

Neoadjuvant Therapy—A treatment before surgery, such as radiation, hormone therapy or chemotherapy.

Neoplastic—Malignant, cancerous.

Nephrostomy Tube—Small tube placed into the kidney through the skin that allows drainage of urine from the kidney.

O

Obturator Nerve—A large nerve that travels in the pelvis and controls some leg movements.

Oncologist—Specialized doctor who has taken several years of additional training after internal medicine and who deals with the evaluation and treatment of cancer.

Orchiectomy—Surgical removal of the testicles.

Organs—Tissues that work together for a specific function, such as bladder, heart or kidney.

Outpatient—Describes a surgery or treatment that does not require an overnight stay in the hospital.

P

PAP—Prostatic Acid Phosphatase, a chemical once used to try to tell when prostate cancer had spread outside of the gland.

Pathologist—Specially trained doctor who looks at tissues under a microscope to determine what they are and if disease is present. Pathologists also oversee laboratory tests such as the PSA blood test.

Pelvis—Part of the skeleton that forms a bony girdle joining the lower limbs of the body.

Penile—Relating to the penis.

Penile Prosthesis—Surgically implanted device to provide erections for men who have become impotent, such as through prostate-cancer treatment.

Perineum—Area just behind the scrotum, in front of the anus.

Permanent Section—Formal preparation of tissue by a pathologist for microscopic analysis. *See also* Frozen Section.

PIN (Prostatic Intraductal Neoplasia)—An abnormal area seen on biopsied tissue. Is not cancerous but may become cancerous. May indicate that cancer is present in neighboring tissue.

Placebo—Fake medication or treatment with no interaction with the body. Often used in research studies to test a new medication.

Ploidy Status—The genetic status of cancer cells; similar to the grade.

Pneumatic Sequential Stockings—Inflatable stockings that squeeze the legs intermittently to help reduce the risks for serious blood clots.

Poorly Differentiated—High-grade, aggressive cancer, as determined by pathologic analysis of tissue.

Positive Biopsy—The detection of cancer in a biopsy.

Positive Margin—Condition in which cancer cells are found at the cut edge of tissue removed during surgery. A positive margin indicates that residual cancer may be remaining in the body.

Posterior—Behind or toward the back.

Prognosis—Act of foretelling the course of a disease. The long-term outlook or prospect for survival and recovery.

Progression—Continued growth of the cancer or disease.

Prostate—Gland located at the base of the bladder.

Prostatectomy—Surgical removal of part or all of the prostate gland.

Prosthesis—Artificial device used to replace the lost normal function of a structure or an organ.

Protocol—Research study used to evaluate a specific treatment or medication.

PSA (Prostate Specific Antigen)—Protein secreted by prostate cells, used to help detect and follow prostate cancer.

Pulmonary Embolus—Blood clot that travels along the large veins of the body up to the lungs. These can be instantly fatal if large enough.

R

Radiation—Treatment utilizing X-rays to destroy cancerous tissues.

Radiation Therapist—Specially trained doctor who treats cancers with radiation therapy.

Radical Prostatectomy—Removal of the prostate gland and surrounding tissues and structures to eliminate cancer.

Radioactive Seeds—Small pellets of various substances that are treated to become radioactive, intended to kill adjacent cancer cells.

Radiologist—Specially trained doctor who specializes in performing and interpreting various types of X-ray studies.

Randomized—Term used in experimental studies to indicate treatment is randomly
decided.

Recovery Room—Area in a hospital to which patients are transferred after surgery to
recover before being sent to their rooms or homes, depending on the type of operation.

Rectum—Last few inches of the intestine leading to the anus.

Recurrence—Return of a disease.

Regional Recurrence—Return of cancer in the same general area where it was first located. *See also* Local Recurrence.

Regression—Shrinking of a tumor, either because of treatment or without
obvious cause.

Remission—Disappearance of the signs and symptoms of cancer. This can be temporary
or permanent.

Resectoscope—An instrument used to cut out prostate tissue through the urethra, under
direct vision.

Resistance—Ability to fight off a challenge. Some germs have developed a resistance to
certain antibiotics. The body has a resistance to fighting infections.

Retention—Inability to urinate.

Retropubic—Behind the pubic bone.

Risk—Chance or probability of something happening.

S

Sampling Error—In testing, when a problem exists but is not detected by the test.

Scrotum—Sac that holds the testicles.

Selenium—An element found in small amounts in food; may have anti-cancer effects.

Semen—Fluid containing sperm that comes out of the penis during ejaculation.

Seminal Vesicles—Glands at the base of the bladder that add nutrients to the semen.

Sepsis—Infection which causes high fever and shaking chills.

Side Effect—A secondary, usually adverse, reaction to a medication or treatment.

Signs—Physical changes that can be observed by the patient or doctor. Signs occur as
a result of a disease or disorder.

Simulation—Technique using X-rays to plan radiation treatment for prostate cancer.

Soy Products—Products made from soy beans (a legume).

Spasm—Rhythmic squeezing that can be painful, such as with a bladder spasm.

Spermine—Substance found in the prostate that slows down the growth of prostate cancer.

Sphincter—A bundle of muscles surrounding a tubular organ and controlling passage
of fluids.

Spinal Anesthesia—Loss of sensation below the level of injection of medication on the
spinal cord.

Stage—Description of the size or quantity of a cancer and the extent of its spread from
its original site.

Stent—Tube that allows drainage from one place to another.

Stricture—Scarring that squeezes down on a channel, such as the urethra.

Suprapubic—Above the pubic bone, as in a suprapubic incision or catheter.

Symptom—Condition that accompanies or results from a disease or disorder. The
individual feels or experiences a symptom.

Systemic—Throughout the body.

T

Testicles—Two glands located inside the scrotum. They produce sperm, testosterone and
other sex hormones.

Testosterone—Primary male hormone.

Therapy—Treatment for a disorder.

Tissue—Specific type of material within the body, such as muscle, cartilage or hair.

Total Androgen Blockade—Total blockage of all male hormones, using surgery and/or medications.

Transferrin—Chemical in the body that has been shown to stimulate prostate cancer growth.

Transperineal—Through the perineum, just under the scrotum and above the anus.

Transrectal—Through the rectum.

Transurethral—Through the urethra.

TRUS (Transrectal Ultrasound)—Technique used to visualize the prostate and guide biopsies.

Tumor—Abnormal tissue growth that can be cancerous (malignant) or noncancerous (benign).

Tumor Markers—Chemical substances that can be used to detect and follow the treatment of certain cancers.

Tumor Volume—Amount of cancer present in an organ.

TURP (Transurethral Resection of the Prostate—Surgical technique performed under anesthesia through a fiberoptic instrument that is placed up the penis. Looking through the instrument, the physician can see prostate tissue that has grown and is blocking urinary flow through the urethra. This prostate tissue is removed with the instrument, leaving only the shell of the prostate behind.

U

Undergrading—Term indicating that grade of cancer is worse than that found in biopsied tissue.

Ultrasound—A technique of visualizing internal organs by measuring reflected sound waves.

Unit—Term referring to a pint of blood.

Ureters—Muscular tubes that drain urine from the kidneys down to the bladder.

Urethra—In men, the muscular tube that drains urine from the base of the bladder to the opening at the tip of the penis.

Urgency—A sense of needing to urinate right away.

Urinary Retention—Inability to urinate, with the bladder filling up with urine.

Urologist— Specially trained doctor who deals with the medical and surgical aspects of the genitourinary tract in men and women. This is the specialist who deals with prostate cancer.

Urostomy—An surgically made opening that allows urine to drain directly to the skin of the lower abdomen, and then into a collection bag. This is performed when the bladder is removed.

V

Vas Deferens—Tiny tube that conveys sperm from the testicles to the prostate gland.

Vasectomy—Minor operation to make a man sterile by cutting the vas deferens so that no sperm can pass through into the semen.

W

Well-Differentiated—Low-grade cancer as determined by pathologic analysis of tissue.

Z

Zoladex®—LHRH medication in the form of a pellet. It is inserted just under the skin every 28 days to drop testosterone level for the treatment of advanced prostate cancer.

Appendix

PATIENT INFORMATION & CONSENT FORMS

The following pages include printed materials that I give out from my office. They are similar to those you might receive from your doctor or an agency such as the Red Cross. They are included only for your information.

Autologous Donation

1. Call the American Red Cross Blood Center nearest you to schedule your donation appointment(s). Your autologous blood donations must be completed at least three working days before your surgery but no more than 35 days before surgery.

2. Your doctor will give you the Autologous Donation Request Form. Please bring this form with you for your first donation.

3. When you donate blood you decrease the amount of iron stored in your body. Your doctor may prescribe iron tablets for you to take to compensate for this loss. You may also wish to include foods in your diet that are high in iron. The Red Cross can provide you with a list of iron-rich foods.

4. Please eat a well-balanced meal before donating. It is important that you drink an adequate amount of fluids daily during the days between your donations. Adequate hydration (enough fluid in your body) is important for a comfortable donation. Four to six 8-oz. glassfuls per day of water or fruit juice are strongly recommended. Coffee and tea are not recommended due to their diuretic effects on the body (they cause the body to lose water).

5. If you are taking any medications, take them as you would normally.

6. Because you may feel weak or lightheaded after your donations, we strongly suggest that you have someone accompany you to the Red Cross for your appointments.

7. You will be given a card with the numbers of your autologous blood units. Please give this card to your nurse when you are admitted in the hospital for your surgery.

8. If you have any questions concerning your autologous donations, or if you are unable to come in for your appointments, please call us. We will make every effort to answer your questions or help you in rescheduling your appointments.

Instructions Before Prostate Ultrasound & Biopsy

To minimize the risks of infection and bleeding, we ask that you follow these instructions. If you have any questions or concerns, please call us. Our goal is to obtain the information necessary from the study while trying to make the experience as safe and comfortable as possible.

For most men, the procedure is uncomfortable. Though the potential serious problems are rare, following these guidelines significantly reduces any risks.

1. Avoid ASPIRIN or aspirin-containing products for TEN (10) days before the biopsy. You should also stop similar medications such as ibuprofen (Advil, Nuprin, Motrin, Anaprox) for THREE (3) days before the study. These medications can increase the risks for bleeding by interfering with normal clotting mechanisms. Tylenol (acetaminophen) is okay to take. If you have any questions about what should or should not be stopped, please call us.

2. Take a Fleets enema at home several hours before the biopsy. This can be obtained at any drug store.

3. Take the antibiotic just as you leave your house to come to the office for the study. This will allow time for the medicine to be absorbed into your system and will reduce any chances of infection. At the time of the procedure you will also receive an antibiotic.

4. Though not absolutely necessary, having someone else drive you home is the best plan.

5. Following the study, you should plan to take it easy the rest of the day. You should avoid golf, swimming, tennis, traveling, etc. The next day you may resume normal activities. Avoid alcohol until the following day, as well.

Transrectal Ultrasound & Biopsy of the Prostate

Transrectal ultrasound is a relatively new technique used to assist in the evaluation of the prostate. This technique allows visualization of the internal architecture of the gland, allowing identification and localization of any areas or lesions that may be suspicious for cancer. Using ultrasound guidance, prostate biopsies can now be obtained of areas that were previously not detected on simple rectal examination.

As in all aspects of medicine, this technique is not perfect. Some cancers will not be detected by ultrasound. This is why biopsies are performed even if no suspicious areas are identified, if there is reason to be suspicious. This way, by obtaining an adequate sampling of the prostate tissue, we can identify some cancers which might otherwise remain hidden.

This technique is performed in the office with a minimum of discomfort. No anesthesia is necessary. Using a high-speed biopsy device, several hair-like slivers of prostate tissue will be obtained and sent to a pathologist who specializes in the microscopic evaluation of tissue to determine if any cancer is present in the samples or if there are any other abnormalities.

Because cancer could be present but not seen on ultrasound or missed on biopsy (sampling error), it is important to follow-up regardless of the biopsy results.

Prior to the study you should have taken an antibiotic tablet. At the time of the ultrasound, you will also receive an injection of a powerful antibiotic as well as several additional antibiotic pills to take following the biopsy: one pill twice a day until all are taken. This regimen will help to minimize the risk of infection in the urine, prostate or bloodstream.

Following the procedure, you may notice some blood in your urine, semen or bowel movements. This usually will pass within a few days but can persist off and on for up to a few weeks. Blood or discoloration can be seen in the semen occasionally up to a few months after the biopsy. Very rarely, some men will notice significant difficulty urinating after prostate ultrasound and biopsy. This can require a catheter to be placed, but usually only for a short time.

This procedure is usually very well-tolerated. If you have any questions, please ask prior to beginning the procedure.

CONSENT: I have read the above description of the proposed rectal ultrasound and prostate biopsy. I am aware of the most common potential risks and complications and agree to proceed.   (signed) _____

Instructions After Prostate Biopsy

The main risks following transrectal biopsy of the prostate include infection, bleeding, and difficulty urinating. These guidelines should help minimize these risks and answer the most common questions and concerns. If you have any questions or problems, please do not hesitate to call at any time.

1. Take the antibiotics as directed: twice a day with a full glass of water until all are taken.

2. Blood in the urine, semen or bowel movements is common. This may be seen off and on for several days. You may also notice clots. There may be some blood or discoloration in the semen for several weeks or more.

3. There may be some burning or irritation with urination, which should last only a day or two.

4. Do not take aspirin or aspirin-containing products for several days after the biopsy, as this may increase the risk of bleeding.

5. After the biopsy, go home and take it easy the rest of the day. Tomorrow you may resume your normal activities.

6. Do not drink any alcohol until you have taken all of the antibiotics.

7. If you should experience a high fever, shaking, chills, severe abdominal or pelvic pain, heavy or prolonged bleeding, or difficulty or inability to urinate, please call me immediately. In the unlikely event you do not receive a prompt response and you feel that you are ill, go directly to the nearest emergency facility.

8. As soon as the pathology report is completed, I will notify you on the telephone. This can take from two to four days. If you have not heard from our office, please call us.

After Radical Prostatectomy Instructions & Care

Following initial recovery from your radical prostatectomy in the hospital, you will be discharged home with a Foley catheter in place. This will need to stay in for approximately 2-1/2 to 3 weeks from the date of surgery. This allows the urethra and the area of the bladder-neck reconstruction to heal adequately and minimizes the risks for any leakage or scarring. The catheter will gradually become more uncomfortable. The following points will help to minimize the discomfort.

First, wash the urethral opening where the catheter comes out, at least once a day with soap and water. This will minimize any crusting and adhesions. You may want to apply a dab of Neosporin® ointment once or twice a day to the opening as well, both to reduce any crusting and to minimize any infections.

It is important that the catheter is not tugging on you. For this reason, the catheter drainage bag should be secured high on the thigh. The straps provided with the leg bag will keep the leg bag against the leg but will not keep it up on the leg, so I recommend putting several large safety pins through the holes in the top of the leg bag and attaching them to the elastic in your underwear. Be careful not to poke any holes in the bag portion as this can result in leakage as well as contamination and possible increased risks for infection.

If you choose to switch between the daytime leg bag and the larger night drainage bag, it is important to keep your hands clean. Always wash with soap and water prior to handling the connections. It is also important that you not handle the connections themselves. Dab some rubbing alcohol on each end of the connections to minimize any risks for contamination during bag changes.

If you sleep with the leg bag, set an alarm clock to wake up once or twice a night to empty the bag so it will not fill to capacity and possibly rupture.

It is important that every day, after you bathe, you alternate the leg bag from the right leg back to the left, etc. If left in one place for very long, it can result in significant skin irritation or even blistering because of chronic irritation from moisture.

Some people find that using tape in various ways to secure the catheter makes it more comfortable. This is something you will have to experiment with to find out for yourself.

As far as incision care, when you are discharged home most likely you will have a stitch holding the skin on the surface together. This needs to be removed about one week from the day of surgery. This is not a fixed time, however, and if for some reason there are delays, this will not be a problem. We expect the incision to be somewhat red and the area along the incision to be firm. Over a period of time this will gradually resolve, though there will be some thickening and firmness for several months. The incision will gradually become a fine red line and ultimately will turn skin color if kept out of the sun the first year.

Some people will have some stretching or even thickening of the scar. This is, unfortunately, oftentimes unpreventable and has to do with some genetic predisposition or sometimes the particular location of the incision which can result in enlargement. If this ever becomes painful or uncomfortable, please come in for a follow-up check on it, as there are some things we can do to minimize this.

If the incision ever becomes quite red with increasing tenderness and pain, or there is discharge of pus from the incision, you should be seen right away. This also holds true for the drain site which should heal quickly.

Some men will experience swelling of their scrotum following the surgery, probably because of interference with the normal lymphatic drainage. This can be minimized by simply wearing an athletic supporter. If this swelling increases, then try lying down with your scrotum elevated for several hours per day to see if this reduces the swelling. If there are any questions or persistence, you should be seen in the office.

It is common for there to be blood in the urine intermittently following the surgery. Sometimes there can be blood clots in the urine. You might also note leakage of blood from the catheter. This is quite common. As time goes by, in preparation for removal of the catheter, you may even notice occasional urine leakage around the catheter. This is quite common because the catheter does not totally close the urethra, but is there to divert the urine. As the bladder begins to heal, it tries to expel the catheter and this results in urine leakage.

If you wear an adult diaper such as Depends® when you go out, the leakage will be of less concern to you when it occurs.

One concern that always comes up is risk of infection with the catheter. It is true that most catheters, if left in place for long enough, will develop colonization (growth of bacteria) that may ultimately turn into infection. This is unlikely, but it is possible. If you begin to notice signs of an infection—fever, chills, or generalized aches—please let us know. We have provided you a prescription for antibiotics to start taking 24 hours before your scheduled catheter-removal time. This will provide adequate time to sterilize the urine and then we will have you continue antibiotics for an additional nine days after catheter removal. This should prohibit any significant risks for infection. If you are concerned, or if there are any problems before the catheter comes out, please let us know and we can recheck the culture.

The following is a sample of a consent form to give you an idea of what you will be asked to sign. The one you are shown will undoubtedly be different.

CONSENT PROCEDURE:
Bilateral Pelvic Lymph Node Dissection
Radical Retropubic Prostatectomy

I, (patient or guardian) authorize Dr._____, associates, and assistants of his/her choosing, to perform the following procedure: bilateral pelvic lymph-node dissection and radical retropubic prostatectomy. I understand the reason for the procedure is prostate cancer and the alternatives include observation, radiation or hormone therapy. If general anesthesia is required, the risks associated with your anesthesia should be discussed with your anesthesiologist.

In some cases the procedure may not be successful and you could be no better or even worse than you are now. For this reason, no guarantee can be given concerning the results. The result may be affected by complications that may occur.

This authorization is given with the understanding that any operation or procedure involves some risks and hazards. Some of the significant risks of this particular procedure include but are not limited to impotence, no ejaculation, incontinence, bladder-neck or urethral scarring, lymphatic fluid collection requiring additional surgery, nerve or blood-vessel injury, risk of transfusions, injury to adjacent organs including ureters, bladder, sphincter or rectum, risk for colostomy, and the possibility of residual cancer requiring additional treatments.

I also understand that the more common risks of any procedure include infection, bleeding, nerve injury, blood clots, heart attack, allergic reactions, seizures, coma and pneumonia. These risks are serious and possibly fatal.

If you have any unanswered questions, please let us give you the answers prior to your signing this form.

Certification: I have read or had read to me the contents of this form and I understand the risks and alternatives involved regarding this procedure; I have had the opportunity to ask any questions I felt necessary, and all of my questions have been answered. I consent to the performance of this procedure.

(signed)_____

PROSTATE CANCER EVALUATION LOG

DATE /	PSA /	EXAM /	BIOPSIES /	PLAN FOR FOLLOW-UP

Bibliography

Altman, Roberta. *The Prostate Answer Book*. Warner Books, Inc., 1993.

American Cancer Society. *National Conference on Prostate Cancer*. Philadelphia, Pennsylvania: September/October 1994.

Gillenwater, Jay Y., M.D.; Grayhack, John T., M.D.; Howards, Stuart S., M.D.; Duckett, John W., M.D., editors. *Adult and Pediatric Urology*. Mosby Year Book, 1991.

Goldstein, Irwin, M.D. *The Potent Male*. The Berkley Publishing Group, 1990.

Gomella, Leonard G., M.D.; Fried, John J. *Recovering from Prostate Cancer*. Harper Paperbacks, 1993.

Griffith, H. Winter, M.D. *Complete Guide to Prescription & Non-Prescription Drugs* (1995 edition). The Berkley Publishing Group, 1995.

McEvoy, Gerald K., Pharm.D., editor. *American Hospital Formulary Service Drug Information*. American Hospital Assoc., 1994.

Meyer, Sylvan; Nash, Seymour C., M.D. *Prostate Cancer: Making Survival Decisions*. The University of Chicago Press, 1994.

Morganstern, Steven, M.D.; Abrahams, Allen, Ph.D. *The Prostate Sourcebook: Everything You Need to Know*. Lowell House, 1993.

Rous, Stephen N., M.D. *The Prostate Book*. W.W. Norton & Co., 1992.

Shapiro, Charles E., M.D.; Doheny, Kathleen. *The Well-Informed Patient's Guide to Prostate Problems*. Dell Publishing, 1993.

Siegel, Mary-Ellen, M.S.W. *Dr. Greenberger's What Every Man Should Know About His Prostate*. Walker and Co., 1988.

Taguchi, Yosh, M.D. *Private Parts: A Doctor's Guide to the Male Anatomy*. Doubleday, 1993.

Walsh, Patrick, M.D., Editor, *Campbell's Urology*. W.B. Saunders Co., 1991.

INDEX